THE SUICIDE INDEX

Also by Joan Wickersham

The Paper Anniversary

THE
SUICIDE
INDEX

*Putting My Father's
Death in Order*

JOAN WICKERSHAM

HARCOURT, INC.

Orlando   Austin   New York   San Diego   London

Requests for permission to make copies of any part of the work
should be submitted online at www.harcourt.com/contact or mailed
to the following address: Permissions Department, Harcourt, Inc.,
6277 Sea Harbor Drive, Orlando, Florida 32887-6777.

www.HarcourtBooks.com

Portions of this book have been published in slightly different form in
the following: "act of . . . attempt to imagine" as "What About the Gun?"
in *AGNI*, 2004; "act of . . . bare-bones account" and "act of . . .
immediate aftermath" as "In the Heart" in *The Hudson Review*, 1997;
"intrafamilial relationships re-examined in light of . . . Munich" as
"Munich" in *The Hudson Review*, 2002; "life summarized in an attempt
to illuminate" as "An Attempt at a Biographical Essay" in *AGNI*, 2006;
"other people's stories concerning" as "The Woodwork" in
Ploughshares, 2006; "psychological impact of"
as "Psychological Impact" in *The Hudson Review*, 2006.

Grateful acknowledgment to the MacDowell Colony,
where much of this book was written.

Library of Congress Cataloging-in-Publication Data
Wickersham, Joan.
The suicide index: putting my father's death in order/
Joan Wickersham.—1st ed.
    p.   cm.
1. Wickersham, Joan.   2. Adult children—Psychology.
3. Children of suicide victims—Psychology.   4. Suicide.
5. Suicide victims—Family relationships.   I. Title.
HQ799.95.W53   2008
155.9'37092—dc22   2007029299
ISBN 978-0-15-101490-3

Text set in Adobe Garamond
Designed by Cathy Riggs

Printed in the United States of America
First edition
A C E G I K J H F D B

THE SUICIDE INDEX

Suicide:

act of
    attempt to imagine, 1–4
    bare-bones account, 5–6
    immediate aftermath, 7–34

anger about, 35

attitude toward
    his, 36–42
    mine, 43

belief that change of scene might unlock emotion
concerning, 44–47

day after
    brother's appearance, 48–53
    concern that he will be viewed differently now, 54–55
    "little room" discussion with his business partner, 56–58
    search warrant, 59–60
    speculation relating to bulge, 61–66

deviation from chronological narrative of, 67–71

factors that may have had direct or indirect bearing on
    expensive good time, 72–87

Suicide:

   factors that may have had direct or indirect bearing on *(cont.)*
      pots of money, 88–102
      uneasy problem of blame, 103–104

   finding some humor in
      ashes, 105
      Valentine's Day, 106

   glimpses of his character relevant to, 107–115

   information from his brother sparked by, 116–123

   intrafamilial relationships reexamined in light of
      Munich, 124–138
      my grandmother, 139–151

   items found in my husband's closet and, 152–156

   life summarized in an attempt to illuminate, 157–195

   numbness and
      Bullwinkle, 196–198
      chicken pox, 199–200
      duration, 201
      food, 202–203
      husband, 204–206
      psychiatric response, 207–211
      various reprieves, 212–213

   opposing versions of, 214–215

   other people's stories concerning, 216–223

   other shoe and, 224–228

Suicide: *(cont.)*

    philosophical conundrums stemming from
        first, 229
        second, 230

    possible ways to talk to a child about
        family tree, 231–233
        full disclosure, 234–235
        not yet, 236–237
        rational approach, 238–242
        weapons god, 243–246

    psychiatry as an indirect means of addressing, 247–255

    psychological impact of, 256–273

    readings in the literature of, 274–277

    romances of mother in years following, 278–296

    "things" folder and, 297–301

    thoughts on method of, 302–304

    where I am now, 305–316

THE SUICIDE INDEX

Suicide:
act of
attempt to imagine

IN THE AIRPORT, COMING HOME FROM VACATION, HE STOPS AT a kiosk and buys grapefruits, which he arranges to have sent to his daughters. They will stumble over the crates waiting on their porches, when they get home from his funeral.

It's the last week of his life. Does he know that? At some point, yes. At the moment when his index finger closes on the trigger of the gun, he knows it with certainty. But before that? Even a moment before, when he sat down in the chair holding the gun—was he sure? Perhaps he's done this much before, once or many times: held the gun, loaded the gun. But then stopped himself: no. When does he know that this time he will not stop?

What about the gun?

Has it been an itch, a temptation, the hidden chocolates in the bureau drawer? Did he think about it daily, did it draw him, did he have to resist it?

Perhaps the thought of it has been comforting: Well, remember, I can always do *that*.

Or maybe he didn't think about the gun and how it might be used. There was just that long deep misery. An occasional flicker (*I want to stop everything*), always instantly snuffed out (*Too difficult, how would I do it, even the question exhausts me*). And then one day the flicker caught fire, burned brightly for a moment, just long enough to see by (*Oh, yes, the gun. The old gun on the closet shelf with the sweaters*). He didn't do it that day. He put away the thought. He didn't even take the gun down, look at it, hold it in his hands. That would imply he was thinking of actually doing it, and he would never actually do such a thing.

Some days the gun sings to him. Other days, more often, he doesn't hear it. Maybe, on those stronger days, he has considered getting rid of it. Take it to a gun shop, turn it in to the police. But then someone else would know he has a gun, and it's no one else's business. He hasn't wanted to deal with their questions: Where did you get it? How long have you had it? Besides, how long *has* he had it? Twenty years? Twenty-five? And never fired it in all that time? So where's the danger? What's the harm in keeping it around, letting it sleep there among the sweaters? He doesn't even know where the bullets are, for God's sake. (But immediately, involuntarily, he does know: he knows exactly which corner of which drawer.)

We have to watch him from the outside. He leaves no clues, his whole life is a clue. What is he thinking when he gets up that last morning, showers, and dresses for work? He puts on a blue-and-white striped cotton shirt, a pair of brown corduroys, heavy brown shoes. A tan cashmere sweater. He has joked to his older daughter that all the clothes he buys these days are the color of sawdust. Might as well be, he said, they end up covered in the stuff anyhow, in the machinery business. So he has shaved, patted on aftershave, and climbed into his dun-colored clothes. He's gone to his dresser and loaded his pockets: change, wallet, keys, handkerchief. Maybe he thinks he's going to work. Or maybe he knows, hopes, that in forty-five minutes he'll be dead. It's Friday morning. He's just doing what he does every morning, getting ready.

He may be thinking about it on the walk down the long driveway to get the newspaper. The cold dry air gripping the sides of his head, the ice cracking under his feet as he tramps along this driveway he can no longer quite afford. It is a dirt road, unpaved; in this town, as his wife is always pointing out, dirt roads have more cachet than fancy landscaped driveways. A dirt road means you are private and acting to protect your privacy. Your house cannot be seen from the road. Your real friends, that delightful, sparkling, select bunch, will know you're in there, hidden in the woods, and they will know your dirt road's ruts and bumps by heart.

Is there something in the newspaper? The front page is the only one in question, since he leaves the paper on the kitchen table folded and unread. More bombings. All this week he's been sitting in front of the television in the evenings, staring at the news. Silent films of Baghdad buildings, fine white-lined crosses zigzagging dizzily over their facades, zooming in and centering. Then a long moment, just that white cross holding steady; and then the building falls down, no sound, no smoke or flash of light, just caves in. And that's it. The screen goes blank; the camera doesn't wait around to gloat. Then another building, another filmed implosion: we're getting all these places, relentlessly. We're hunting them down and getting them.

What has he been thinking about this week, watching these films over and over? The silent buildings that simply implode.

The front page of the paper is full of the war. But nothing else that's major. No market crash. Nothing that would lead, directly or indirectly, to his losing more than he has already lost, which is virtually everything.

Maybe that's it, maybe that's what he is thinking, not just on this last morning but all the time: you've lost everything, not at a single blow but gradually, over years, a small hole in a sandbag. You see the hole clearly but you have no way to fix it. No one but you has been aware of that thin, sawdust-colored stream of sand escaping, but now enough sand has leaked that the shape of the bag is changing, it's collapsing. It will be noticed. You will be caught. And then, and then—you don't know what. You want not to be here when that happens.

He makes the pot of regular coffee for his wife, fills a cup, carries it upstairs to her bedside table. The fact that he doesn't make his own usual pot of decaf might mean that he's already decided—or it might mean that he generally makes that second pot when he comes downstairs again. And this morning, he doesn't go downstairs again. He stands at his wife's side of the bed and looks at her, sleeping. He looks at her for a long time.

Or maybe he doesn't look. Maybe he puts down the saucer and goes for the gun and is out of the room before the coffee stops quivering in the cup.

Suicide:
act of
bare-bones account

THIS IS WHAT MY FATHER DID. HE GOT UP, SHOWERED, SHAVED, and dressed for work. He went downstairs and made a pot of coffee, and while it was brewing he went outside and walked the long driveway to pick up the newspaper. He left the paper folded on the kitchen table, poured a cup of coffee, carried it upstairs, and put it on my mother's bedside table. She was still in bed, sleeping. Then he went into his study, closed the door, and shot himself.

My mother heard a popping sound. She was up by then, on her way into the shower. The coffee wasn't hot; she drank it anyway. When she was dressed, she took the empty cup down to the kitchen. He wasn't there, but she didn't think he would have left for work without saying good-bye, and there were no breakfast dishes in the sink. Usually he made two pots of coffee, a big one with caffeine for her and a smaller one of decaf for himself. But the smaller pot was empty, cold, clean. She called his name. She saw the paper on the table, unfolded it, and read the front page.

She went upstairs to her study, next to his, and rummaged in the closet for a tablecloth she meant to iron. She set up the ironing board and called his name again. His hearing was bad; sometimes he didn't answer when she called. She went and knocked at his study; she pushed the door open.

She found him.

She called Ted Tyson and told him to come over. She called the police.

Suicide:
act of
immediate aftermath

I THOUGHT I KNEW WHY TED TYSON WOULD BE CALLING ME AT eight in the morning. My mother had said that he was planning to come up to Boston soon, and I had said he could stay with us. "Really?" my mother had said. "Really?"

"Sure, why not?" I had answered. I was always trying to think of ways to prove to her that I liked him. But I had never really expected him to take me up on my offer.

"Ted!" I said warmly now. "Ted, how *are* you?"

"I have some bad news," he said.

"Oh?" I said.

"Yes," he said. "Your father has taken his own life."

We didn't say anything in the car, driving to Connecticut. It took three hours. My husband drove, and I looked out the window. Our three-year-old son sat in the backseat, looking at his truck books, murmuring to himself. He had a music box with him, one that my father had brought him from Switzerland. There was a little man inside, dressed in a clown suit. My son kept passing it to me through the gap between the seats; I kept winding it up and passing it back to him, with the little man dancing, his arms and legs flailing loose and wild.

At Waterbury we got off the highway and pulled into the parking lot of a new hotel. We were early; my husband's step-father was meeting us at 11:45. We went inside. We wandered through the lobby, along corridors carpeted in undersea green. Men in suits were going into the restaurant. I looked at their faces. My son stood in front of a glass shelf of stuffed animals in the gift shop, looking but not touching.

"Isn't he a precious," said the old lady working there. "Isn't he a love." She smiled at me. "I have a little grandson just that age," she said. "He comes to lunch with me every Tuesday."

"Really?" I said.

"There's Neil," said my husband.

"What happened?" Neil asked us in the lobby.

"We're not sure yet," I said. "We think it must have been a heart attack."

We handed him our son's overnight bag, and we all went back out to the parking lot. We moved our son's car seat into Neil's green Rolls-Royce. I watched Neil strap our son in and drive away; the car was so big that I couldn't see even the top of my son's head in the window.

When we got back into our own car, I asked my husband if he thought the body would still be in the house when we got there. I looked at the dashboard clock. "It's been over four hours," I said. "Four and a half by the time we get there. He'll be gone by then, won't he?"

"Oh, I'm sure," my husband said, clearing his throat.

"What do they need to do?" I said. "Look around. Talk to my mother. Take pictures. Do you think they take pictures?"

"I don't know." He cleared his throat again. "Probably."

My parents' house was in a cold pocket. The town was in a deep, rocky valley, and their house lay in a dip in the road. A police car sat at the entrance, between the low stone walls, red and blue lights flashing. We turned in and stopped, and the policeman got out and started walking toward us.

"Get out," I told my husband. "Go talk to him over there."

I didn't look at them while they were talking. I looked out my window, at a white opaque patch of ice on the driveway. My husband got back into the car and rolled down the window.

"You can't go in there yet," the policeman said. He was talking to me. I looked at his black belt, sagging with the weight of a gun in its black holster. "Your mother's over at Mr. Tyson's house. We asked her if she wouldn't rather be with a woman friend, if there was someone else we could call, but she said no. She wanted to be with him."

My mother was sitting in a big blue-and-white striped armchair, in front of Ted Tyson's kitchen fireplace. There was a fire going. There was a plaid blanket over her, and Kleenex in her fist. She held out her hand to me, and I went down on my knees in front of her.

"Oh, the horror," she said, "do you know? The horror."

She was shivering. I rubbed her hand between mine; her skin was loose and very dry, like crumpled tissue paper.

"Can you imagine what I went through, finding him like that?" she said.

I kept on rubbing her hand. There were shelves behind her, built into the corner, filled with square glass bottles of Ted's herb vinegar. He had given me a bottle of that vinegar for

Christmas six weeks before. Ted was standing at the counter, stirring something on the stove.

"He was at the desk?" I asked my mother.

"No, in the chair."

"What chair?"

"The armchair."

"There is no armchair in that room."

"Of course there is," she said. "Why would I invent an armchair?"

I couldn't get it out of my head that he'd been at the desk, slumped over the piles of paper that had killed him. "What color is it?" I asked.

"I don't remember," she said.

"Where was the gun?"

"I don't know," she said. "I didn't see the gun. He was sitting in the chair, with his feet on the footstool. His feet were like this." She stuck her own feet out from the blanket, crossing them at the ankles. "He looked so peaceful. You know how they always say that, 'He looked peaceful'? Well, he did. I shook him. I kept saying, 'Paul, wake up.'"

"But you knew he was dead."

Her hand was shaking. "There was all this blood."

"Where? Where was the blood?"

"Here." She took her hand out of mine and drew a shape on her chest, like a bib. "He shot himself in the heart."

I looked over at Ted. There was a woman in the kitchen with him, helping him cook. That must be Annette, the cabaret singer who was always coming up from New York to stay with him. Ted paid her rent when she was short of money, my mother had told me. He got her jobs, he introduced her to people in the record business. She was lazy, she used him, my mother said. Annette saw me looking at her; she smiled at me and raised her hand in a limp little wave. I looked at my mother again.

"Why there?" I said. "Why in the heart?" My hand went to my chest, feeling around for my own heart. "How did he know exactly where to aim? That's risky, the heart. You could miss, or hit a rib. Why not the head?"

The blanket was slipping down; she pulled it up to her chin again. "I guess because he thought it would be less messy. He was trying to spare me. You know how considerate he was."

Ted came over and handed us coffee, in big white china mugs. My mother drank some of hers. "You want to hear something weird?" she said. "He cleaned his closet before he did it. I was asleep, but I heard him. I must have opened my eyes for a second. He was straightening out his sweaters on the top shelf. Isn't that strange? But he was so neat. In thirty-five years I never had to pick up after that man. Not one dirty sock. I want you to say that, at the funeral."

"He was getting the gun," I said.

"What?"

"Was that where he kept it?"

She didn't answer me for a moment. Then she said, "I don't know. I guess maybe it was." Then, "You think so? Oh, my God, why didn't I just wake up? Why didn't I sit up and say good morning? Then he wouldn't have done it."

"Yes he would," I said. "Maybe not this morning, maybe not right then. But sometime."

"No," she said. "The moment would have passed. I could have gotten him through the moment."

She drank more coffee. She told me about the coffee he'd made, how he only made one pot.

"So he knew," I said. "It wasn't just a moment." I thought of him bringing her coffee up the stairs, putting it on the night table, knowing. Apologetic, I thought, like a dog bringing its master's slippers when it knows it's done something bad.

"He tried so hard to take care of me," my mother said.

"How can you shoot yourself in the heart with a rifle?" I asked. I remembered that rifle; long ago, at our old house in the country, my father and I used to go out to the big field behind the house and shoot targets. We would lie in the grass. My father showed me how to slide back the bolt and put the bullet in and lock it into place, as I balanced on my elbows to steady the gun. I remembered lining up the sights and squeezing the trigger, the gun's small jump as it went off, the satisfying click of the bolt as I released it to let the spent golden shell spring out. The targets, when we went to collect them, were pockmarked with small holes—some wildly isolated at the outskirts of the black concentric rings, but most clustered at the center. Both of us had good aim.

Would you ever use it for hunting? I asked him.

No, he said. Once as a boy I shot a rabbit, and it was so terrible that I decided I'd never kill anything again.

Then why do you have the gun?

For protection, he'd said.

"A rifle?" my mother asked, surprised. "Why would he use a rifle?"

"You think he went out and bought another gun?" I didn't agree with her that he'd done it in the impulse of a moment, but this amount of premeditation was too much for me.

"He had another gun."

"He did?"

"A little one. A handgun. He'd had it for ages. He bought it in the summer of 1964. The summer of Watts. When everyone was saying there were going to be riots all over suburbia."

"But that's crazy," I said.

My mother shrugged. "It didn't seem so crazy back then."

I looked up and smiled in the direction of Ted and his friend. "You must be Annette," I said, in a loud voice.

"That's right," Annette said, smiling sadly at me. She had long pale hair that lay like yellow satin ribbon on either side of her chest.

"Well," I recited in polite exaggerated singsong, "it's nice to finally meet you."

We laughed.

"I'm sorry about your father," Annette said. "He was a lovely man."

"Thank you," I said. "What are you making?"

"Soup."

"Chicken soup," Ted said. "Your father's chicken soup, as a matter of fact. He made it for me a few weeks ago when I had the flu, and I asked him for the recipe."

"Fresh dill," I said.

"That's the secret," said Ted. The phone rang, and Ted answered it and brought it over to my mother. "Eric Parsons calling you back."

"Who's Eric Parsons?" I asked.

"The lawyer," Ted told me.

I went and stood at Ted's kitchen window while my mother left the room to talk to the lawyer. I looked out at the hillside where his back garden was. When I'd come here at Christmas, my mother had walked me up the hill through the garden, which was studded with dozens of metal rings supported by wires, like haloes in a school Christmas play. Peonies, my mother had told me. Ted's put in thirty-seven different varieties of peonies.

I didn't know there were thirty-seven different varieties, I'd said.

Well, apparently there are. Even Daddy's impressed, she'd said.

The garden now looked exactly as it had that day: a bare rocky brown hillside caked with ice, each peony waiting invisibly beneath its frozen glittering cage.

The floor trembled under my feet; my mother was walking into the kitchen, replacing the phone in its cradle.

I turned to look at her. "What did he say?"

"He was appalled. That's what he kept saying, *I'm appalled.* Fuck him."

"You need a different guy," Ted told her. "Call my guy. He's terrific."

"Who is he to be so fucking appalled?" my mother said.

"He was appalled," Ted said. "Gee, that's too bad."

"Fuck him," I said.

"Yeah, fuck him," said Annette.

We went on like that: for a few moments Ted's kitchen was filled with "appalled"s and "fuck"s, murmured over and over until all of us were smiling, as if at some distorted message in a game of Telephone.

Finally I said, "But did he have any advice?"

"Advice?" my mother said. "What about?"

"I don't know."

"Call my guy," said Ted.

The doorbell rang and Ted went to answer it. My sister came into the kitchen. She was carrying a suitcase. Her face was puffy and her eyes were red. I stared at her. She and I hugged for a long time. I didn't want to let go of her; I didn't want to start talking again.

"You poor girls," my mother announced. "Your father."

"Well," I said, releasing my sister. "Your husband."

"But *your father,*" my mother said. She sat down in the striped armchair and pulled the blanket up over her lap.

My sister said, "What happened?"

My mother told her. *He got up, showered, shaved, and dressed for work . . .* She put in all the details I'd prodded her on before—the handgun, the blood on his chest, his feet crossed at the ankles. When she finished, my sister was crying, soundlessly. My mother stroked her arm and got up and went into the bathroom.

My sister whispered to me, fiercely, "He brought her the coffee."

"I know," I said. I told her what I'd thought before, that it was like the dog bringing the slippers.

"No," she said, "it was like 'fuck you.'"

When my mother came back, my sister said, "Was there a note?"

"A note?" my mother said. "No, there wasn't any note."

"On the desk?" I said.

"I didn't look," she said. "The desk was a mess. You girls don't know. He hadn't cleaned it for months. I used to say to him, 'Let me help you, I'll sit down with you and we'll spend an evening sorting it out.' But he wouldn't." Her voice was rising. "He was so damned secretive. He never told me anything. I was always saying to him, 'I really should know what we have and where it is. What if something happens to you?' But he would never tell me. You know what he said finally? He said he was afraid that if I knew, I would leave him. Can you believe it? He thought if I knew where the money was I would take it and leave."

My sister looked at me and I could tell we were both thinking the same thing: maybe there wasn't any money. Maybe that's what he didn't want you to find out; maybe that's why he thought you would leave.

"That desk is such a mess I don't know how anyone could find anything there!" She was screaming now. "Oh, my God. You think there was a note? You think he left me a note and I didn't see it?" She looked at my sister and me. "What if the police find it and read it? What could it say?"

"I thought Monday for the funeral," my mother said. We were back in our places: she in the armchair, without the blanket now, my sister and I on what looked like ancient wooden milking stools that Ted had produced from somewhere.

"Daddy wouldn't want a funeral," I said.

My mother shook her head, blinking. "Yes, he did. He wanted them to play the Mozart *Requiem.*"

"Well, we're not having the Mozart *Requiem,*" I said loudly. Then, trying to explain my vehemence, "If we do anything, we have to make it something we can get through, and that's something I couldn't bear."

"I agree," my sister said.

"I mean, Ma, whatever he may have said to you about wanting a funeral, these circumstances—"

My mother cut me off. "He's dead. Never mind how. A lot of people are going to miss him."

"I know that, but—"

"There's a Unitarian church. It's very simple inside. We could do it there, Monday morning."

"You mean with a coffin and everything?" My voice was rising, beginning to shake.

"No," my mother said calmly; it seemed we were taking turns, the three of us, being the calm one. "He wanted to be cremated."

I took a breath and tried to match my mother's tone. "We can wait until spring, then, to scatter the ashes. We could do it in Long Island Sound, where he sailed."

My sister said, "I don't want him in the water. There needs to be a place."

"There's an old graveyard up on Diamond Rock Road," my mother said.

"Why?" I said. "Why does there need to be a place?"

"So we can visit it," my sister said. "I want to be able to take my kids there."

"Well, I'm not going to visit it," I said.

"Don't," my sister said.

"If he's dead then let him be gone," I said, my voice cold, hard.

My mother put her hand on my wrist, fingering the end of my sleeve. "We'd better start calling people. Get Ted to give you some paper. We'll make a list."

The paper Ted gave me had a tiny red pineapple printed at the top, with his initials underneath. I wrote down names with a black felt-tip pen: my mother's brother and his wife and their grown children. My mother's other brother. I chewed on the top of the pen for a moment and then wrote down the name of my father's business partner.

"Let's see, who else," my mother said.

"Kurt," said my sister.

"Kurt?" My mother frowned. "God, I forgot about him. I suppose you have to call him."

"Of course we do; he's Daddy's *brother*," I said, annoyed; I'd forgotten about him, too, but my hand, writing his name, was shaking. "You should call him, Mom. You should be the one to tell him. I hardly know him."

"No, no, you do it. I can't deal with him now."

"Well," I said. I looked at my watch. It was nearly three o'clock. He must be gone by now, I thought; they must have finished and taken him away. I didn't want to make the phone calls; there was something limbo-like about sitting there in Ted's warm kitchen. My father was sort of dead, but not all the way yet; we hadn't told anyone in the family; something might still change.

"Use the phone in the study, upstairs," my mother was saying. "Ted will show you where."

All these studies, I thought. I said, "Do you want me to tell people how?"

"What do you mean?" my mother asked.

"I mean when they ask what happened. Should I say it was suicide, or should I say a heart attack or something?" I was aware, suddenly, that I was trying to pick a fight: my mother would say heart attack, and I would argue for telling the truth. My sister, I thought, would back me up.

"Why should we hide it?" my mother said.

"I just thought—you know, because Daddy was so private—"

"We've got nothing to be ashamed about," said my mother, and my sister said:

"If he hadn't been so private, maybe he'd still be alive."

My husband came with me to make the phone calls. I let him do the talking, pulling people out of meetings. It's an emergency, he said.

Yes, it is, I thought; and there was something of a relief in hearing him say it. This was not a debatable emergency, like calling the pediatrician on a Sunday morning when our son had a fever; this was emergency in its starkest, purest form. We had a perfect right to interrupt meetings, to shock people out of the ordinary progress of the day. I liked it that they came to the phone a little ruffled, a little worried, but unprepared for what my husband was about to tell them. I listened to him explaining over and over that my father was dead and how it had happened, and I felt a startling calm sense of power that was almost a thrill, as my cousins and aunts and uncles went over the road that I had already traveled that morning. They were innocent, then they were shocked and saddened; they were out on that rainy, windy road but I was farther along than they.

"What did they say?" I asked my husband after each call was over.

He told me: They were upset.

No, no, I wanted details. How did their voices sound, what words had they used exactly? They were mobilizing, he reported. One cousin would drive up from the city tomorrow, another was leaving the office right now to go break the news to my mother's eldest brother and his wife. My uncle was sick, he had heart disease; he and his wife had adored my father, and the cousin thought someone had better tell them the news in person. Good, I said, pleased to have set so much in motion. Things were happening, after the eerie stillness of the morning;

people were scurrying, waves were rippling out from the spot where the stone had hit the water.

The sky was getting dark behind the bare tree branches at Ted's study window. The lights of the rooms below made pale wedge shapes on the frozen stones of the terrace. The day was receding; the last daylight my father had seen would soon be gone.

"Who else?" I asked.

"Just Kurt."

"Try him at the theater." I flipped though my mother's black address book and found the number. I stood up and wandered around Ted's study while my husband dialed. The silvery barn-board walls were covered with photos of Ted when he was younger, chiseled and aloof, leaning on a Jeep, running on a beach. A series in black-and-white, Ted standing in jeans and a white shirt against a crumpled paper backdrop. My mother had told me that Ted had been a model when he first got to New York. He must have been gorgeous, my mother had said. He looks like Montgomery Clift in those pictures.

"Oh," my husband was saying, "well, do you know where I can reach him?"

At the top of Ted's stairs, in the corner, there was a stair-climbing machine. I went over to it and held on to one of its chrome railings. There was a lamp next to it; I switched it on and the room was filled with stark yellow light, throwing huge sudden shadows among the eaves high above.

My husband hung up. "He's not there. They said he's probably on his way in, for tonight's performance."

"Try him at home anyway, just in case." Let him not be there, I thought; please make him be out. But I heard my husband say, "Oh, hi, Kurt. Listen, um . . ." He went on to tell Kurt who he was and why he was calling. Then, "Yes, he's dead . . . No, nothing like that. He killed himself . . . no, with a gun . . . no, we're pretty sure it was instantaneous . . . Yes, this morning . . . sometime before seven." There was a long silence; then my husband said, "Kurt. I know . . . I know. Kurt." He took the phone away from his ear and covered the receiver. "He wants to talk to you."

I shook my head and walked quickly to the stairs.

"She can't talk right now . . . Well, because it's been a long day, and everyone is tired." His voice rose. "I know, but we didn't call *anyone.* There's been a lot to do, and—Kurt. Kurt, calm down." His voice was rough, angry.

I started down the stairs. Behind me my husband said, "No. In the heart."

The police were there, in Ted's kitchen. Three of them, two wearing uniforms and one in a khaki raincoat. "You're the older daughter?" one of them said to me. "Do you mind coming with us into the other room?"

They took me into the living room. There was a fire going in there, too. I sat on a green velvet couch. The man in the raincoat sat down on a spindly wooden chair and asked me to tell him my name, my address, whether I was married, how many children I had. He said, "Can you think of any reason why your father might have done this?"

"He was having some business problems," I said.

"What kind of problems?"

"He was in the machinery business, and they weren't selling any machines. It's a low-volume, high-end business—if you sell one or two a year, you're fine, but if you don't . . ."

One of the uniformed policemen was sitting in another spindly chair, writing down what I said on a small yellow pad.

The third policeman wasn't there; he must have stayed in the kitchen.

"And there were some product liability suits," I said. "Some people had gotten hurt, using the machines. They didn't use them right, they were careless and they got hurt. Or maybe they weren't hurt—maybe they were faking. You know how people get when they want to do a lawsuit."

"Uh-huh," said the detective. His tone was neutral, but it made me scrutinize my own words; I was telling him what my father had told me, but now it sounded defensive, rationalizing.

"Anyhow," I said. "My father kept having to go to court and testify, and I think it was very upsetting to him. I think he took it personally."

"Right," he said. "Your mother told us the same thing. How was the marriage?"

I folded my hands together and looked past him, at Ted's big black piano topped with silver-framed photographs.

"Fine," I said.

"They didn't fight or anything?"

"Nope." In the corner of my eye I saw the other policeman silently making notes.

"Never?"

"Well, sometimes," I said. "But it was always—like she would say, 'I'll clean up the kitchen,' and he'd say, 'But you made dinner, let me clean up the kitchen.' And she'd say, 'But you've been working all day, you're tired, let me do it.'" This particular fight was dredged up from my childhood; it had happened probably twenty years ago, but the policeman didn't have to know that. I looked at him and smiled: See how benign?

He didn't smile back at me. I took a breath and said quickly, "But there's something else, something my mother doesn't know. There was a loan, a big one, not for the machinery business but for this other company he was starting, with three other guys. They took out this big bank loan and they'd been making the payments, but then they missed a couple of payments. It wasn't their fault—the bank didn't bill them for a couple of months so they stopped paying, but they would have paid if they'd realized—" I stopped myself; both policemen were looking at me curiously, with that same solemn pity I thought I'd seen when I was telling them about the product liability suits. I clasped my hands together more tightly. "Anyway," I said, "a few weeks ago the bank called the loan."

It was as though we'd all let out our breaths, invisibly, silently. A collective sigh was in the room. *Oh, dear,* it whispered, and at the same time, *Thank God. Now we can say: We know why he did it.*

"And how big was this loan?"

"I don't know. He wouldn't tell me. But I know it was big. And I know he didn't tell my mother."

I sat and the uniformed policeman wrote. How gentle these policemen were; they probably had families. They would go home tonight and someone would ask, How was your day?

"Should I tell my mother now, do you think, or would it be too much for her?" I asked.

"That's up to you," the detective said. "When was the last time you talked to your father?"

"Two days ago. Wednesday night."

"What did you talk about?"

I looked away from him, over his shoulder, blindly. For the first time that day, I felt as though I might cry. But it occurred to me as an idea, rather than a sensation—huh, I might be about to cry—and the instant it surfaced, it was gone.

(I had been talking to my mother, and then, on impulse, I'd asked to speak to him. He was hurt, sometimes, I knew from my mother, when my sister or I called and didn't ask for him; but guilt hadn't been driving me that night: I had suddenly wanted—needed, it now seemed to me—to talk to him.)

"Not much," I said. "I was planning to grow some roses this summer, so I was asking him for advice."

"He sounded normal?"

"Oh, if anything, he sounded better than usual. Sometimes we'd have these long conversations but he didn't talk—whenever I asked him a question he'd turn it around so we were talking about me instead of him. But Wednesday I asked him how he was, which usually he wouldn't really answer—he'd say, 'Okay—how are *you*?' But this time he said, 'Lousy,' but he said it in this kind of, I don't know, cheerful, funny kind of way. I asked him what he meant, and he said, 'Oh, I spilled Mom's coffee all over myself going up the stairs this morning, and the day was just downhill from there.'" I smiled at the detective: You see how elegant, the way he just laughed at all these disasters? And I felt the smile dissolving, falling off my face.

"That's all? He spilled the coffee?"

"Well, but there was more than that. The business stuff." I frowned. *Literal, this fellow, isn't he?* The thought came to me in my father's voice, the faintly English-accented one he used for irony and puns; for an instant it was as though my father and I were sharing a joke.

"But nothing specific? What else did you talk about?"

"Oh. My son. We talked about him for a while, and my father said he thought my husband and I were doing a wonderful job with him . . ." I looked at the piano again. That was the good-bye, I thought.

The policemen were getting up. The quiet one had shut his pad. I said, "Is he—I mean, have you finished up at the house?"

"No, not yet. It shouldn't be much longer. We'll let you know."

"And do you know of any—is there some kind of cleaning service we could get in there tonight? And I want that chair out of the house before my mother goes back."

The detective said, "We can remove the chair, but I don't think you'll need a cleaning service." He cleared his throat. "It's really not that bad."

We all stood for a moment, looking down at the floor.

The detective said, "We asked your mother if there was a woman friend we could call—you know, someone to be with her now. But she seemed to want Mr. Tyson."

"Uh-huh," I said.

In the next room, my mother was screaming. "Oh, my God! Oh, my God!" I pushed open the door and ran in. "Oh, my God!" my mother cried, holding out one hand to me and pointing with the other at the third policeman, the one who'd stayed in the kitchen. "He was on the *woodchipper* murder!"

"What's the woodchipper murder?" I asked.

"It's the *book* I've been reading. You know how I like those true crime books? I just *finished* it. The man who killed his wife and then put her body into the woodchipper. It happened just north of here. And I just remembered why his name was familiar—he was the policeman in the book!"

I nodded politely at the policeman, who looked down and shifted his weight from one foot to the other and then back again.

———

When the police left, I felt tired, or disappointed—I couldn't tell exactly what the feeling was, the loss of momentum, perhaps. The day had gone along as a procession of things that needed to be done; the prospect of the next task had felt, oddly, like hope. But now the tasks were completed; the anticipated relief had not come. There was no obvious next step.

It was the dinner hour. Ted and Annette were setting the long dining room table with heavy peasanty ceramic dishes, blue-and-white checked place mats, blue linen napkins. My mother was ladling the soup into a big flowered tureen. My husband was mixing a salad.

"What is this, a dinner party?" my sister muttered to me in the little passageway outside the kitchen.

"Ted's been cooking all day. It's his way of trying to help," I said; but my sister's face was dark and her red eyes glittered.

I went into the dining room and stood by the table.

"That's where your father spilled the wine on New Year's Eve," Ted said softly behind me. I looked down at a dark splotch on the porous blond wood of the table; I put my hand on the stain.

At dinner my mother and Ted did witty repartee, as though their dialogue were being documented—Look at us, we're doing witty repartee! My sister's face was frozen. Annette lit candles, handed dishes, silent and beautifully grave, a Vermeer maidservant. I couldn't eat, but occasionally I joined in the talk, casting apologetic glances at my sister: I know it's horrible to talk and laugh, but Mom and Ted are trying so hard, and if this is how they want to play it, then it's our job to help them out.

We were all still at the table when the phone rang; it was Kurt.

"You'd better talk to him," I told my mother. "He was upset before. I think he feels shut out."

"I can't help how he feels," my mother said, but she got up and took the phone from Ted and went with it into the kitchen.

The rest of us cleared the table. I put down a stack of plates on the counter and heard my mother say, "No!" a couple of times; then, "Kurt, I don't think you understand, we don't *have* the body, the police have it, I don't know where it is." Then, "Kurt, there's nothing to see, this is not a body you'd want to see . . . Kurt. No. Kurt." She held the phone away from her. "He wants to drive up here tonight."

"Tell him no," I said.

"He hung up," said my mother.

"Call him back," I said. "I'll talk to him."

"Don't bother. He won't come."

"What if he does?"

My mother shrugged. "He doesn't know where to find us."

"Mom," my sister said. "Let's at least call him back and tell him where we are."

"He won't come," my mother said again. "He always gets lost. He always says he's coming—Christmas, Daddy's birthday—and then he doesn't show up. If he cares so much, then where was he when Daddy was alive?"

"This is different," my sister said.

"He's hysterical," my mother said.

"It's his brother," I said.

"Well, it's my husband," she said.

A few minutes later I went upstairs and tried calling Kurt at the theater, but they said he had just gone onstage. I left a message saying that I hoped he'd drive up and see us tomorrow.

But all that night I wondered if he was in his car, driving along dark, frozen, unmarked roads, winding up by blind instinct at my parents' house, banging at the door.

"So, should we tell her about the loan?" I asked my husband. We were back upstairs, whispering, in Ted's study.

"I don't know," he said. "There's nothing she can do about it tonight. It might just upset her."

"It might make her feel better, to know that's why he did it."

"We don't even know how much it is." He took a deep breath. "We need to call Neil."

"Maybe we should."

I stood beside my husband as he made the call. I listened as he told Neil that it wasn't a heart attack; it was suicide. My husband said, "We know there was a loan that you guys took out to start the door company. We know that the bank had called the loan—is that right? We need to know how much it was."

I pushed a piece of paper under my husband's hand, and gave him a pencil from the silver cup on Ted's desk. I waited for the figure to appear: millions, a number that would throw my mother into debt, that would clang like a giant bell tolling, a number that would explain everything. I watched as my husband wrote down: *$220,000.*

I said out loud: "His share?"

My husband shook his head and wrote: *The whole thing.*

I divided in my head by four, for the four partners in the door company. I said, "You mean his share was fifty-five thousand?" I wrapped my arms around myself; I went into the next room, Ted's bedroom. I sat down on the big bed, which was the only piece of furniture in the room. The walls were lined with built-in drawers and cupboards, one of which gaped open to show a row of hanging shirts, grouped by color. I saw white shirts, blue ones, striped ones, dark plaid flannels. My husband came in. I said, "We could have given him that. We could have taken out a second mortgage and given him a check. *He* could have taken out a second mortgage. My God. *Neil* could have covered it, without blinking an eye."

"Maybe that's what he was afraid of, that Neil would have to cover it," my husband said. His face was white. "Maybe he was ashamed at having gotten Neil into the deal."

"I thought when we knew how much the loan was, we'd understand," I said. "All day I've been thinking that was the reason."

"Maybe it was," my husband said again.

I stood up. "Fifty-five thousand? That doesn't explain anything." I began to walk around the room; I slammed the cupboard door shut. "That is not a reason."

"Sssh." My husband came toward me with his arms out. I ducked away from him.

He said, "Should we tell your mother?"

I shrugged. "Sure."

"There's something else," he said. "Something the police told me. There was a note. Well, not a note exactly."

"What do you mean?"

"Something on the desk. An envelope. He'd written your mother's name on it."

"What was in it?"

"I'm not clear exactly. Financial information. A list of bank accounts. Should I tell your mother?"

"I don't know," I said. I went over to the window, saw my own reflection, turned away. Behind us, in the study, the phone was ringing. "I want this day to be over," I said. "I want things to stop happening."

"I know," my husband said. Then: "So, should we tell her?"

I said, "Well, now she'll know what she has and where it is."

My husband moved to leave the room. I said, "Wait," and I stood for a moment on Ted's threadbare Persian carpet, trying to purge myself of meanness before I went downstairs.

My sister and Ted were trying to talk my mother out of going home for the night.

"What are you making such a big deal for?" my mother was saying. "I don't have any problem going back there."

"Sleep here tonight," Ted said.

My sister looked at me.

"Go home tomorrow," I said. "Not tonight."

"I'll stay here with you," my sister said.

"We can't go back there anyway," I said. "The police are there."

"They've finished," said my mother. "They just called, to tell us they're leaving."

"Okay," I said slowly. And I felt another, final, surge of organizational energy. I looked at my husband. "You go over there and pack a bag for my mother. Get a nightgown and her toothbrush and—and, Mom, you tell him what you need."

"I'll go with you," Ted said.

"Oh, that's all right," said my husband.

"No, let him go with you," I said. "Mom, give Ted a list." I pulled my husband into the back hall and whispered to him, "Make sure the chair is out of there. The police told me they would get rid of it, but make sure they did. And take some paper towels and some, I don't know, Windex or Fantastik or something. All right?"

"All right," he said, and I could see that he knew what I meant, but I didn't want to take any chances.

"Get rid of all the blood," I said. "I mean it. Check the baseboards, the stairs. They probably took him out in one of those bags, but check anyway."

"I will," he said.

Annette had finished in the kitchen and gone to bed. I sat with my mother and sister by the dying fire waiting for my husband and Ted to come back.

"He always took such good care of me," my mother said sleepily. "Even today. Did you hear about the list he left?"

"How do you know about that?"

"The police told me," my mother said. "Do you think he sat there this morning, making the list?"

We didn't answer her.

"No," she said, "this morning he acted in the moment. He must have made that list some time ago, and this morning he just put it into an envelope for me and left it on the desk." She looked at me. "Are you planning to stay here tonight?"

"Of course," I said.

"It's just that I don't think Ted has enough beds. Annette's in the guest room, and there's the other little guest room down here, for me." She looked at my sister. "And you can sleep on the couch."

"Oh," I said. The thought of going back to my parents' house frightened me. I did not want to be there, sleepless, where my father had slept the night before; I did not want to be there tomorrow morning, watching the clock creep around to the last minute of his life. Yet I also knew that if I went there I would be as close to him as it was still possible to be.

"And you must want to see the baby," my mother went on. "You could drive there tonight and still be back here in time for breakfast."

"Drive where?" I asked.

"To Katherine and Neil's, of course," my mother said.

She was right. I could get in the car and drive to my husband's parents' house, an hour away; they would take care of me. I could be someplace safe for a few hours and then come back to all this, because I had that child fifty miles away: a perfectly honorable excuse, a flight from responsibility disguised as maternal duty.

There was a noise at the front door, and I got up and went out to intercept my husband and Ted in the hall.

"Was the chair gone?" I asked.

"It was out on the front porch," my husband said.

"That's what they call taking it away?"

"We're going back first thing in the morning, with the Jeep," Ted told me. "I'll get rid of it."

"Before my mother sees it," I said.

"Of course," said Ted. He was holding my mother's overnight bag.

I took it from him and opened it up. Inside there was a pale green nylon nightgown, something I had never seen my mother wearing. I took it out and unfolded it; it was narrow and silky, nearly transparent. I looked at my husband. "Where did you find this?"

"In her dresser."

"Was it in a satin case?"

"Yes."

"You can't let her see this. This is the nightgown she wore on her wedding night. She's saved it all these years; she showed it to me once."

"Oh, God," he said.

The three of us looked at each other, and the horror on their faces made me, suddenly, want to laugh.

I crumpled up the nightgown and stuffed it into the pocket of my husband's jacket. "Just tell her you couldn't find a nightgown."

"I'll lend her something," said Ted. "A shirt, or something."

I said to my husband, "Listen, the plan is for us to drive up to your parents'. We'll come back tomorrow morning."

"All right," he said, and his face mirrored my own relief.

In the car, driving along the dark roads, my husband asked if I had told my mother about the bank loan.

I shook my head in the darkness. "I'll tell her tomorrow. Or the next day." Then I asked, "Was there any blood?"

I looked sideways at him. His face was still and tight, his eyes on the road. "A little," he said. "Not much."

"But you—"

"I got it."

"Did you turn on the lights and check really carefully? Because—"

"I got it all."

"Where was it?"

He glanced at me, then back to the road. "On the baseboard. A little on the closet door."

"And the police were gone, when you got there?"

He hesitated. "No, they were still there."

"My father? Was my father—"

"No, they'd taken him away. There was just a van, I guess it was a crime-scene van, still in the driveway."

"Did you go inside it?"

"Yes, for a minute."

"What were they doing in there?"

"Drinking coffee, filling out reports." His voice grew softer. "It was sort of cozy. Like a little ship."

We didn't talk, then, for several minutes. I thought of the police, in their little lighted ship in front of the dark, empty house.

"Kurt wasn't there, was he?" I asked suddenly.

"No," my husband said, surprised.

We were on the highway now, driving fast, passing other cars. I tried not to think of my father lying in the back of some police conveyance, traveling over these same roads to wherever they were taking him. I tried to think of Katherine and Neil waiting up, in their big calm house, with my son sleeping upstairs. I looked out the window and ahead of us I saw a white Toyota Camry, exactly like my father's car, in the left-hand lane, just enough ahead of us so that I couldn't see the driver.

"Can you go a little faster?" I said to my husband. He glanced sideways at me, and then we went a little faster. But the white car was speeding up, too, as if it sensed that we were chasing it. I watched it pulling farther and farther away. And I saw that no matter how fast we went, the white car would always go faster. We would never catch up to it; I would never know who was inside.

Suicide:
anger about

I COULDN'T SUMMON ANY UP. NOT FOR THE LONGEST TIME afterward. Not at him, anyway.

Suicide:
attitude toward
his

MY FATHER DISAPPROVED OF SUICIDE.

It's odd, considering how much I don't know and will never know about him, that I should know this. I know because he talked about it.

When I was about twelve or thirteen, a friend of my grandmother's died with his wife in a suicide pact. He had been a Danish ambassador, and that's how my parents referred to him, when I heard their somber voices one evening and asked what was wrong.

Often when I tried to find out what was going on in our house, my parents would tell me it was none of my business. But this time my father sighed, and answered me. "You know the Danish ambassador?"

I didn't. I'd never even seen him. I knew vaguely that my grandmother had such a friend, but I'd never known his name, or where he lived, or whether he was a Dane who'd been an ambassador to this country or an American assigned to Denmark. But I nodded.

"Well, he was very sick," my father told me. "He knew he

was going to die soon, and he and his wife had agreed that nei-ther of them wanted to live without the other. So they killed themselves, in their apartment."

"How?" I asked.

"They—" my mother began; but my father frowned.

"Never mind how," he said. "The point is that what they did was wrong."

I didn't understand why. If he'd been dying anyway, and if they'd both agreed that the idea of one of them dying while the other survived was not only unbearable but unnecessary since they could simply choose to die together, then what was so wrong about it? I didn't ask. I was still stinging from his "Never mind how," the implication that my asking "how" was either tasteless or irrelevant, or both.

He went on to say that suicide was always wrong, because you were cutting off the possibility that things might improve. "People assume they know what the future is going to be like," he said, "but those assumptions can be wrong. I've known people who've been sick and been told they were dying, but they got better. Either the sickness went away, or the doctor made a mistake in the diagnosis.

"You can't throw away your life, no matter how hard it gets," he said, "because it's all you have."

I was in college, home for a weekend, when my parents told me that Ricky Shellenberger had killed himself.

The Shellenbergers had been friends of my parents, with two kids about the same age as my sister and I. It was one of those friendships that is actually based on the compatibility of two people—in this case, my mother and Karen Shellen-berger—but that insists on the compatibility of two entire families. Look, we're parallel! Look how well we fit together! Only we weren't, and we didn't, quite.

We were always going over to the Shellenbergers' house. While the grownups sat in the living room or out on the patio talking—my mother and Karen in animated, laughing voices, on and on; my father and Sherm Shellenberger quieter, more reticent—my sister and I were upstairs with Rachel and Ricky Shellenberger, uneasy and awkward. "What would you like to do?" they would ask, and we'd say we didn't know. They were polite, deferential, kind. Their rooms were neat and organized, and attested to the worthiness of their pursuits: Rachel's violin case and music stand; Ricky's stamp albums and terrarium.

It wasn't as if there were no playthings. There were board games, neatly stacked on shelves. There were baseball gloves, jump ropes, a badminton set which was still kept in its original packaging, taken out and then put away again each time it was used, net neatly furled and tucked into its original indentation, shuttlecocks lined up in their individual slots. We had similar toys and games at home, but ours were always in disarray—stray backgammon tiles in the checkers box; a joker in the card pack redesignated in ink as the two of clubs; a suspicion that there weren't really enough "U"s left to properly serve the "Q" in the Scrabble box, though no one ever sat down to actually count them.

Rachel and Ricky, with their respectfully maintained toys and their careful manners, were simply too good. My sister and I always felt that our mother was saying, "Why can't you be more like Rachel and Ricky?" ("Did I tell you Rachel Shellenberger got a scholarship to take lessons at the Hartford Conservatory? If you practiced more, I bet you could get one too.")

But though Rachel and Ricky's goodness certainly appealed

to the grownups, it wasn't just decorative. It was real. Once we were invited to the Shellenbergers' house on a Friday night. We all stood around the table, and Sherm Shellenberger suddenly began half saying, half singing some words in Hebrew. He went on and on and on. It was formal and fervent. I'd never heard anything like it: my mother's family was Jewish, but no one ever celebrated anything. The unfamiliarity of it made me nervous, and I started to laugh. I tried to stop, which only made it worse. My parents glared at me; Karen and Rachel ignored me; Sherm kept on going. But Ricky, standing across the table, gave me a long mild look, vastly kind and a little amused, that seemed at once to understand the reason for the laughter, to sympathize with my embarrassed inability to stop it, and to forgive me for it.

When my mother told me that Ricky had killed himself, alone in his college dorm room, I remembered that look he'd given me, the detached generosity of it.

"He must have been very sick," she was saying. "Because what he did was—he had a knife, and basically what he did was to commit hara-kiri."

"It's a terrible thing," my father said.

"The perfect family," my mother said, shaking her head.

I was trying to imagine how anyone could disembowel himself. I was remembering Ricky's calm brown eyes looking at me across that dinner table.

"Didn't you always think they were the perfect family?" my mother asked. "What went wrong, do you think?" She kept talking; she kept using the word "perfect," as if perfection, the thing that had blessed and elevated the Shellenbergers, was the thing that had now undone them, or the thing they were being punished for.

"Well, I guess there is no such thing as the perfect family," she concluded. Her voice was hard and brisk; she sounded almost relieved. "Right?" she asked.

My father and I looked back at her.

I didn't say anything. I was just dazed, by the violence and loneliness and mystery of Ricky's death. I didn't want to analyze it with my mother, or guess about it, or make emotional observations.

"It's a terrible thing," my father said again. His face was impassive, blank. "It shouldn't have happened."

That was all he said. It wasn't like with the Danish ambassador, whom he'd disapproved of for committing suicide. He didn't seem to be blaming Ricky. It was the suicide itself—not the person who had done it, but the act, the fact that it had happened—that was terrible.

A year or two later, my grandmother was taken to the hospital, in a coma. She was found lying unconscious on the floor of her apartment by some of her students, on the morning when she was to go into the hospital to have her foot amputated, something she'd been fighting against for months.

My grandmother lived for another six weeks, never regaining consciousness. While she was in the hospital, my mother told me that there was a rumor (originating where? With my grandmother's students? With my mother herself, whose habit of emotional speculation could be reckless and often uncannily accurate?) that my grandmother had made a botched suicide attempt. That she'd taken pills, but not enough to kill her.

I asked my father what he thought. His mouth tightened. "Absolutely not," he said, coldly. "Mother would find the idea of suicide absolutely unacceptable."

No discussion. No gray areas; no equivocating. No entertaining, however uneasy, of the possibility that life might, under certain circumstances, become unbearable; and no metaphysical questioning about what the person who found it unbearable was or was not morally entitled to do.

So what happened?

Did he change his mind at the end, discarding his long-held principles when he finally discovered, for himself, what it was like to hit the wall of a hopeless and terminal misery, when his own life became unbearable?

Or maybe he needed to make clear pronouncements against it because he was secretly, helplessly, attracted. Maybe he was like one of those Victorian clergymen who preached against vice and then went out after dark into gaslit London, in search of a streetwalker.

And although I certainly heard him use the words "wrong" and "terrible" and "unacceptable" in connection with suicide, I also heard him speak of it quite differently.

"My grandfather killed himself," he told me once, apropos of nothing. We were sitting together in the living room, listening to music. It was a Sunday morning; I was grown up and married, visiting my parents for the weekend. It was years before he died. This wasn't foreshadowing; it was just conversation.

"Really?" I said.

"He was getting to be an old man, and he decided he didn't like being an old man and he was going to like it even less as it went along. So he went upstairs, ran a bath, and cut his—"

I don't remember anymore what he cut: his wrists or his throat. My father told me this a long time ago. What I do remember is the tone of my father's voice: matter-of-fact, almost approving. Putting oneself out of the way like this, he implied, using a razor in the clean privacy of one's bath, had a kind of self-reliant, nineteenth-century honor and dignity about it. A choice was made and was acted on, without dithering or discussion. This act was not one of cowardice or abnegation; it was an adult, fully cognizant assumption of responsibility, the rational culmination of a well-lived life now beginning to decline.

So here we are, in the kind of paradoxical muddle that seems to be the destination of much of what I write about my father. I thought he disapproved of suicide, but now I'm not sure if that was true; and even if it was true, I'm not sure what it tells me about his death. I'll never know whether, for him, suicide was a long-considered, maybe even long-resisted, possibility or a sudden brainstorm. I'll never know what he would have said if I had been able to ask him, a day or an hour or a minute before he died, whether he thought suicide was wrong.

"Always"?

"Sometimes"?

"It depends"?

"Yes, but I'm going to do it anyway"?

This is what I do know, or what I believe. When someone dies this way, you're left with unanswerable questions, unresolvable paradoxes. You have to become a posthumous mind reader. You have to look at the things you know, those small, possibly unreliable and often contradictory scraps of memory, and come up with your own version of the truth.

Here's mine. My father disapproved of suicide, except for the times when he thought it admirable. And except for the one time when he found it necessary.

Suicide:
attitude toward
mine

IT WAS SOMETHING TERRIBLE AND ROMANTIC THAT POETS DID. It was extreme. It was sad beyond imagining. It was out there, somewhere—I knew it existed, I knew that people did it— but it was remote. It had nothing to do with us.

Suicide:
belief that change of scene might unlock emotion concerning

IMAGINE A WOMAN, ASLEEP, WITH HER HUSBAND SLEEPING NEXT to her. The quilts are pulled up around their shoulders. It's very early, still dark, a cold February morning. The phone rings.

Her husband passes her the receiver. She learns that her father has shot himself.

Here's what she feels in the first minutes.
Nothing.

They pack a bag and drive to Connecticut, where it happened. They go through the day. Time moves slowly, but still it is moving, carrying her in unnoticed, unwilled increments away from her father. Carrying not just her, but also her mother and her sister and her son and her husband, everyone who knew him. They are all moving forward, away from the place where he stopped.

That night, she and her husband drive to his mother's house. For a moment, as they come up the dark driveway, the sight of her mother-in-law, silhouetted in the open doorway, fills her with something that is almost a feeling. Not quite comfort, but the anticipation of what comfort might feel like: an imagined yielding, the luxury of collapsing against something detached and solid. She likes her mother-in-law. But it's also that this house is neutral, out of the path of destruction. A different place. Things will feel different here.

But nothing is different. Her mother-in-law is kind. She has some cigarettes in the drawer of her desk. They sit on the couch in the enormous kitchen and smoke them. Brandy is brought. Questions are asked. How did he do it? Did anyone know he was thinking about it? Why do you think he did it?

She smokes, drinks, answers.

The house isn't neutral. The relationships are complicated. Her father and her husband's stepfather were in a business deal together. Money got lost. Her father felt ashamed and guilty.

Did you know he had a gun? her husband's stepfather asks her, bending to refill her brandy glass.

I knew he had a rifle a long time ago, but not a handgun, she answers. Her voice is gentle, numb. No point in blaming her husband's stepfather; it wasn't his fault.

Later, when they are upstairs undressing for bed, her husband puts his arms around her. She just stands there. She says: It's like he busted through the guardrail. It's like there was a sign that said DO NOT GO BEYOND THIS POINT, and he went beyond that point.

Her husband is unbuttoning her sweater. You're so tired, he says. Come to bed. I'll hold you.

You loved him, she says to her husband. Didn't you?

Yes, her husband says.

They go into the bathroom, brush their teeth, spit together into the sink.

Their son, who is three, is sleeping in the room next to theirs. They stand looking down at him. He is lying in his portable crib, holding his stuffed white bear. His head is turned to the side, his lips flared out like a flower.

She almost whispers: Will he remember my father, do you think?

But doesn't say it. She and her husband both know he won't remember.

All day long, she's been dully curious about the next thing. *What will it feel like to see my mother?* she thought in the car driving down to Connecticut.

Then, after she saw her mother: *How will it feel when it gets dark?*

Driving to her mother-in-law's house: *Will it be different when we get there?*

But it keeps feeling the same, everywhere. It feels like nothing.

Now she's sitting on the floor of her mother-in-law's guest room, leaning her back against the bed, wondering how she'll feel when her husband, who is lying in bed struggling valiantly to stay awake to keep her company, finally loses the struggle and falls asleep. *Then I'll be alone,* she thinks. *Maybe I'll feel it when I'm alone.*

The TV is on: *Marcus Welby.* The actor who played him tried to kill himself last month. Something had gone wrong (or right—the attempt failed, anyway), they'd found him and gotten him to the hospital in time. She remembers reading an article in a magazine, earlier this week. Reading it and thinking, if she thought anything at all: *Poor man, his poor family.*

Marcus Welby looks paternal, rock-solid. (Although those things don't really fit together anymore, do they?) He is taking care of a troubled teenager. Marcus Welby talks to the boy's parents, his teachers, his sister. No one can figure out why the boy is sick; no one understands why he is miserable. Then suddenly, on the screen: a gun. The boy has it. Black and stubby.

She reaches out to shut off the TV, but she's not quite fast enough. The shot has been fired, with a shattering crack. The gun's tiny dark mouth is pointing at her, and then it vanishes, sucked into a blue dot in the center of the now-black screen. The dot hangs there for several seconds. Then it fades and disappears.

She turns around to look at her husband, to see whether he found the image disturbing. He's asleep. Deep oblivious breathing. She's alone, for the first time since her father's death.

Now, she thinks.

Now nothing.

Suicide:
day after
brother's appearance

THE DAY AFTER MY FATHER DIED, MY MOTHER'S HOUSE FILLED up with people. Neighbors bringing turkeys. Cousins nobody remembered, who'd driven up from New Jersey. My husband's father spotted my husband's mother across the living room, and went over to say hello to her. They'd been divorced for twenty-five years. She saw him coming and turned her head away, refusing to speak to or even look at him. My mother, standing near me, seeing all this, muttered, "She can't even be nice to him in my house? Today of all days? I should have to worry about smoothing this shit over?"

"Leave them alone, they're grownups," I said, but she was already moving across the room, smiling stiffly at my husband's father, her arm stretched out in compensatory welcome. The doorbell rang again, and I went to answer it.

At first I thought it was my father standing there. My mouth began to relax, to grin: I imagined the stunning relief of saying, "You won't believe it when I tell you what we're all doing here."

Then I realized it was his brother, Kurt.

He put his arms around me, and I buried my face in him. He was tall and warm and solid. He resembled my father—not exactly, but more closely than anyone else on earth. The same mouth, the pale blue eyes—Russian eyes—under thick wiry brows, the big bony nose. He had that unmistakable brother-look of having hatched from the same egg. His physical presence was so powerful that the minor differences between them—he was a little shorter, he had more hair left—didn't matter. Oh, God, I thought, so that's what my father looked like. I had already forgotten; and the forgetting was only going to get worse with time.

My father had not been close to Kurt, and I barely knew him. But I just stayed there, folded against him. He held me and said my name over and over, in my father's voice.

Finally we let each other go. He ran a hand through his long, thin white hair. He was wearing an old black corduroy jacket; the pile was thinning at the elbows, and some of the cuff buttons were missing. He and his wife had come once to visit for a weekend, when I was a child. They were supposed to arrive by lunchtime but they hadn't shown up until late afternoon, and they'd slept until noon the next day. "Actors' hours," my parents had sniffed. They hadn't made their beds, or offered to strip the sheets; their wet towels littered the bathroom floor.

I had another memory of Kurt coming to visit, when I was even younger. He was playing Ariel in a production of *The Tempest* in Hartford. We went to the matinee, and he came to our house for an early supper before the evening performance. I hadn't understood the play, but it had been exciting to see my uncle, simultaneously familiar and unrecognizable, leaping around the stage in white tights, his blond hair goldened and standing up in peaks like sun rays all over his head. He kept his makeup on when he came to our house—there wouldn't have been time to remove and reapply it. His face was painted white, with black and gold lines around the eyes. He was glamorous, an uncle and not an uncle, a spirit and not a spirit, gilded, but wearing an ordinary blue button-down shirt and gray slacks, talking to my parents about the recent blackout and the New York transit strike.

When I'd seen him last, ten years ago at my grandmother's memorial service, he had still been blond. It was only the startling sight of his white hair now that made me realize how long ago that had been.

The living room had gotten very crowded. "My mother's here somewhere," I murmured. Kurt put his hand to his forehead and worked his fingers back and forth; apparently he was no more eager to see my mother than she was to see him. "Could I get a cup of tea, do you think?" he asked.

"Of course."

I led him toward the kitchen. I wanted to stay close to him, to take care of him. And I was ashamed of my reluctance to talk to him on the phone the day before. I'd been afraid that he might be too emotional. But what could "too emotional" possibly mean, in a situation like this?

In the kitchen, Kurt dropped into a chair at the table, pushing aside a bakery box someone had brought from New York. "I never thought he'd do it," he said, as if doing it had been a possible choice all along, a plainly visible brush in the paint box that the artist had never yet had occasion to use.

Maybe he knew my father better than I'd realized. Maybe he was going to explain why this had happened.

I went over and shook the teakettle. It was nearly empty; I took it over to the sink and filled it. Kurt was talking. He was saying that he'd always known my father was damaged, but that he had never realized how deep the damage had gone. He said that my father had put up a strong front. His willpower had been incredible, Kurt said. "He thought that if he willed everything to be all right, then it would be. He thought if he could make it all look a certain way—solid and healthy—then it actually *would* be solid and healthy. He thought he could change deep feelings, erase old injuries, just by deciding: *Enough already.*"

I sat down at the table with him. He was speaking in my father's voice—those eerily familiar deep tones, the slight hint of nasality, the slow, carefully assembled diction hinting that English hadn't been their original language—but he was saying things my father never would have said. It was illicitly fascinating and morally queasy. I was torn between wanting to listen and wanting to preserve my father's privacy. He would have disapproved of this conversation. "Psychobabble," he would have said.

The teakettle began to whimper and then to shriek. I got up and put a tea bag into a mug. "Do you take milk or sugar?" I asked Kurt.

"Do you have any honey?"

Heavy footsteps were coming into the kitchen: my mother. "Are you making tea?" she asked me. Then she caught sight of Kurt.

Kurt stood up and went over to her, and kissed her cheek. "This is a terrible thing," he said.

"Yes, Kurt, it is," my mother said, as if she'd figured this out long before and was peeved at him for only now arriving at the realization.

I got down a second mug from the cupboard, and reached for another tea bag.

My mother and Kurt stood just inside the kitchen doorway, facing each other. "So this happened yesterday morning?" he asked her.

"Very early," she said. "I wasn't even up yet."

Kurt sighed. "You know, Lee, I wish someone had thought to call me earlier. I don't really understand why it took until three o'clock for me to hear about this."

"We were busy, Kurt," my mother said, loudly. "We had a lot on our minds."

"I know," Kurt said then, and he touched her shoulder. "I know you did, Lee."

"Do we have any honey?" I asked.

My mother looked surprised. "No. Why?"

"For Kurt's tea."

My mother tightened her lips. "Everyone else is having sugar or Sweet 'N Low."

Other people came into the kitchen, and my mother and Kurt were happy enough to be separated. He and I had been interrupted, but I didn't mind. If there were sides to be taken here—open discussion of feelings versus a stoic resolution to keep one's own counsel—then I was going to side with my father. Much as I wanted information and explanations, I was going to abide by his preference for silence.

I don't think I understood yet that what he had done was final. I think I believed that if I proved I was a good enough daughter—loyal enough, discreet enough—I could get him back.

I made a big pot of tea, put it on a tray with some cups, and carried it out to the living room. In the course of the afternoon, I passed near Kurt several times. He was moving around, talking to different people, asking them what time yesterday they had been notified of my father's death.

Suicide:
day after
concern that he will be viewed
differently now

ANOTHER MOMENT, FROM THAT SAME AFTERNOON. PEOPLE were saying things to me like "My God, your poor father. The pain he must have been in." And I was saying things like "Yes, I know. So listen—how's grad school going?" I was in loony high-hostess mode. I had my aunt Irene backed into a corner, and I was asking about her vacation plans. She was going to Italy in a couple of months. Where? I wanted to know.

She looked troubled, and embarrassed. "Florence. And Venice, and Ravenna. We're not going to make it to Rome this time."

I smiled and nodded. I wanted to show her that, yes, my father had killed himself, but that didn't mean we couldn't still have a normal conversation. I said, "My father always said that Venice is a much better city than Rome."

Irene's shoulders tensed in her little dressmaker suit. "Yes, well, that's what we've decided. For this trip at least." Her voice was gentle, but I knew that there was distaste there. Maybe it was for the strangeness of me and my chirpy small talk. But more, I thought, for my father. Irene had loved him. But I could see, in that moment, that he'd been permanently shifted from one category to another. From the world of people whose opinions about various Italian cities were worth listening to, to the world of crazy people.

What difference did it make that he'd liked Venice better than Rome? He killed himself—what did he know?

Suicide:
day after
"little room" discussion with his business partner

MY FATHER'S BUSINESS PARTNER AND HIS WIFE WERE PUTTING their coats on, getting ready to leave. I went over to them and thanked them for coming. "I'm sorry I didn't get a chance to talk to you, Gil."

Gil shook his head. "I've been wanting to talk to you, too. Or your mother. I wanted to tell someone about what happened Wednesday."

"What?" I asked.

"It just wasn't like him. We were out on the turnpike together. Your dad was driving. It was rush hour, snowing a little, getting dark. Your dad went to change lanes, he pulled out, and there was this big truck bearing down. It almost hit us, the guy sounded his horn—and Jesus, was Paul upset. I never saw him so upset. He pulled over into the breakdown lane, he stopped the car, and he just sat there. I said, 'Paul, you almost got us killed.' And he wouldn't answer me. He just sat there behind the wheel, just kind of staring at nothing. It was like he was in a trance. And then he wouldn't drive anymore. He made me get behind the wheel."

"Oh," I said.

"Not that I think that caused his death, or anything. But sometimes there is a straw that breaks the camel's back. Or at least it might be a clue to his state of mind this past week."

"Right," I said. "Thanks for telling me, Gil." I was beginning to see that there was never going to be a straightforward sentence: *He did it because* . . . It was all going to be fragments, a snarl. All these bits would keep coming, and that's all they would ever be, bits. Nobody knew the whole of it. It was as if one person was saying, "Well, I knew he had matches, but I didn't think he'd ever light them," and someone else was saying, "I knew he lived in a house made of paper, but I didn't know he had matches."

Gil was still talking. "I kept asking him, after that, 'Hey, Paul, what's the matter, are you okay?' But he wouldn't answer me. It's not like I didn't *try* to find out what was bugging him."

"No, no, I'm sure you tried," I murmured. I felt sorry for Gil. The business was such a mess, and now he'd have to try to clean it up alone. I put a hand on his coat sleeve. "But listen, how are you? Are you doing okay?"

"I don't know," he said. "Yeah, I suppose. I'll be all right." Then he laughed. "Too bad I can't just walk away, isn't it?"

"Gil," said his wife.

"You think I haven't thought about it, too? You think I haven't wanted to do what your dad did, just go into that little room and close the door and take myself out of it? Your dad doesn't have to worry anymore. He's out of it all right. All right for him. But what about the rest of us? We can't just go into the little room, can we?"

"Stop it," his wife said. She opened the door, threw me a quick embarrassed look, and got him outside.

The door closed behind them. I stood there looking at it.

I had assumed that all the people closest to him would still love him—would maybe even love him more, because now we were all beginning to understand how secretly fragile he had been all along, or had become at the end.

The little room. As if it were a cozy, tidy place.

Or a yearned-for destination.

Shit, Gil, you make it sound like he packed a suitcase and jetted off to Bermuda.

Suicide:
day after
search warrant

MORE FOOD SHOWED UP: A FRUIT BASKET, A PIE. THERE WAS NO room left for them on the kitchen countertops, so I went into the laundry room and set the basket down on top of the dryer. As I turned to leave, I saw a piece of paper lying on the washing machine.

SEARCH WARRANT, it was headed.

I didn't read it carefully. My eyes jumped around and found the word MURDER, under the heading REASON FOR SEARCH.

I was leaning over it, scanning the rest of the document trying to make it make sense, when my mother came in.

"Oh," she said.

"Why a search warrant?" I asked.

"It's a formality," she said. "That's what the detective told me."

"But what were they searching for?"

"Nothing. I think they needed it in order to take things out of the house."

She put her hand on the orange cellophane covering the fruit basket and then bent down to sniff the outside of the pie box. When she straightened up she said, without looking at me, "There was a word on that paper that really upset me. I'm sure you know which word I mean."

"Do they think Daddy was murdered?"

"No. No. The detective told me 'no.' No, they know he wasn't murdered. I mean, what, do they think *I* did it? 'Is *that* what you think?' I asked him. But he said no, no, of course not. That's just the word they use when something like this happens. They have to investigate it as *if* it's a murder, even though they know he killed himself."

"They shouldn't throw around a word like that."

My mother put a hand over her mouth and said behind it, "Can you imagine what it was like for me, seeing that word?"

I nodded, and followed her back into the kitchen.

Suicide:
day after
speculation relating to bulge

AT DINNER THAT NIGHT MY MOTHER SAID SUDDENLY, "THERE
was a bulge on his head."

We all looked at her. "What?" I said.

"A bulge. This funny . . . bulge." She touched a spot on the
top of her head. "Right here. I noticed it when I found him."

There was a silence. The cousins and friends had gone
home. We were sitting around her kitchen table—my mother,
Ted, my sister, my husband and me—eating a turkey one of
the neighbors had brought. There were sweet potatoes, too,
which no one in our family had ever liked. They were mounded
up, glowing, sprinkled with herbs, in a little blue pottery bowl.
I had been thinking about the solemn, lavish trouble someone
had gone to, cooking and mashing the potatoes for us with
some careful seasoning that no one would ever taste. I felt sorry
for those unwanted potatoes, and for the hands that had pre-
pared them. I hoped someone in our house knew whom to return the bowl to.

I had been thinking about all this when my mother spoke
up about the bulge; and the residual melancholy about the blue

bowl of glowing potatoes stayed with me for just a moment, fondly: such a foolish simple thing to feel sad about.

I cleared my throat. "Maybe," I said, "he was sick."

My mother, seemingly carefree now that she had made her announcement, speared a piece of broccoli with jaunty energy and ate it.

The rest of us were all looking at one another.

Ted said, "Was it possible that he had a brain tumor?"

My mother frowned, as if Ted had said something incredibly vulgar. She shook her head and ate another big hunk of broccoli.

"Had he seen his doctor recently?" I pressed. I had become sure, already, in these few moments, that here was the explanation for my father's death. The missing puzzle piece that would make the whole picture clear. He had gone to the doctor, been told he had untreatable brain cancer, and decided on a fast, private death. He hadn't told us about the diagnosis because he knew we would try to talk him into treatments he didn't want. Also, I thought, he'd been unable to bear the prospect of seeing us react to the news: the sorrow, the fear, all the big emotions heaving messily within the family. If his situation was really hopeless, then what was the point of going through all that? Better to duck out through a side door, and to trust that once we discovered the reason for his swift exit, we would understand and forgive him.

I said to my mother, "Do you think there's a chance he might have gotten some really awful diagnosis?"

"How would I know?" my mother said. "He never told me anything."

I was taken aback at her choosing this moment to go into

this particular riff. "You could call his doctor, and ask. Find out if he'd been in recently, if they'd found something wrong with him."

"What difference does it make? He's dead."

My sister looked at me, and then asked my mother, "But aren't you curious? If that bulge was a brain tumor, and if that's why he did it, wouldn't you want to find out?"

My sister, my husband, Ted, and I kept glancing at one another. We all thought she was being strange, obstinate, obtuse.

"You know, Lee," Ted said, "it would make sense, wouldn't it? Maybe he got the diagnosis and just decided the hell with it. Can't you just hear Paul saying 'The hell with it'? Don't you think that's what he would have said?"

My mother bent her head, shaking it from side to side and gripping the rim of her dinner plate as if it were a steering wheel.

"How do you know what he would have said?" my sister asked Ted.

I didn't want there to be a fight. Especially not a scuffle in an alley that was somewhere off the main avenue where this whole brain-tumor thing was happening. But I knew why my sister was annoyed. I felt it too. I wanted to tell Ted: Stop making my father a character. We don't need you to interpret him for us.

"How do *you* know?" my sister said again.

"I don't know," Ted said mildly. "I'm just saying, it's not unheard of. As a reason for suicide."

We poked around at our turkey for a few moments, passed the salt, looked at the potatoes. The scuffle was averted.

"Mom," I said finally. "Why don't we call his doctor after dinner?"

My mother put her elbow on the table, her forehead against her palm. "Next week. Maybe I'll talk to the doctor next week."

"It might be better to do it tonight," Ted said, lightly stroking the surface of his plate with his fork. My mother closed her eyes. Ted looked at me again.

My father's body was still at the state coroner's office. It still existed; it hadn't yet been released for cremation. If we had any questions about it, we needed to ask now.

"Are they supposed to call you, after the autopsy?" I asked.

My mother flinched at the word "autopsy." "Why should they? It doesn't take a genius to figure out the cause of death here."

"No," I said, looking down at my hands knotted in my lap, turning over and over. "But that bulge you saw on his head— maybe tonight is the best time to follow up on that."

"Maybe," my mother said.

"Because there might have been a brain tumor which he knew about, and that's why he did it. Or maybe that bulge was a brain tumor he *didn't* know about, which was pressing on some nerve or behavioral center. Maybe it affected his mood, his personality even—"

"I don't have to know tonight," my mother said, picking up her fork again.

She looked at her plate and ate. The rest of us looked at each other. That was as far as we could go. We'd been as brutal as any of us had felt able to be. None of us had felt able to say: *The coroner would have looked at the chest wound but he may not have paid any attention to the head. Tonight is probably the last chance to cut him up some more before he is burned.*

We finished dinner. My mother went and sat in the living room with Ted. My sister carried some plates into the kitchen, where my husband and I were washing up. "I hate him," she said.

"Daddy?" I asked.

My sister jerked her thumb toward the living room. "No. Him."

I took the plates from her and started rinsing them.

"I mean, what is he doing here? Doesn't he ever go home?"

"Apparently not," I said, airily; and again I was aware of something that had started happening in the day since my father's death: I was speaking in his voice.

We kept talking about Ted while we cleaned up the kitchen. We spent a lot of time on the turquoise sweater he was wearing. "Aggressively bright! Aggressively!" we kept saying. We decided he'd worn something aggressively bright on purpose, just to make clear his stance that any kind of mourning was tacky. The word "aggressively," repeated so many times, started to seem funny. Little bits of spit flew out of our mouths, visible under the halogen ceiling lights, making us laugh. My husband watched us, with a gentle sad look on his face. He wasn't laughing, and he did most of the kitchen cleanup.

None of us mentioned the bulge, or the doctor, or the coroner. My mother had staked out the response to the brain-tumor question, and the rest of us had lined up meekly behind her.

My husband offered to pursue it. Later that night, when we were lying together in the single bed in my mother's study, next door to the room where my father had killed himself, my husband asked me whether I would like him to call the coroner in the morning.

I was lying stiffly in his arms. After a while I shrugged. The bulge speculation had been so dazzling, so plausible at dinnertime, but now, at midnight, it had burned itself out. I didn't want my husband to check with medical experts, to dig for a definitive answer. I was already pretty sure what the answer would be, and I didn't want to hear it. I wanted to hold on to the very slight possibility that the brain-tumor theory might be true—that there might be a simple, rational explanation for what my father had done.

Suicide:
deviation from chronological narrative of

UP UNTIL NOW, I'VE PRETTY MUCH BEEN STICKING TO A STAN-
dard linear way of telling the story of my father's suicide.
I've adhered to chronology: first this happened, then that
happened.

I'm not going to be able to keep it up.

Late in the afternoon, on the day after my father's death,
my husband and I drove to the local Unitarian church to see if
we could arrange to hold a memorial service there in a few days.
We met with a young minister who was solicitously eager to
let us use the building.

"Was your father's death sudden?" she asked me.

I said that it had been.

"Oh, how hard for you. Was he very old?"

"Sixty-one," I said. By this point I was bracing myself.

"Oh, dear," she said. "That's young. What did he die of?"

"He shot himself." I said it fiercely, almost proudly, with
childish defiance. Take that, you earnest minister, you. I wasn't
seriously worried that she might rescind the offer of the church
once she knew we were going to use it to eulogize a suicide; it

was more the simple playground need to find someone to punch after having been punched myself.

She winced. I could see her squaring her shoulders, preparing to wade in with some pastoral counseling. "Do you know why he did it?" she asked.

People had been asking me that all day, at my mother's house. I had tried, obediently, to respond. Um, he was having some business problems. Um, we don't really know yet.

In one sense, I knew exactly why my father had done it. I felt as if I were standing on a mountaintop looking down at the entire topography of his life, a landscape of hurts and failures and physical ailments and disgraces and shames and exhaustion and hopelessness that was suddenly—from this new, high vantage point that had become accessible only with his death—fully visible for the first time. I realized already, looking back at the moment yesterday morning when I had first learned of his death, that in addition to my genuine disbelief, I had also known that what I was being told was true—had known it so deeply and clearly that his suicide didn't even seem like news. It felt like something I'd known about for a long time, which was only now being confirmed by an official source. At the same time that I'd been thinking, "Oh no!" I had also thought: "Of course."

I knew, but I didn't know.

I knew, but I couldn't explain what I knew.

I knew, but I also thought it was possible that what I knew was wrong.

When the minister asked if I knew why he'd done it, I shrugged. "I think there were a number of different reasons."

Poor woman, she kept trying. "Do you think he might have been depressed?"

I snapped, "Gee, I guess he must have been."

All of us—she, my husband, and I—stood there for a moment and let this piece of rudeness dissipate in the air, like cigarette smoke. It hadn't made me feel any better to respond with sarcasm to what had seemed like a spectacularly stupid question. But I couldn't find the energy or grace to apologize, either. She and my husband went on talking, about what time on Monday the church was available and where people could park once the lot was full. I stood there feeling a new kind of loneliness. I saw that the question that would accompany my father from now on, asked by people who had known him and by people who hadn't, was going to be "why?" It was a naïve, simplistic question. There could never be an answer—certainly not a neat answer that began with the word "because."

"Because he was depressed"?

"Because he had business problems"?

"Because he had business problems and family problems, and was depressed"?

All of the above. None of the above.

I might figure out all the reasons and add them up, but I still wouldn't get the answer my father had gotten when he'd done the same piece of math.

What was it about him that made him add up the reasons and come up with dying as the right answer?

Had he been adding up reasons? Was it possible to arrange rational causes in a column and arrive at an irrational result?

Was his death a rational act, or an irrational one?

Was his suicide a decision he made, or a force beyond his power to control?

Did he have a choice?

But let's be honest here. I did not stand in the church vestry formulating all these questions while my husband and the minister discussed parking arrangements. The only question I recognized and acknowledged that day was the simple, dumb, inescapable "why" that the minister had raised. It was a question I scorned because it seemed beside the point, a question only an outsider would ask.

And yet it's the question that has obsessed me for the past fifteen years.

The other questions—whether or not he was rational, whether he had a choice—came later. They didn't appear suddenly, or in dramatic settings. If they had—if I'd been driving on a snowy highway one night and had narrowly missed being sideswiped by a truck, and had pulled my car over to the side of the road and sat there shaking and suddenly remembering what my father's business partner had told me about how my father had nearly been sideswiped two days before his death, if I had sat there and thought My God, now I know exactly how he felt!—if there had been a lot of incidents like that, then I could write this as a chronological narrative. If my understanding of my father's death had been a straightforward pilgrim's progress, a journey from bewilderment to insight with well-marked stops along the way, then it would make sense to start at the beginning and continue to the end.

But it wasn't like that.

The story of my father's death—what I think led up to it, and the impact it had on my family—is a messy one. A lot of things bore down on him for years, and a lot of things changed after he died. If you take it year by year—chronologically—not much happens. It's when you begin to look at it thing by thing that the story starts to emerge.

It's a crooked, looping, labyrinthine story. You walk into the maze, pick a path, and follow it as far as you can, until you hit a dead end. You realize: no, that's not it; or that was partially right, but not entirely. Or maybe you don't hit a wall—maybe you make it all the way through to the exit, but then you start wondering if there are other paths that would have worked, too. You realize you haven't figured out the entire maze yet, and that's your goal. You want to know the whole of it.

So you keep going back to the beginning. Or to a beginning, anyhow. The fiendish thing about this particular maze is that there are so many different beginnings, and an infinite number of possible places to end.

Suicide:
factors that may have had direct
or indirect bearing on
expensive good time

MY MOTHER IS SEVENTY-NINE; MY FATHER HAS BEEN DEAD FOR fifteen years.

"Sometimes I dream about him," she said, the last time I went to visit her.

"What kind of dreams?" I asked.

She shrugged and shook her head.

I asked her what he was like, in the dreams.

"He's okay," she said, after thinking for a moment. She sounded faintly surprised. "He's young. He's okay."

She is in a rehab place. She woke up one morning about three weeks ago, got out of bed, and fell. Her legs were numb. At the hospital they found swelling around the spine, pressing on the nerves. They decided it was a virus, maybe a rare reaction to a flu shot. They pumped her full of steroids, antibiotics, and tranquilizers. After a week they moved her over to the rehab wing. Every day she has to dress herself, and a big pulley hauls her from her bed over to a wheelchair. "They really push you here," she says, annoyed. She still can't walk or stand.

"How did I get to be an old lady, alone in this terrible place?" she asked me over the phone last night.

I said, "I know, it must be really scary." I thought, Stop trying to make me feel guilty. "But I thought you said the care there was good."

"I don't mean that this hospital is a terrible place," she said. "I mean in life. How did I get to be alone in such a terrible place?"

She would sometimes call me in the morning, after he died, to tell me she'd dreamed about him the night before. "It was terrible," she would say.

She is sitting at a table in some business place, a conference room. One of the walls is made of glass, and he is standing on the other side of the glass, in his raincoat. The other people at the table tell her: He's a codfish salesman.

She cries out: But I don't want to be married to a codfish salesman!

Behind the glass, he turns and begins to walk away from her.

No, come back, I didn't mean it, it's all right. I don't mind if you're a codfish salesman!

But he keeps walking away.

"Then I was awake. And I wanted to go back in and fix it?" she said, as if asking a question: did I know what she meant? "But the dream was like the glass wall. I couldn't find a way to get back in."

Ted Tyson started off as a customer. My mother had been working in real estate for a few years, since my father's string of

73

business failures had convinced her that she needed to make some money of her own and build up a bank account, separate from his. She was in her early sixties then; Ted was probably ten years younger. He came up from New York to look at houses and told my mother he didn't want to ride in her station wagon, no fun; instead he'd drive her, in his Jeep.

She called me that night. "It *was* fun," she said, a little breathless. "You're high up, and you feel like you're going to fall out. And you know how twisty the roads here are? Well, he was talking away the whole time—and *looking* at me while he talked. I'm surprised we weren't killed."

Ted was a handbag designer. He made leather purses, with gold interlocking "T"s for clasps. And he made little jeweled evening bags that were shaped like things: dragonflies, and teapots, and slices of watermelon. His bags showed up in *W* and *Vogue* a lot, my mother said. Actresses were sometimes photographed carrying them.

"Have you heard of him?" she asked me.

"No," I said.

"He's very well known. Huh. Daddy hadn't heard of him either. I said, 'Paul, *everyone's* heard of him.' And Daddy said, 'Well, I haven't. So shoot me.'"

Ted bought an old farmhouse and then asked my mother to help him decorate it. She said she didn't know anything about decorating, and he said, "Oh, sure you do. Look at your house." She said that he must know tons of professional decorators in New York, and he rolled his eyes.

"He told me to stop being boring," she said to me over the phone.

The next thing I remember her telling me was "Daddy really likes him."

Ted was coming over for dinner fairly often—"He's a bachelor, he gets tired of cooking for himself"—and after dinner he and my father would sit in the living room and talk. About history, about music.

"Ted looks up to Daddy," my mother said. "His own father is horrible—cold and distant. And then of course Daddy knows so much. Ted is sensitive about never having finished college—he left after a year to be a model in New York. So he got one kind of education, but not the, you know, not the conventional *school* kind. I think he admires Daddy's erudition."

"I really want you to meet him," she kept telling me, on the phone. "I think you'd really like him."

"She said it again," I told my husband. "How we're going to really really like him."

"I can't wait," he said.

We met him that year, at Christmas. He was there on Christmas Eve. We got there late; we'd had a long drive down from Boston, with bad traffic and fog and the baby crying a lot of the way. And for the last five or six miles, I told my mother, we'd been stuck behind a red sports car that had been going so slowly I wanted to scream.

"I hope it wasn't you," I said to Ted, who looked startled. I was startled too—at what I'd said, and at the tone in which it had come out.

My mother called me a couple of days later, when I got back to Boston. "Ted thinks you don't like him," she said.

He started inviting my mother to come in to New York. To the ballet, to a concert, to have dinner at Windows on the World, to hear his friend the cabaret singer performing in the Bemelmans Bar. Sometimes my father went with her, and other times she went alone. Ted would go to a hotel and let her stay in his apartment on Eighty-third Street. "It's small, but perfect. Like a jewel box," she said of it, each time.

She would take the train in, and Ted would arrange for a car and driver to meet her at Grand Central. That was how he did things, she said: you came out of Lincoln Center at midnight in the rain, and there was the car and driver waiting to take you across town.

"Sometimes it's not enough just to have a good time," my mother said. "I've been trying to explain this to Daddy for years. Sometimes what you need to have is an *expensive* good time."

I was visiting my parents, and I asked my mother if I could borrow a sweater. When I opened her closet, I saw that the shelves were full of turquoise-and-black boxes with little interlocking "T"s all over them.

"Some he's given me, some I've bought," my mother said. She had followed me into the room. She was smiling. "At a deep discount, of course. But it's an addiction. Like smoking. It's ridiculous. I've got to quit."

Each box was labeled with the bag's material and color.
Patent: Black.
Kid: Green.
Sequins: Multi.
Alligator: Wine.

"Alligator wine," I said to my husband later. "Doesn't it sound like some really sleazy drink?"

"A potion," he said.

Ted moved in with them, because he was having his house redecorated.

"I thought he decorated it when he bought it," I said.

"That was nothing, compared to this," my mother told me. "Like, guess what, he's having new windows made, because we think the mullions need to be more substantial."

"*We* do?"

"He consults me. That's what he calls me now, my nickname. The consultant. Even Daddy's picked it up—like when we're trying to decide if the roast beef is done, Daddy'll say to Ted, 'Let's ask the consultant.'"

"I wonder why he's never married," she said. We were sitting at an outdoor table at a restaurant, under an umbrella, eating chicken salad sandwiches.

"Ma, he's gay," I said.

She had been about to take a bite of her sandwich, but she stopped. "He is not."

I nodded. "Yes he is."

"I think he's very masculine," she said.

"I didn't say he wasn't."

I fed the baby a spoonful of applesauce.

"Besides," my mother said, "there was a woman once, a long time ago. Someone in New York. He almost married her, he said."

"So?"

She picked up her glass of iced tea and stirred it with the

straw. She shook her head. "I think he's kind of shut down, that way. Or has been, anyhow. I'm not sure why." She frowned and drank some tea. "I don't think it's really men *or* women. That's what I think."

When I went to visit my parents the following winter, Ted was still living with them, and my mother had begun to redecorate, also. Not on the scale of having floors ripped up and replaced with old salvaged wide-board ones, or installing dropped canvas ceilings—both of which were going on in Ted's house then. She was re-covering furniture, buying lamps. And she had bought, at Ted's urging, a huge French armoire for her bedroom, lined its worm-channeled insides with shirred Provençal fabric, and fitted it out with compartments for sweaters and a slide-out shelf for the TV.

"Way, way too expensive," she told me, "but he made me do it."

He had also made her remove the doors from the closets, hers and my father's, which lined the narrow passageway leading to their bathroom. He'd said the doors were a nuisance, that they took up too much room when opened, and that it was much chic-er this way.

"How does Daddy feel about all this?" I asked my mother, when she showed me the improvements in the bedroom.

She shrugged. "Fine, I guess. I don't think he really cares, one way or another."

The day after my father died, when we all went back to the house for the first time, I went upstairs into their bedroom. The bed was unmade, the pillows dented. I thought of him getting out of bed early yesterday morning, and of my mother getting up an hour later; he was already dead by then, but she didn't know it yet.

I thought of her having to come back into this room, later today; of how she would look at the rumpled bed and think of his head lifting from his pillow while she still slept; of how she would have to decide whether to make the bed, and when to change the sheets.

At least if I changed the bed she might not have to think so much.

I stripped the sheets and blankets off and slid the pillows out of their cases. I gathered up the linens, and when I went to put them in the bathroom hamper, I walked by my parents' closets. I saw my mother's clothes, and all the little boxes with the interlocking "T"s; and my father's suits, and his shoes neatly lined up on the floor, and his sweaters folded in the shelves up above, where his hands had rummaged yesterday morning, groping for the gun.

And then I thought, without pity, in fact with a momentary coldness that was almost pleasurable, of how my mother would have to see all this every time she walked past on her way to the bathroom, because there weren't any doors to shut it all out.

But I'm jumping ahead. A few more things, from before he died.

The swimming pool.

My mother had gotten estimates, and the work was going to be done in the spring. The pool would be an irregular curved shape, so that it would look natural; and the water would be a dark, dull blue, not that fake Caribbean color. There would be stone paving around it, and then gardens. Ted had suggested grading the land, and putting in some rocks and a waterfall, but my mother had drawn the line there: too expensive. As it was, the pool was going to cost eighty thousand dollars.

I heard about these plans that year at Christmas. On Christmas Eve, I was outside with my father, helping him to stack firewood. "So you're getting a swimming pool," I said.

He gave me a sweet, odd, rueful smile, and shrugged.

I said, "Don't let them shove it down your throat."

"Ouch," he said. "That would certainly hurt."

We piled up some more logs. It was late afternoon, very cold. The light was clear and weak and thin. I thought of what I knew: the problems he was having with his business, the balloon payments that were going to be due soon on the loans. The way he never would tell me, really, what was going on, but once recently on the phone I'd wondered if he was crying.

"What I mean," I said, "is don't let Mom and Ted just decide about the pool. You should be part of the decision."

Again that odd little smile, and then he looked away, at the sky. "Apparently," he said, "it's already been made."

A late-night conversation between my father and Ted, which my mother told me about.

"We'd had Ted over for dinner, but it got late. I'd gone to bed," she said, "and they were sitting up, drinking cognac. And they were talking. I know this from Ted. Daddy suddenly looked at him and said that I was the most important thing in the world to him. Why do you think he said that?"

"I told her I didn't know," I said to my husband.

"What do you really think?" he asked me.

"What do I think he meant? 'Back off.'"

"But your father knows they're not having an affair, right?"

"Yeah," I said. "But he's not sure if my mother knows it."

The cake.

My mother went to a fancy bakery to pick up a cake for Ted, whose birthday was the next day. When she got out of her car, she saw my father coming out of the bakery carrying a cake box. She laughed and said to him, "Great minds think alike."

He just looked at her.

"Maybe he wanted his cake to be a surprise," I said when she told me. "Maybe he was disappointed that you'd seen him."

"No, it was weirder than that. He didn't recognize me. I said, 'Paul, it's me.' I said, 'Paul. It's your *wife*.' He just looked at me. And then he got in his car with the cake and drove away."

This thing with the cake happened on Monday, four days before he died. She told me about it Saturday night. We were sitting in the dark, on the love seats in my parents' living room, trying to figure out if my father had shown any sign that something was wrong.

After my father died, my mother kept asking me what I thought.

I had to be careful about what I said to her. I said, "I don't know."

But here's what I really thought: my father kept needing to prove that the thing with my mother and Ted was safe.

I think he went to the bakery to show that, see, he had no problem with Ted—in fact he was so at ease with the situation that he was buying the guy a birthday cake.

I think that when my mother showed up at the bakery, my father thought, Christ, they don't even need me to do that.

Another dream she told me, in the months after my father's death:

She is in an office building, a big one, in New York, she thinks. She is running down the corridor, and my father and Ted are ahead of her. They are getting on the elevator to go down, and she keeps yelling, Wait! Wait for me!

But they don't wait. They ignore her. The doors close just as she reaches them.

"And then you want to hear something weird?" she told me. "I woke up, and then when I fell back asleep I had the exact same dream again."

That dream came later, after the thing with Ted was over.

On Monday we were getting ready to leave for my father's memorial service when a truck pulled into our driveway. The driver said he was there to deliver a chair.

For one wild moment I thought it was the chair that my father had died in, which my husband and Ted had taken to the dump on Saturday morning. I thought maybe it was making its way back to us in some mysterious, obstinate way, like a lost animal.

"No!" From behind me, my mother was yelling at the driver. "This is not a good time. You'll have to come back."

The driver said he couldn't do that. She'd asked for delivery on the eleventh and this was the eleventh. He'd driven up specially from New York. She needed to take delivery of the chair.

"My husband is dead!" my mother screamed. "Leave me alone about the chair!"

"What chair is this?" I asked.

"It's the one from my bedroom. It used to be yellow. It was getting re-covered. Ted made me do it." She screamed at the driver, "I don't want it now!"

I told the driver to just bring it in.

Ted was around a lot, the week after my father died. My mother had asked him to do a eulogy, and he said he would. But then he changed his mind. He said it would make him uncomfortable.

He offered to take charge of the food, for when people came back to the house after the service.

After everyone had left, my mother said to me, "Didn't you think the meal was *elegant*? I think Ted did that as a labor of love for Daddy, instead of speaking at the service. It was too hard for him to put his feelings into words."

A few nights later I came downstairs and she and Ted were in the kitchen, laughing.

"What's so funny?" I asked.

My mother pointed at Ted, who was holding the salt shaker in one hand and its lid in the other. "Daddy," she said, gasping, her face red, "always insisted that the one with the *big* hole was for pepper, and the one with all the *little* holes was for salt—"

"—and *I* always said," Ted continued, laughing, breathless, "I said, 'No, Paul, it's the other way around.' And so just now I happened to notice the salt and pepper shakers sitting there, so I said—"

"—and so he said, 'Aha! Finally *I can just switch them!*'"

———

After I went back home to Boston I called her every day. "Ted is being wonderful," she said each time.

"I'm glad," I would say.

One night she told me that the strangest thing had happened.

"Before Daddy died, he started to put some wire fencing around the edges of the property. So deer couldn't get in this summer, and eat the garden. Well, today I looked out the window and there was Ted, at the edge of the woods, and he was finishing the deer fencing. He didn't even ring the doorbell to tell me he was going to do it; he was just there, doing it."

"That's nice of him," I said.

"I went outside to thank him. And he said something really weird."

"What?"

"He said, 'Don't thank me. I have my own guilt, you know.'"

A few days later, she asked me what I thought Ted had meant, about feeling guilty. "Guilty about what? What would he have to feel guilty about?"

I knew what I thought. Guilt because he'd imagined his friendship with my mother was harmless. Guilt because he'd believed my parents were secure people happily opening their arms to him. Guilt because he hadn't seen that my mother had been using him to get at my father, and that my father was not okay.

"I don't know," I said.

"You don't think," she said, and then there was a pause, and she lowered her voice. "You don't think he's in *love* with me, do you?"

There was a surface layer of skepticism and horror, but underneath was tremendous excitement.

"No. I don't," I said.

It must have been a few months after that, the night when she called me and then couldn't talk, because she was crying. Heartbroken, gulping sobs.

"What?" I said. "Mommy, what is it?" I hadn't called her "Mommy" in decades.

"He called me a cunt," she whispered.

"Who did?"

"Ted. He called me a cunt in King Neptune's Palace."

That was the name of the seafood place where they had dinner together once or twice a week. "Sssh," I said. "Tell me."

"I can't."

"Oh, Mom."

"I didn't mean—I was just trying to *empathize,*" she gulped out. She told me: Ted's father, to whom he had not spoken for years, had died the week before. And so at dinner she had said something to Ted about how they both had enormous losses now to deal with; and he had asked her how she could even begin to think of comparing those two losses.

"And he looked at me. Such a look, the coldness of it. And he said, 'You are such a cunt.'"

It was after that, I think, that she began telling me over and over how much she missed my father. And began to say sometimes that she felt guilty, but when I would say, "Guilty about what?" she would say, "A lot of things."

That was also when she began telling me about the dreams.

———

I am remembering now that the last time I saw Ted, before their friendship ended that night at King Neptune's Palace, I tried to thank him for whatever it was he was giving my mother. I told him a little stiffly that he'd been great.

He gave me a funny look and said, "I don't know how long I can keep it up."

I'm not sure what happened, why he pushed her away so hard. Maybe he had liked her as part of a couple, but didn't want to be stuck with her alone. Maybe between the two of them, Ted had, in fact, been more deeply attached to my father. My mother believed that for Ted she was the sun and my father the moon, but maybe she got it backwards. Certainly my father's death sobered Ted. Certainly he and my mother had been giddy together, and in their giddiness they had missed my father's despair. Maybe after he died Ted felt chastened, and was repelled because my mother seemed to feel only abandoned.

I don't know. What I know is: She's my mother. My love for her has very little to do with liking. It's a fierce, dumb love. It's a love compounded of anger for all the things she could never see, and desire to protect her from ever seeing them.

When I called her at the rehab place at lunchtime today, she sounded tired and subdued. She told me some of the sensation in her legs is starting to return.

"That's good," I said.

"It hurts," she said.

She told me another dream.

My father is dead, but he is back with our family for a while, on a kind of furlough. We all know he is dead, but no one is supposed to mention it. He is very tall, wearing a dark suit and the kind of brimmed felt hat he used to wear a long time ago, when he was on his way up in business.

He is sitting with my mother. She is holding his hand, which is warm. She keeps meaning to ask him where the steel platter is, the one he used to carve the meat on. But she keeps saying other things instead.

He gets up, and she knows he is leaving.

Where's the steel platter? she tries to say. This time she can't say anything. No words come out.

But just before he leaves, he looks at her and he is smiling.

And he tells her: Don't worry about the steel platter. It's all right. I know where everything is.

Suicide:
factors that may have had direct or indirect bearing on
pots of money

MY HUSBAND'S FAMILY WAS COMPLICATED, AND VERY RICH.

When I met him in college, his parents had been divorced for years and had both since married other people. His father and stepmother lived in Connecticut with their two young daughters, on a gentleman's farm fueled by old family money that seemed to be astronomical and inexhaustible. They had boats and yacht clubs, horses and hunt clubs, and a huge shingled summer house on Cape Cod that had been in the family for three generations. They drank a lot, fought a lot, and threw large, raucous parties for the handsome young guys who crewed on their racing yawl and the girls who mucked out their stables and schooled their ponies and rode in horse shows up and down the East Coast.

One of these parties was going on the first time I visited their house, shortly after my husband and I met. His father and stepmother, Cal and Abby, greeted him in a way that was at once hearty and distracted, and they shook my hand and said, "Ah, another potential daughter-in-law." Then they sent us into the library to get ourselves drinks.

"Let me show you the paintings," my boyfriend said. Over

the library desk, which was crowded with liquor bottles and monogrammed glasses, was a Boudin seascape. I looked at the signature and then looked at my boyfriend, shocked. A Boudin was something you saw in a museum, or in an art history slide show; you didn't have one hanging around in your house. My boyfriend laughed at my face, and told me that his grandparents had bought a bunch of paintings on a trip they'd taken to Paris in the 1920s. "A Boudin!" I said, and he said, "Yeah, but for the same money they could have been buying Monets." Then he offered to show me the Corot, and when I gasped about that he said, "It's not a very good one."

"How could a Corot be not very good?"

He took my hand. "I'll show you."

The Corot was hanging in a corner of the dining room. A gray country landscape with a cow in one corner.

"Oh," I said.

I was giddy, even though I'd only had a couple sips of my drink. Everyone else at the party was laughing and hollering and arguing about who got hit by the boom during last year's Bermuda Race. My boyfriend and I were gliding around invisibly, snickering at his family's inferior Corot.

His mother, Katherine, lived with her husband Neil in New York. They worked in a Wall Street brokerage firm; Katherine was in the marketing department, and Neil was on his way up, putting together deals buying and selling companies and looking to buy one of his own someday. They must have been making good salaries at that point, but they weren't really rich yet. They lived in one of those bland, boxy white buildings east of Lexington Avenue.

Out of their small, flimsy apartment, Katherine had made

something glamorous. Cocoa brown walls. Old rugs on the floor, faded tans and golds. A fur rug draped over the back of a damask settee. Silver boxes, red leather picture frames. Huge salmon-pink amaryllis, green leaves splayed over the rims of blue-and-white Chinese pots. Books and newspapers piled everywhere. Old travelogues, biographies of English statesmen. Gardening memoirs. Architectural histories.

We would come in to the city from college on the train, and they would take us to the theater and then a late dinner at Christ Cella's or the Russian Tea Room. Or we would all get into their car—it was small and very fast—and drive up the Hudson, to look at Washington Irving's house and have lunch at the Culinary Institute. They were warm and self-contained; they simultaneously coddled us and left us alone.

By the time my boyfriend and I got engaged, at the end of our senior year, my parents had grown friendly with Katherine and Neil. We would all have dinner in New York or at my parents' house in Connecticut. My boyfriend and I sat close together on my mother's blue love seat, or on Katherine's needlepoint bench. My mother and Katherine talked about art and spread goat cheese on crackers to pass around. And my father and Neil would sit on a sofa, slightly separate from the rest of us, talking in low voices about business.

By this point my father had had a couple of professional failures, which had devastated my mother and had some effect on him, I thought at the time, though it was impossible to tell what the effect was or how deep it went. He was very quiet.

Neil had an assurance about himself, and about the ups and downs of business, that seemed to scoop up my father and include him and suggest that the two of them were comrades in the trenches, out there every day fighting the same you-win-some-you-lose-some battles. Watching them as they had these rational-looking, inaudible, murmured conversations brought me a comfort I didn't even know I'd been seeking, in answer to a fear I didn't know I had. Neil found my father credible; they were two executives on a couch.

My parents' relationship with Cal and Abby never got off the ground. My boyfriend and I had a brief, grubby, awkward engagement summer; we were jobless, inept, and so young and fiercely austere that the hoopla of planning a wedding mortified us and bemused our friends. Once during the engagement, my parents invited Cal and Abby over for dinner. They lived in the next town, and my mother knew people who knew them. "*Pots* of money," she said, with frank relish and awe.

She was nervous about having them over. What should she cook? What should she wear? She and I were peeling or chopping something on the day of the dinner, when my father came into the kitchen and said he was going to call Cal. "It's such a hot day, I'm going to tell him not to bother with a coat and tie." But Cal, on the other end of the phone, didn't seem to know who my father was. My mother and I heard my father repeating his name several times, and then finally saying baldly, "Your son is marrying my daughter." Then he laughed and said, "Yes, well, I'm glad we've finally got *that* straight." He came back into the kitchen afterward to hang up the receiver, and with a kind of wobbly dignity and a faintly English accent said, "An interesting conversation," and then he went out again and my mother hissed at me, "He didn't know who Daddy was?" and I made vague murmurs excusing Cal's behavior but my hands were shaking.

After we were married, my husband and I would some-times go out sailing with Cal, and I would wish that my father had been invited, and feel relieved that he hadn't been. Cal's boat was a fifty-two-foot racing yawl, sculpted and sleek. There was a picture of it one year in the sailing calendar my father liked me to give him for Christmas: an aerial view, taken off the coast of Nova Scotia, the sails ballooning out like pregnant bel-lies and the deck littered with a dozen tiny figures in orange foul-weather gear. My father had shown me the picture and said, wistfully, "That must be some boat."

My father had only recently taken up sailing. He had all the passion of a newcomer, and the careful reverence for ter-minology. He had joined a boat club on Long Island Sound, and on weekends he liked to take out one of the twelve-foot dinghies. Sometimes my husband went along too ("It makes me feel much better when I know you're with him," my mother muttered into his ear, "because you actually know what you're doing").

Cal sailed with a cigarette in his mouth, his fingers on the wheel, his squinting eye on the wind and the compass and the crew and the horizon. He expected everyone on his boat to be expert and offhand. The first time I went out with him, he shoved a line into my hand, and when I just stood there he shouted, "Tail, damn you, tail!" Then when I still didn't know what he meant, he grabbed the line away from me and tossed it to his nine-year-old daughter, and after that he ignored me.

I imagined my father as a guest on the boat, avid and de-liberate and too slow. It would have been humiliating to see Cal size him up and then dismiss him as a sailor—one kind of humiliation if my father was aware of the dismissal, and a dif-ferent, equally excruciating kind if he was ignorant of it. Better, maybe, that he was never invited. But the lack of an invitation, which could have been extended with such ease and would have been received with such delight, ate at me. So did my father's telling me that he'd seen Cal and Abby once or twice in the Parnassus Diner on the Post Road but that they never seemed to recognize him when he waved at them.

Meanwhile, my parents' friendship with Katherine and Neil had developed to the point where they would get together on holidays even if my husband and I weren't there. When our son was born, nine years into our marriage, the four of them jumped into a car and drove from Connecticut to Boston to spend a thrilled, doting half-hour with us in the hospital.

The following year, at Christmas, my mother and I were in her kitchen, checking on the roast beef, when she said, "So did they tell you about the sixteen million dollars Neil is going to get from the sale of his company?"

"*How* much?" I said, straightening up from basting the meat. I remember that my necklace, heated from the open oven, swung against my throat and burned.

"Just wait. You'll hear her in there, going on about it." She glanced through the open doorway into the living room, where my one-year-old son was sitting on the floor pulling at the large wooden fire truck that Katherine had brought for him. "So," my mother said, "now there'll be a rich grandmother and a poor grandmother."

"Cut it out," I told her.

We went back into the living room. Neil was talking about the Rolls-Royce he was buying. "I made a vow, when I was a scholarship kid in business school, that someday I'd have a Rolls."

"That's great," my father said. He was smiling.

"And a sable coat for me," Katherine said. "That was always our deal, darling, right? The car for you and the coat for me. But I have to tell you two what I did." She looked back and forth from my mother to me, her face glowing. "It was so bad of me. They showed me a mink, which I just fell in love with. And I thought, what the hell, and got both. I mean, what's another ten thousand for a mink when you're already spending a hundred for a sable? Right?"

"Right," my mother said.

Back in the kitchen, alone with me, she hissed, "You see?"

I did, but I didn't want to talk about it. I didn't want to hear what she was going to say. I poured some wine into the roasting pan and started scraping the drippings off the bottom.

"What's the *matter* with them?" My mother was mashing potatoes; white chunks were leaping above the rim of the pot. "I didn't think they were *like* this."

"They're just excited," I said. "It's brand new; they're drunk on it. It'll die down."

"I don't know why she can't just say, 'He sold his company,' and leave it at that. I don't know why she thinks we need all the specific *dollar* figures." The masher kept thudding up and down, very fast. "There's a *reason* why it's considered rude to talk about money. Because it makes other people feel bad."

"I'm sure she didn't mean to make you feel bad."

"Well, maybe she should be a little more considerate."

"She's excited," I said again. "They both are. They've worked very hard for this."

"*Daddy* works hard," she said. She banged the masher a few times on the rim of the pot, and then dropped it into the sink. She stood there, looking out the window, though it was dark outside and she must have been looking at herself and the reflection of the kitchen.

After a minute she said, "Daddy vowed to buy a Rolls-Royce, too, you know."

Later, after dinner, I went into the kitchen, where my father was loading the dishwasher, and asked if I could help. He said I could get the coffee started. "And maybe put some cookies on a plate?"

I did both of those things, and then I went over and put my arms around him. I laid my cheek against his soft blue-gray sweater.

"You okay?" he said.

I nodded. "You?"

He held me for a moment.

"I hope there are enough of those cookies," I said.

His arms tightened, and then he let me go. "If not," he said, in his stagey fake-English accent, "then let them eat cake."

Sometimes he said things like that, where I didn't quite know what he meant; but the jaunty gallantry of the remark, as well as the obscurity of it, would break my heart.

It was in Antigua, the next winter, when Neil laughed and told me about the ulcers. We were walking on the beach together. He was repeating a remark that had been made to him by a man who had lost his job as a result of a leveraged buyout Neil had done. "So the guy says to me, 'Some people get ulcers, and some people give 'em. And you're one of the ones who gives 'em.'" Neil imitated the man's grim tone and then laughed. "He thought he was insulting me. I told him I considered it a compliment."

My husband and I were in an awkward position. On the

one hand, we hated all the talk about money. On the other, Neil and Katherine were giving us some. Enough to replace our crummy old car, enough to put in an upstairs bathroom, enough to feel that we might actually be able to afford to send our son to college when the time came. My husband was an architect and I was a writer, and neither profession paid well. We were in our thirties now, but still austere and fierce. My husband felt guilty about taking the money. He thought we should stand on our own, and that Neil only respected self-made men.

"So what?" I said. "We need it; he's offering it; just take it."

"The more we take, the less he'll think of us," my husband said. "I guess I just have that classic trust-fund guilt."

"Yeah, except you don't have a trust fund," I pointed out: Cal may have had pots of family money, but my husband didn't have even a small saucepan.

Neil had a kind of straight-shooting pragmatism that was tough but bracing. You knew where you stood with him. That was what my father said, when he told me Neil was investing in the door company that my father and his partner, Gil, were starting. They were planning to import doors made cheaply in Korea and sell them to builders here. Neil, my father said, had looked over the paperwork and thought they all stood to make a nice return on their investment.

"But are you sure it's a good idea to go into business with someone in the family?" I asked.

My father shrugged. "Ordinarily, I'd say it's a terrible idea, because the feelings in families tend to run so high. But I'm not worried about that with Neil. Business is business and family is family. He's tough, but he's out in the open. It's all perfectly straightforward."

At the time I must have thought, of my father: He knows what he's doing.

Now I think: Oh, my God. His dignity, and his incompetence. His haplessness.

The door business flopped. The bank called the loan. Neither my father, Gil, nor the third investor could come up with the money.

It looked like the bank was going to turn its sights on Neil.

My father got up early one morning, went into his study, and shot himself.

Of course that wasn't the only reason why he did it. Nor does it justify what he did; people withstand greater pressures, and worse disgraces. But my father had a code of honor. He was proud. He must have felt responsible for getting Neil into the mess. A debt had been incurred, which was now going to fall with disproportionate heaviness on Neil since my father couldn't repay his own share. Paying with his life must have seemed (oh, such cockeyed, pompous, macho, fucked-up logic) like the right and noble thing to do.

Two days after my father died, my mother said she wanted to talk to Neil about money. She was worried about whether she'd have enough to live on, and whether she could afford to stay in her house.

My husband and I looked at each other. My father had never told my mother about the bank calling the loan. She didn't know that Neil was having to cover my father's share, and that he would be one of the creditors looking to be paid back out of the estate.

Her house was full of people, making tea and hugging and crying and washing dishes. We took her into the small, dark laundry room behind the kitchen, so we could talk privately. I told her about the loan. I expected her to start screaming. That same expectation, I knew, combined with his own shame, was what had prevented my father from telling her. But she just said, "All right." She asked what my father's share of the debt was. We told her: fifty-five thousand. Then she said, "So you think it's a bad idea to talk to Neil about my finances?"

"That's up to you," my husband said.

She thought for a minute, then shrugged. "I trust him. And he knows about money. I would value his advice."

We all went upstairs and sat in her bedroom. She told Neil how much money she had. There was almost nothing left in my father's brokerage accounts, but there was several hundred thousand dollars' worth of life insurance. Some of the policies had suicide clauses, but Neil looked at them and said she'd be all right; the clauses had lapsed. My mother also had some money of her own, which she'd saved from her years working in real estate.

"How much?" Neil asked.

"About two hundred thousand."

"Great," Neil said.

"So you think I'll be all right? The kids just told me about this big bank loan."

"I'm covering it for now," Neil said.

"But the money's there, in the estate, right? So you'll get your share back?"

"Right," Neil said.

"Thanks for helping me sort this out," my mother said. She kissed Neil.

"Okay, kid," he said.

Cal showed up at my father's memorial service, alone; Abby had filed for divorce several years before. He listened to all the nice things people said about my father: how kind he had been, how considerate, how loving. When the service was over, Cal went and hugged my husband and said, "I guess I haven't been a very good father to you."

"And what did you say?" I asked coldly that night, when my husband told me this story.

My husband looked at me helplessly. "What the hell could I say? I told him he'd been fine."

A few months later, Cal called my husband and asked if it was okay to sell the Boudin. It was hanging in his house, but since the divorce it was officially in trust for his three kids. Things were tough financially, he told my husband. He'd had a bad year in business and he owed a lot in taxes.

"I can't give you permission to sell it," my husband said, "because it isn't in trust just for me."

"If I talk to the girls, they'll tell their mother. And Abby will bring the lawyers down on my head."

My husband said he was sorry, but he couldn't tell Cal to go ahead and sell the painting without talking to his other children.

Cal got mad then, and said, "I'm desperate. Don't you get it? I'm telling you I'm desperate."

"Look," said my husband, "I can't stop you from selling it

if that's what you want to do. But I can't tell you it's okay, either."

When my husband told me about this conversation that evening, I said, "You could stop him, if you wanted to. You could pick up the phone and call Abby."

"I know," he said.

"But you won't, will you?"

"No."

I was scrubbing out a pot, scouring in big, angry circles. "How desperate can a man with a fifty-two-foot boat be?"

My husband shrugged, and looked at me. I didn't say anything else. I turned on the water so hard that it splashed the front of my shirt. Desperate, I said to Cal in my head, you don't even know what desperate means.

Then I thought that maybe he'd used that word on purpose, knowing the terrible power it would have with my husband in the wake of my father's death.

Or maybe he really was desperate.

I looked at my husband, who was wiping down the counters briskly and dazedly. Despite the distance in their relationship, I knew that he loved his father—but that wasn't what was going on here. What was going on was a careful decision not to take any action, because the consequences of that action were unpredictable. My father's death had made a permanent shift in how we saw the world, in what we were certain of and what we were aware of not knowing. There really was no way to tell for sure if a man was in a corner. And what that man, if he ever got into a corner, might do.

Then one afternoon my husband called me from work, more upset than I'd ever heard him. Neil, he said, wanted my mother to pay him back for covering my father's share of the bank loan.

"I told him the estate would cover it, if he could just be patient," my husband said, "but he wants to be paid now. And he says he knows your mother has the money to do it."

"But the only reason he knows is because she confided in him," I said.

"I know. I said, 'Neil, this is family. This is my wife's family. You've sat across from these people at the dinner table.' He said he didn't see what that had to do with anything. He said that when they signed the loan agreement, your father looked him straight in the eye and promised that he was good for his share."

"And he killed himself because he couldn't make good."

"I said that. I said he'd paid the debt in the only way he knew how. And Neil said the debt hadn't been paid, because he still doesn't have his money back."

My husband thought he could protect my mother from all this. He told Neil to back off, and he drove to Connecticut and took Katherine to lunch and asked her to tell Neil to back off.

Within the year, my mother told me that the estate had been settled and Neil had been paid. But recently she said to me, after a Thanksgiving dinner at which Neil had annoyed her, "Sometimes I think he is literally heartless. Remember after Daddy died, when he came after me for that money?"

"He did? We thought we'd nipped that in the bud."

My mother shook her head. "He called and said he wanted the money right then. Can you believe it? I told him he could just wait, along with the other creditors. I said, 'Neil, take a number.'"

Families spend years eating meals together, chatting, sniping, listening, not listening, concealing unhappiness, leaning on weak spots, eroding the mortar. You get through time. You don't say, "I never want to see you again."

You invite everyone for Christmas, or Thanksgiving, or the birthday. You baste the meat, and light the candles, and open the presents. You get up to make the coffee and put the cookies on the plate, and then you go back and sit down at the table again.

Suicide:
factors that may have had direct or indirect bearing on
uneasy problem of blame

GO AHEAD, READER. SAY IT. CLEAR YOUR THROAT, LOOK EMBAR-rassed, and say, "Um, excuse me, but how come you're blaming everyone else for his death?"

Good question.

It was my mother's fault, for getting carried away with Ted.

It was Cal's fault, for being rich and heedless.

It was Katherine and Neil's fault, for being rich and heartless.

All the parents had failed, except for my father. In the months after he died, I felt like I'd lost all of them, except him. I knew it was crazy, but that was how I felt.

Here's another crazy thing: I thought that if only he were around, he might console me for the loss of the others.

I was merciless toward them—not in my behavior, but in my thoughts. There are glib explanations for this:

Ah. I resented them because they were the parents who were left.

Ah. It was safer to get mad at them than it would have been to blame him.

Ah. Scapegoating.

In the months—more than months, decade—after my father's death, I was angry at a lot of people, but not at him. He needed my protection, I thought. The world had found him unacceptable. He had found himself unacceptable. I was different, loving, loyal. I accepted his weakness; his despair; his secrecy; his pride; his failure; his shame; his beautiful, stupid, addled ideas about honor; his love for me, which might possibly have been there even in the last instant of his life.

I accepted everything about him, except that he was the author of his own absence.

Suicide:
finding some humor in
ashes

A FEW DAYS AFTER MY FATHER DIED, MY MOTHER GOT A PHONE call from a man she knew who was lobbying to get curbside recycling in town. He was calling to invite her to a meeting. She explained that she couldn't come, because her husband had just died.

The man said he was sorry to hear that.

As they were talking, my mother suddenly remembered that he was the person in charge of the little graveyard where she wanted to bury my father's ashes.

"Listen, Ralph," she said, "speaking of recycling . . ."

Suicide:
finding some humor in
Valentine's Day

MY MOTHER AND I WENT OUT TO LUNCH TOGETHER ABOUT A week after my father died, and the waitress asked, "So, did you have a good Valentine's yesterday?"

My mother stiffened, managed a shrug.

The waitress was instantly alert with sympathy. "Didn't he give you what you wanted?"

And my mother said, "Not exactly."

Suicide:
glimpses of his character relevant to

AFTER MY FATHER DIED, I COULDN'T SEE HIM CLEARLY ANYMORE. My memories all seemed to say one thing about him; his death said another.

In my memory, he is gentle. He is tolerant, witty, judicious. He smiles. He's kind.

He takes me shopping for my birthday, and when I can't decide between two jackets, he says, "I'd like to get you both."

When my husband is rejected by a graduate program he'd set his heart on, my father takes a day off from work and walks in the woods with him, not saying a lot, mostly just listening. He also writes a letter to the president of the university, chewing out the institution for passing up such a terrific candidate.

He comes to my house the week after my son is born and cooks Thanksgiving dinner, a gorgeous, complicated meal that he gets on the table with no help and no fuss.

He's warm and patient with a crying baby; he walks up and down the room with my son, sings to him, whispers Edward Lear's nonsense rhymes into his ear.

Then one day he picks up a gun and pulls the trigger.

All right, maybe he's not the world's smartest businessman. He feels like a failure at times. He's proud, and perhaps more easily hurt than he ever lets on. His wife has gotten carried away with another man.

But: *He picks up a gun?*

He pulls the trigger?

Hearing the news an hour after it happened, I felt that I'd just missed being in time to stop it. Without ever having admitted it to myself, this was what I'd been afraid of for a long time. I had sort of known—occasionally, dimly—that something might be wrong, but I'd accepted the superficial reassurances that nothing was. When he died, it was as if he'd finally been caught, literally, red-handed. He had come out into the open and we had finally spotted him, an hour after spotting him could have made any difference. We saw it an hour after it was too late.

I had never seen it clearly before. But I came to wonder, as I tried in the months after his death to piece together why he'd killed himself, if perhaps I had glimpsed it—that dark hidden thing that killed him—a few times in the past. It was always far away, hidden in the trees. I was never sure if what I was glimpsing was a dangerous and wild creature or just a big dog, someone's pet, turned into something menacing by fear, and a trick of light and shadow.

Once he hit me. Only once. I must have been about ten. My mother and I were screaming at each other, and I told her to shut up. Then I went running up the stairs to my room and slammed the door.

My door flew open. My father charged across the room and he hit me so hard that my glasses snapped sideways and broke in half, and blood started pouring out of my nose.

I remember that he kept apologizing, as they cleaned me up. They dabbed at me with a cool, wet washcloth. The fight had incinerated itself, burned in a fiery instant down to nothing. "I'm sorry," my father kept saying. "I'm so sorry." I was sorry, too, that I'd provoked him to become unrecognizable, to do something that hadn't even seemed in the range of possible things he might do.

I didn't know that night, or indeed until after he died, that he'd been beaten by his father, sometimes to the point of broken bones.

I remember my bathrobe: white terry cloth, with appliquéd gingham flowers down the front. I remember the blood on the flowers. I remember the numb, tender feeling of my nose and lips, and the chill of the washcloth, and my father's voice saying over and over, "I'm sorry."

I was twenty-three and had just started a job in a Boston advertising agency. It was my lunch hour; I was in the Lord & Taylor on Boylston Street, buying shoes.

Seeing the other women in the agency had made me realize that my wardrobe was nonexistent. I needed everything, and I was having fun. A white blouse with pleating down the front. Another in lavender-gray silk, with small abalone buttons. A narrow red skirt. And now, today, two pairs of shoes: dark-red leather flats, and black suede pumps with heels. I handed the salesman my MasterCard.

"Sorry," he said, "we don't take this one. Lord & Taylor charge? American Express? Or you could always pay by check."

I knew there wasn't enough money in our checking account to cover the shoes. I hadn't gotten my first paycheck yet, and my husband and I had wiped ourselves out with the move to

Boston, but my salary was a good one and the money would be there in a week or two.

My father had given me an American Express card on his account, to use in an emergency. I'd had the card for several years and never used it, but I was sure he wouldn't mind; I would send him a check as soon as I got paid next Friday, so he would have the money before he even got the bill. I pulled the card from my wallet and handed it to the salesman. He was fiftyish, nervous, with long strands of graying hair combed across a mostly bald scalp; he'd scurried around, bringing me the shoes I had asked to try, and I had thought, How sad, to be that age and selling shoes; could he possibly be supporting a family that way?

He came back holding the American Express card in front of him, between thumb and forefinger. "There seems to be a problem with the card."

"What kind of problem?"

"The charge is being declined."

I'd never heard of anything like this. "But what does that *mean*?" My voice had gotten shrill.

The salesman didn't say anything; he just looked at me over the tops of his wire-rimmed glasses. It suddenly occurred to me that he thought I was trying to get away with using a defunct or stolen credit card; it probably happened a lot, and he'd been trained to deal with us crooks politely. He was still standing there with his eyebrows raised, holding out the card. I took it, and said in a regal voice completely new to me, "Is there a telephone I could use? I'd like to straighten this out with American Express immediately."

I sat in the wooden phone booth with the door open, one leg crossed over the other and jutting imperiously out into the shoe department. I read off the card number to the American Express woman. "Just a minute," she said. She came right back. "I'm sorry, that account is delinquent."

Delinquent. I digested the word for a moment. "Are you saying the bills haven't been paid?"

"That's right," the woman said. "There's an unpaid balance of eighteen thousand dollars."

"But it's my father's account," I blurted out. Then I realized that of course this meant nothing to the American Express woman; she didn't know my father. "I'm sure it's a mistake. I guess I should call him?" Meant as a statement, not as a question; but the uncertainty of it seemed to elicit a little sympathy from the American Express woman.

"That's probably a good idea," she said.

I called my father at the office and told him the whole story. "And *then*," I said, and, "Can you *believe* it?" My indignation was audible proof of my faith in him. "They said the account's *delinquent*," I finished, and waited. My father would laugh in annoyance, I thought. He'd say, Oh, Christ. And then he'd say, Let me call them and straighten this out.

But there was a long silence.

Finally he said, "It's being taken care of."

Surprise made me stupid. "You mean the bill really hasn't been paid? Why not?" I regretted this the moment it came out. I should never have made this phone call. I should have taken the card back from the salesman, put it in my wallet, and never told my father I'd tried to use it.

His shame came over the phone wires as clearly as his breathing. He was explaining: it's a business account, we ran into a little cash-flow problem, it'll all be straightened out at the end of the month—

I interrupted him. "It's okay. You don't have to tell me."

"Well," he said. "You know how it is."

But I didn't know. And I didn't want to. I'd caught a glimpse into some frightening, uncertain business world where my father spent his days, and which he tried to keep private. It was something I shouldn't have seen, and it was my clumsiness that had knocked down the partition.

"I'm sorry," I said.

"What for?"

"Well, for trying to buy the shoes. I know that's not why you gave me the credit card—"

"That's exactly why I gave you the card," he said. "Of course you should use it to buy shoes."

A silence, while the echoes of this magnanimous boom died down and we both remembered that no, I couldn't buy the shoes.

"Listen," my father said finally. "One thing."

"What?"

"Don't tell Mom."

"But doesn't she have a card too? Shouldn't you warn her not to use it?"

He sighed. "She probably won't. Let's hope not, anyway."

I got off the phone, told the salesman I wasn't going to take the shoes, and walked back to the office.

Nine years later. Only a year or so before he died. My parents were visiting us in Cambridge, and my father and I went out for a walk. It was a cold, gray winter afternoon. We threaded our way through streets of houses where the lights were already coming on, and eventually came out onto Massachusetts Avenue.

"You're cold," my father said. "Let's find you a cup of tea."

We stopped at a little café, got our drinks at the counter, and carried them to one of the small tables at the back. We stirred in milk and sugar.

"Really hits the spot," my father said. He smiled at me.

"So how are you?" I asked.

"Not too bad." He smiled again. Then he said, slowly, "It's been a rough week." It was unusual for him to say even that much.

"You want to talk about it?"

He shook his head. "You know. The usual."

"Would it help to tell me?"

"Tell me about you."

I looked at him, then bowed my head and drank more tea.

Finally he said, "Oh, let's see. Debts. Angry customers. Unfilled orders. Maybe a lawsuit."

We took it item by item: I asked him about each of those things, and he told me. At some point while he was telling me, the owner of the café, who was notoriously mean, came over and yelled at us for sitting at a table with just drinks; the tables were for people who had something to eat. I almost started arguing with him—the other tables were empty, we weren't preventing anyone with food from sitting down—but then I just asked him for two slices of linzer torte. He brought the plates and slammed them down in front of us.

After he walked away, I asked my father, "Do you ever think of getting out?" I meant: getting out of his business.

"It's complicated," he said, after a moment.

"But it sounds like it's complicated to stay in."

"That too."

We both tasted our cake, which was excellent.

"Sometimes I feel like everything I touch turns to shit," my father said.

He had never said anything like that before. Probably not to anyone; certainly not to me. I think it terrified both of us. The silence went on and on. We kept eating our cake, by small forkfuls. When the cake was gone, we smashed the crumbs with the backs of our forks and slid them between our teeth. We kept picking up our cups and sipping from them even though all the tea was gone.

"Listen," I said finally. "Let's figure out what else you could do."

He looked at me.

"If you ever did decide to get out of the business." I pulled a napkin out of the dispenser on the table. "Here, we'll make a list."

It was one of those well-meant, bad ideas. You start it, re-alize the folly of it, and keep going, because you don't know what else to do. We wrote down that he could become a consultant to American companies wanting to conduct business overseas, and to foreign companies wanting to do business here. "Not just rules of set-up and operation," I scribbled, "but also subtleties of business climate, culture, etiquette." We wrote down that he could teach in a business school, or teach business courses at a college or even a high school. We started to get far-flung. He could become a history teacher, or a guidance counselor, because he was so good at listening to other people's problems. He could go back to school and get a degree in psychology.

"I could write an espionage novel," my father said, and he went on to outline the plot of one he'd imagined.

"Great! Great!" I said, writing it down.

Finally we got up to leave. When we were outside on the street again, he put his arm around me and squeezed my shoulders. "You're so good for me," he said.

When I went through his dresser drawers after he died, in one of my restless searches for a note, a clue, something, anything, I found the napkins, covered with all those hopeful, useless alternative lives he might think of pursuing if he ever decided to get out of his business, all written down in my panicky blue scrawl.

Three glimpses, of things that were ordinarily hidden.

His violence.

His shame.

His despair and self-loathing.

It's hard to imagine a list any more concise that that, or any starker. It looks like a recipe for suicide.

Or maybe not. If my father hadn't died the way he did, would the events I've set down here have any particular meaning? Don't we all have terrible days, moments when we lose our balance? What about the times when he was happy?

Suicide:
information from his brother sparked by

THAT FIRST SUMMER AFTER MY FATHER DIED, I WENT DOWN TO New York to meet with my editor. I was finishing my first novel. I had a contract and a series of deadlines, which I was managing to meet, although the writing had gotten hard, since my father's death had convinced me that I didn't know anything about anything. When I got to the city, I called Kurt. He invited me to come and see the play he was appearing in that week.

I took a taxi down to the Lower East Side, to a theater that was labeled only with a tiny scuffed sign on a door between a discount beauty-supply store and a taco stand. Up two flights of stairs, the theater space was small and shabby, but full of people.

The play was about a group of passengers on an ocean liner. There was an angry artist, and a pair of young lovers, and a nimble cynical kleptomaniac and his old and very religious mother. I don't remember who the other characters were: the usual ship-of-fools assortment. What I do remember is Kurt, wandering around the stage in a seersucker suit and a bow tie and a small-brimmed straw hat—the sort of pale spiffy outfit businessmen used to wear, decades ago, on the hottest summer days. His character was a professor, a serene and learned man who in the beginning of the play was all knitted together.

Then the play's pivotal disaster occurred: a tidal wave. (A group of stagehands dressed in dark blue leotards thundered forward on bare feet, holding aloft an enormous billowing sheet of blue-gray silk.) The passengers spun around, the stage listed, the ship was crippled. Everyone panicked. Everyone's traits became exaggerated. The lovers clung and quarreled; the religious old woman called more loudly upon God; the thief took compulsive, agile advantage of the general confusion to lift more objects from more pockets. Only the professor—Kurt—remained calm. The other passengers asked him to be their leader, to come up with a plan, and he agreed; but then he didn't do anything. He just kept drifting around the stage, never losing his gentleness, growing vaguer and more lost. The passengers ganged up to accuse him of being ineffectual, of leading them nowhere. By this point he'd lost his mind so entirely that he couldn't respond; he just held on to the sinking ship's railing and looked blankly out to sea. There was a big philosophical argument then: the lovers were blaming Kurt for their fate; and the kleptomaniac was defending him as a fatalist, who had seen and accepted doom long before the rest of them (he extracted a gold watch from Kurt's pocket in the midst of this long speech); and the old lady bleakly and predictably lost her faith. I wasn't paying much attention. I was watching Kurt, standing alone at the front of the stage in his natty clothing; I was watching his frozen, mild face as the ship went down.

Afterward he took me to a small dark Russian restaurant a couple of blocks away. We ordered vodka, and I told him how good I thought he'd been.

Then I said, "The character you played tonight, the professor—were you thinking of my father?"

Kurt's shoulders hunched suddenly; he looked startled, almost furtive, but not displeased. "So you could tell?" He took a quick swallow from his glass.

"Yes," I said. I took a sip of vodka, too, and waited for the slow cold burn of it to travel through my throat and chest. I was confused and shy about what to say to him. I didn't understand how Kurt, who had not been close to my father, had known so much about him. Or, conversely, why, if Kurt had known him so well, the two of them had been unable to be close.

What I finally did say was "You and I saw some of the same things in him." I was thinking of my father's proud, baffled loneliness; his rigid paralysis in the face of crisis; the beautiful manners that concealed deep pessimism; the erudition that brought pleasure but no real solace, animated as it was by intellectual, rather than spiritual, curiosity. The spiritual question had been answered long ago, and the answer was "no."

The waiter brought our blinis, and there was a silence of a few minutes while we began to eat.

Kurt asked me then, lifting and replacing his glass on the tabletop over and over, to make a circle of wet interlocking rings, how much I knew about my father's childhood.

"Some," I said. "I know your parents left you in Germany, while they came to America to get settled. My mother always thought my father must have felt abandoned."

Kurt laughed. "God, no. Abandoned? Are you kidding? That was the happiest time of his life, those three years. We were in the country, with Tante Wanda and Tante Erma. They were our grandmother's sisters, twins; they never married but they loved kids, they adored us. And the school they sent us to, in the Alps—we loved that, too. Your father used to do the most beautiful, sensitive drawings—plants, flowers—"

"We have some of his old notebooks, in the basement. I never knew where they were from."

"So you still have those sketchbooks? I'd love to see them again. I always thought Paul—well, we still called him Boris then—should have been an artist." Kurt ran his hand through his hair. "No, I'm telling you, that part was fine. It was after that the trouble started. After our parents sent for us, and we came to America. Don't you know? He never told you any of this?"

Something—hints my mother had dropped, and a sudden sickening instinct of my own—made me say, slowly, "I know he didn't get along too well with your father."

Kurt said, "Our father was a sick bastard."

This was it: this was what he wanted to talk about.

"Our father thought that no one else in the world mattered, only him. Not his kids, not his wife, no one. Nothing was his fault. He was a brilliant good man alone in the universe, wasn't he? Wasn't he? Wasn't he wonderful, talented, beautiful, amazing? Wasn't it unfair that the world didn't care? More than unfair—wasn't it *sinister*? When he had a call-back for a Broadway show, a good dancing part, whose fault was it that he was reduced to this, having to compromise his talent, forced to whore himself to make money? When he overslept and missed the audition, whose fault was that? Who forgot to set the alarm clock? Here he was trying to make a little money so the family could eat—who was it that had conspired against him by forgetting to set the alarm? No, he couldn't call the producer to reschedule, because if his family was going to conspire against him then let them starve, let them lie in the bed they'd made.

"Our parents were the supers of the building where we lived, in the Bronx. There was a terrible old furnace. Sometimes it went out. Boris would be down there at five in the morning, sweating over it, swearing, praying. Once it just wouldn't start. The building owner came down and yelled at our father, and our father beat Boris. Screaming, the whole time, about how dare Boris humiliate him like that, make him lose face, maybe make him lose his job; we would all be out on the street and it would all be Boris's fault.

"I used to lie in bed at night trying not to hear the beatings, trying not to hear Boris's screams."

I cleared my throat. "Where was your mother while all this was going on?"

"She was in there with the two of them. Maybe he made her watch; I don't know. She was afraid of him. He hit her, too. At one point she was pregnant. I remember her in those big smocky clothes. Then one day he beat her up, and he left us, stalked out of the apartment and didn't come back for days. She started bleeding. Boris was the one who got a taxi; Boris took her to the hospital, this eleven-year-old boy. And then when my father came back and heard what had happened, he gave Boris another beating—it was all Boris's fault that my mother lost the baby; he hadn't gotten her to the hospital fast enough.

"God," said Kurt, pressing the tips of his fingers into his forehead, "God, I just remembered something else; I haven't thought of this in years. They sent us to summer camp one time. And some of the boys saw Boris in his swimming trunks,

120

they saw the marks on his body, and they asked him what all that was from. Anyway, we told them. We'd never told anybody before. But these boys, they helped us come up with this whole plan, to report my father—"

"Report him to whom?"

"We didn't even know. It didn't matter. It seemed so real, such a *plan*. It made us feel safe, all that summer—we were going to have our time at camp, and then we were going to go home and report him—"

"And did you?"

"Of course not. Once we got home we were much too scared. Of him, and of exposing him. He was always talking about how people were trying to humiliate him; we wanted to protect him from anything like that—" He looked at me. "I know, it was crazy. But we were kids. Boris was just a child, eleven, twelve, when my father was doing all this stuff to him. Not just the beating. The words. 'Boris, you're stubborn, lazy, worthless, you can't do anything right, you're evil'—at least once I heard him call Boris evil.

"When you grow up with things like that, you never get rid of them, never. Words like that are a tape that plays in your head for the rest of your life."

We sat there at the restaurant table, looking at each other. Kurt's face was creased, wrinkled, as though all the different characters he'd played over the years had settled themselves in his skin.

"He never told you any of this?" Kurt asked.

"No," I said. "I knew he'd had a bad time with your father, but that was as much as he ever said. And I knew that when your father was dying, my father went to see him in Munich."

"Yeah, the big reconciliation. I couldn't believe it when

Boris told me. I said, 'Well, I'm glad you can forgive him, but I never will.'"

"So he beat you, too?"

People were leaving the restaurant, and new people came in and filled up the tables. The waiters kept gliding by. No one paid any attention to us; we were like two ghosts sitting in some separate shadow-world.

"No. Never. He never touched me. It was always Boris, only Boris. That's what I'll never understand."

We drank some more, Kurt paid the bill, and we finally left the restaurant. I hadn't felt drunk when we were inside. If anything, the vodka had sharpened me: I felt as if I'd been listening to Kurt while balancing on a narrow blade of some kind, and that I hadn't fallen because I'd kept my eyes focused on his face. But outside in the cool June night, Kurt steadied me. Then he went out into the street to hail me a cab. "Be patient, it may take a while, down here at this time of night."

I looked at my watch. It was midnight. I was suddenly very tired.

Recently I had found a photograph at my mother's house. It showed my father as a very young child—perhaps three or four. His arm was stretched upward; he was holding on to an adult's hand, being led away. But he had turned his head back to laugh over his shoulder at the photographer. His hair was wildly curly, so blond it was almost white; it looked like light. That's what you saw when you looked at the photograph: that pale glowing aureole of hair, and the big delighted laugh.

A cab was gliding in, next to Kurt. He opened the door, and turned to hug me. "Be well," he said.

"Keep in touch," I muttered into his shirtfront. Then,

enunciating more clearly, wanting to be sure he heard, I said, "Call me. Will you?"

"I will," he said, and he did. Over the next year or two he would call me sometimes, and we would talk, and he would tell me a little more each time. After a while his calls became less frequent. I didn't mind. I was even glad in a way. As time went on we had less to say to each other, and there were long silences when we were on the phone together. And his voice was so similar to my father's; after a while I began to find the sound of it too disturbing.

Suicide:
intrafamilial relationships reexamined in light of Munich

HIS FATHER WAS DYING, OF A CANCER WHOSE NAME HE DIDN'T understand when his stepmother said it; as soon as she said it, he forgot it. His vocabulary, in German, was still largely that of a nine-year-old, to which had been added a set of fluent phrases and terms needed to do business. Nothing in his German experience had taught him words that applied to sick old men.

Would he have made a special trip from America, just to see his father? Luckily, he didn't have to decide; he had to go to Germany for a board meeting that spring; it would be fairly easy to take the train to Munich for a day. Not even a day—an afternoon. The morning spent on the train, then a taxi through the city, arrive after lunch. Visit visit visit, accept a cup of tea or coffee, decline if they offer dinner: another train to catch.

He called Kurt before he left the States, to tell him he was going to see their father. Did Kurt have any message he wanted to send?

"Are you crazy?" Kurt said.

"He's an old man."

"So?"

"Agathe says he only has a few months to live."

Kurt was silent; then he let out a long, gusty sigh that sounded just like their father's old sighs. "Well, best of luck."

"That's what you want me to tell him?"

"Not him. You."

"So you don't have a message, then?" Stubborn, prosaic: this was the way to deal with melodrama. Ignore it; become willfully dull.

Another sigh from Kurt. "If I think of one, I'll call him myself."

All cities are beautiful at the end of April. But Munich, that day, seemed to have a special, startling loveliness. (He'd never been there before; he'd imagined it gray, steely, Gothic, like falling down inside a church organ.) Soft sunny air, blowing fresh and cool through the half-opened window of the taxi. Beds of red tulips, jaunty and alert. Streets of houses in light, Italianate colors—cream, yellow, pumpkin. Tall old trees, their outspread limbs just beginning to soften beneath a tracery of pale green blossom.

The taxi dropped him in front of a dark red building that looked as if it had been made by a child grimly determined to use every single block in the toy chest. It bulged with towers, arches, bays—and yet it had about it no sense of fun or fancy. It was serious and very German. Inside it was dark, too. He stood in the small lobby for a few moments before his eyes picked out the staircase wrapping around a small elevator in an iron cage. Riding the elevator seemed too passive, too helpless; he walked up to the second floor.

Agathe, his stepmother, hugged him, kissed him on both cheeks, and squeezed his hands. Her blue eyes shone at him;

her downy cheeks were pink; she smelled of some soft cologne that made him nostalgic, though he didn't know for what or whom. She took his arm and pulled him down the dim hallway toward a room full of light at the end. There was an archway, and there was his father coming toward him, walking with a cane.

The first two things his father said were: "Boris!" and "You're looking well, and I'm not."

Both would ordinarily have irritated him. His father would never call him "Paul," and having to remind him, or argue about it, made it seem as if the affectation lay in his own insistence that he be addressed this way, rather than in his father's refusal to adopt a name change the rest of the world had long ago accepted and forgotten. And his father was incapable of making a remark or having a conversation that was not primarily about himself. But so what? These first utterances, so predictable, seemed almost amusing; he had come to this visit so well armored, so overprepared to defend himself in case of a major attack, that these greetings merely bounced off his breastplate and fell softly, harmlessly, to the floor.

His father looked old. He'd looked old for years, had been completely bald since his mid-forties, but he'd always had a kind of fierceness in his face, with its bold black eyes and eyebrows, its audaciously large, bony nose. Now the eyebrows were white, and the real bones of the face had emerged; the forehead bulged, the cheekbones jutted, and between them the dark, dull eyes were sunken, like the eye cavities of a skeleton. The walk, too, was brittle and shrunken; there was an uneasy sense, watching him, of bone grinding on bone. Each step seemed painful, a wince.

There was a picture, done a long time ago, lost now, or hidden in a pile of papers in a drawer: a silhouette of his father dancing. Perhaps he was doing a part out of the Arabian Nights: the head was turbaned, the lines of the limbs were loose, flowing, Eastern-costumed. One arm was across the chest, its palm out, pushing the air; and one leg was lifted across the other, ready to leap and caper. Just a black shape on white paper, but tilted and witty and fluid, full of energy and elegance.

"No, no, Father, you're looking fine," he said, bending to kiss his father on both papery cheeks. "How are you feeling?"

"Hungry. Agathe has done a wonderful meal, and we were very good and waited for you to get here." The voice was the same as ever: booming, theatrical, heavily (almost comically) Russian-accented.

So he had lunch with them after all, at a round table before the big sitting-room window. Agathe had made veal, rolled and stuffed, in a light sauce, potatoes with parsley, and braised endive. There was a white tablecloth, and a bowl of grape hyacinths, and a bottle of gewürztraminer. The room was high and white, filled with sunshine; the window looked down on a small brick-walled garden. "Isn't that nice?" his father said. "Someone grows roses down there in the summer, and it isn't me."

"Oh, yes, those are always the most beautiful roses: the ones grown by someone else." Saying this—the same thing his father had just said, parroted back to show that he understood—he felt a pinch of self-loathing in his stomach. He took a breath and concentrated on stopping it, on not letting himself fall, the way he might have tried to clear his head during an attack of dizziness. He and his father could never just agree; they had to congratulate themselves on agreeing. (And a voice whispering in his ear, Kurt's voice: *You heard what he just said about the roses, didn't you? All the beauty and none of the work. That's his motto. That's the story of his life.* Kurt being devilish.)

(And Kurt, hearing this thought, too, whispering in his ear: *I'm not the devil, you idiot. You're having lunch with him.*)

"Agathe and I have actually been doing some growing of our own up here. We've become very interested in cactus."

"So I see." The windowsills were lined with them, green and brown and gray, growing in polished copper troughs. "They look very healthy."

"That's it. They look always the same. There's no suspense to growing them, no waiting for anything to happen. They're prickly; they stand there; they're always the same. And they can live to be ancient. There are some in America—in the Southwest, New Mexico, Arizona—"

"Yes—"

"Thousands of years old. Have you ever seen them?"

"No."

"I haven't either. I would have liked to. I should have gone, at some point. In all those years when I was living in America."

"But you were living in New York. New Mexico isn't exactly next door."

"I was a lot closer to New Mexico then than I am now. *You* should go." Pointing a finger.

For a moment he recoiled from his father's finger pointed at his face; then he nodded, smiling. "Well, maybe. It's hard to find the time, to get away. And the family—"

"No." His father sat back, crossing his arms imperially.

"Don't be polite. If you don't want to go to New Mexico, don't go, but if you do want to go, then make sure you go."

Agathe laughed. "This is the silliest conversation. What are you talking about, you two? You're all snarled around. Don't make him go to New Mexico; don't put him in a corner about it. He may not even like cactus."

"No, I do, I do like cactus. Agathe," he wiped his mouth with the corner of his napkin, "this is a wonderful lunch. Everything is delicious."

"Yes," said his father. "For a while they had me on a diet, for my heart. Nothing was wrong with my heart; it's just that diet they've devised to punish old men. No cream, no cheese, no butter. Nothing with any taste. But I thought, maybe this will help me live to be a hundred. Now, of course, I eat whatever I like." He reached over and put his hand on top of Agathe's wrist. "Tell him about the—what was in that soufflé you made the other day?"

"Oh, let me remember. Gruyère. Asparagus."

"No, but the flavoring. What was it that made it so—" The pursed lips fluttered, almost kissed the air.

"A little bit of mustard? Nutmeg?"

"Nutmeg. That was it." The eyes closed. "Everything *tastes so good.*"

"He sleeps now." Agathe came back into the kitchen. "Just for a little while, every afternoon. It refreshes him."

"Is he getting any treatment?"

"Not now. He had radiation, but it didn't work. And it made him sick, and exhausted. Very depressed. He's better since it all stopped. He feels better."

"And this isn't something that's operable?"

"We hoped it was, initially. He did have surgery."

"When was that?"

"A year and a half ago."

"Ah." He took the wet plate that Agathe held out to him and dried it with the linen towel, then placed it gently on the shelf. "I wish I had known."

Agathe was scrubbing another plate. "It wasn't the right time, then," she said.

He thought of asking her what she meant, and decided he preferred not to know. But he did know. From where they stood at the sink, they could see his father sleeping on the living room sofa, covered in a moss-green blanket, chest rising and falling, face slack, frowning involuntarily under the sunshine. His cane lay on the floor beside the sofa. One hand trailed onto the floor, palm up, amid the soft blues and reds of the carpet, the fingers loose and open. A sound like a purring cat: steady, faint snoring.

"He seems so tame now."

"He is," said Agathe, handing over a fistful of wet forks. "Now he is."

Cane, belt, broomstick. Shoe. Hanger. Once, when the fire went out in the basement furnace, a poker. Two broken ribs, that time.

"And how is your mother?"

The light had moved; the room, which had been bleached and dazzling, was now blue with shadows. His father sat on the sofa, the green blanket spread over his lap. Paul and Agathe sat at the table, their chairs turned sideways to face him. They were drinking coffee, out of thin green-and-white cups.

"She's fine," Paul said evenly. An hour from now he would be in a taxi, heading for his train. He was at once exhilarated and cautious, like a long-distance runner anticipating the finish line, gauging how much energy was left, how much was still needed. They'd made it through the lunch (now that he'd actually gotten through it, he was touched that they'd waited so late in order to eat with him), and there had been the respite of his father's nap. Some pleasant, hushed talk with Agathe — she'd shown him photographs of the honeymoon trip to Egypt she and his father had taken nine years ago. Now he couldn't stop looking at his watch; there was a sense of precarious accumulation, of all these unexpectedly good things piling up with ease, so that the possibility of dropping them became more and more terrible.

"Her health is good?" his father went on.

"Very."

"She sent a Christmas card, but not much of a note. Right?" turning toward Agathe. "Usually she writes a longer note. But maybe she's too busy for us, these days."

"Stop that," Agathe said sharply. Then, to Paul, "She is busy. She seems to be doing more teaching as time goes on, rather than less. I saw her, you know, in New York last year."

"You did?" But it was his father he was alert to, tense and waiting. You could not speak to his father the way Agathe just had. But his father sat still, smiling mildly, swathed in the blanket, like a baby in a perambulator.

Agathe said, "It was fun. She and I are old friends, you know, school friends; we go way back, long before either of us married—" she jerked her head sideways "—him."

"Yes, she told me. She was so glad when she heard you were getting married."

"We had fun this last time, in New York," Agathe said again. "She invited me to come to a class—to observe, you understand. I couldn't have participated at twenty-five, let alone seventy-five. And there she was in the middle of all these young dancers, and she pointed to one girl and told her to do something, and the girl said, 'I can't. Nobody could. It's impossible.' And then your mother leapt up in the air, and twisted or flew—it was so quick and so beautiful I almost didn't see it—but suddenly she was on the other side of the room, and she pointed back at the girl and said, 'Like that. That's how you do it.'"

Paul laughed. "That's wonderful." He'd heard plenty of these stories about his mother, from people she'd worked with or had taught. "She's amazing." But he was still afraid for Agathe. His eyes kept darting back toward his father, whose very silence was familiar and terrible, a gathering of force before the roar and the spring. Something was said, and the usual response was immediate outrage. How dare you. And escalating from there. But worse was when no response came. Then you thought that maybe the thing you'd said had been received as an innocent remark, or had been overlooked. You'd examined your words before you said them, and your tone; you'd washed them and rinsed them and made sure they came out of your mouth white and sanitized. Maybe this time they had passed inspection. The silence might mean safety. But no, it was just a delay.

How could Agathe just keep chatting away, standing directly under the teetering boulder?

But, "Your mother cooked supper for Agathe," his father was saying, now, in a voice rich with laughter. "I have trouble imagining it. Your mother cooking. Not just a bowl of macaroni, or a cheese sandwich. It was beef Stroganoff, no less."

"And it was delicious," Agathe added, chuckling. His father was chuckling, too.

Paul had a giddy sense that it was time to go. He stood up, slowly. "So—"

"She cooked." Agathe twinkled at him. "I didn't say she ate. She ate only the tiniest—less than a child's portion, and she didn't even finish it."

"Agathe says she's thinner than ever. Funny, when we were first together, she never cooked, would have considered it utterly bourgeois; and she was too fat, for a dancer, anyway. I was always at her about it." Rubbing the side of his face with his fist. "And rightly so, I think. She did lose weight, became quite slender." Opening the fist, rubbing his cheek gently with the palm. "And now she's too thin, and she cooks."

"Make her eat," Agathe said, standing up and taking Paul's hand in both of hers. "Make sure she takes care of herself."

And then a roar from his father. "You're not going now!"

Paul drew in his breath and tensed his hands. He said quietly, "I have a train to catch, and business in Frankfurt tomorrow."

The green blanket thrown back, the cane fumbled for and picked up. His father rising, coming toward him. Still roaring. "Oh, my dear child, I wish you didn't have to go! It's been such a long time since I saw you. And such a short visit! So wonderful to see you." His father's arms were around him; he was being rolled back and forth in his father's arms. "Oh, oh, oh," his father said.

Then the arms released him. "Come with me," his father said. "I want to give you something."

Paul glanced over at Agathe; she raised her shoulders and her eyebrows, a quick shrug, and then began clearing away the coffee cups. He followed his father, who was lurching away down the dark hallway. His father opened a door and stood aside to let Paul pass through it. "In here," he said.

His father turned on a small lamp with a rose-colored shade, which cast a dull light across a wide bed, spread with a plum satin coverlet. Above the bed were three framed watercolors: mountain scenes, with snow-covered rocks and icy skies and dark smudgy fir trees. The walls were the color of a manila folder. The rug on the floor was dim and brown, so worn that it crunched underfoot. Paul, standing just inside the doorway, watching his father rummaging in the top drawer of a tall bureau, thought suddenly that nothing in the entire apartment was familiar to him; there was not one object, one piece of furniture, one picture that he had ever seen before. Everything must be Agathe's.

But then what possessions had ever been associated with his father? They had never had a proper home as a family in Germany: touring with the dance company and staying in rooming houses, the children living most of the time with their grandmother and great-aunts, away from the parents. Then had come the basement in the Bronx, barely and cheaply furnished, then (after his grandmother died and a little bit of her money found its way across the Atlantic) an apartment on the Upper West Side. His mother still lived in that apartment, and all of the broken-down, beautiful pieces in it—the chipped-gilt smoky mirrors, the inlaid French chests with all the drawer pulls loose or missing, the tall dirt-smeared Chinese vases, the tarnished silver trays and hairbrushes—belonged to her, had come from her family. After the divorce, his father had lived in a succession of furnished New York studios, then had moved back to Germany in the early 1960s.

There were only two things Paul could remember, now,

that had belonged to his father, definitely and indelibly: a black wool beret, which his father had worn, year after year, over his bald head in cold weather, and which suited him, made him look elegant and wicked and free. And then that painted silhouette of him dancing, which come to think of it made him look the same way.

"Come here," said his father now, turning from the open bureau drawer, holding out his hands. "I'll let you choose."

Paul went closer. Lying on one of his father's open, upturned palms was a gold pocket watch and chain; on the other was a hunting knife with a gnarled bone handle.

"You choose," said his father again. "I'd really like you to have one."

Paul clasped his hands behind his back and bent his head to look more closely. "Boy oh boy," he muttered, speaking English for the first time that afternoon. "It's a tough decision."

"Take your time," his father answered, also in English, breathing heavily; Paul could feel the warm, gusty breaths on the back of his neck.

Was this some kind of test? If he reached for the watch, would his father think him unimaginative and greedy (both accusations that he'd made before)? If he chose the knife, would his father call him stupid, perverse? (There you go again, Boris; anyone else would have picked the watch. But you can't just do the straightforward obvious thing, you always have to show off. Everybody else goes left so you go right. Who the hell do you think you are?) And he didn't want either of these objects, didn't associate either with his father; and if there had in fact been some object associated with his father, he wouldn't want that either. And at the same time he was thinking: why make me choose? Why not just give me both?

"You choose, Father," he said after a long moment. "Which one would you like me to have?"

"No, no. You."

He took the watch. It was warm from his father's hand. The gold case was engraved with a delicate flowering vine; it opened to reveal a white face, with delicate Roman numerals. "Thank you," he said.

His father closed his eyes, smiled. "It doesn't work. But you could probably get it fixed." He turned and put the knife back into the drawer.

Paul snapped the watch shut and put it into his pocket. His father was still grinning at him, obviously expecting something more to be said. "Thank you," Paul repeated, speaking in German again, enunciating carefully. "Was this—have you had this watch for a long time?"

"Yes, a long time. It was a present."

"Someone has to go," came Agathe's pointed singsong from the doorway. "Someone has to go to the train station. Or he will be late. And miss his train."

"Yes, yes, we're coming." To Paul: "From a lady." A theatrical whisper. "I was always getting presents from ladies."

Paul asked if he could use the bathroom. When he came back out into the bedroom, his father and Agathe weren't there. The top drawer of the chest was still slightly open. Quickly, silently, as if every motion had been oiled, he crept over to it, edged the drawer out a little more.

It was full of knives. The one his father had shown him lay in a nest of others: blades of different lengths and thicknesses, handles made of ivory and leather and bone and wood and steel. There was at least one other pocket watch that he could see, and several wristwatches, and square jeweler's boxes in worn blue and green velvet. He picked one up and opened it—silver cufflinks—then shut it and put it back. His fingers closed around the sinewy handle of the knife his father had shown him, and he lifted it out of the drawer.

He ran his fingers along the blade; it was dull (if he'd chosen it, doubtless his father would have pointed this out, and advised having it sharpened). He slipped the knife into his pocket.

He was pushing the drawer shut, trying to approximate the slight gap his father had left. But then he stopped, slid it open again, pulled the knife from his pocket, and gently put it back where he'd found it.

Agathe and his father were waiting by the front door. Agathe handed him his raincoat and kissed him. Then his father held out his arms and pulled him close. "Thank you for coming. Thank you. Thank you."

"I'm glad I came," Paul said, hugging his father back.

"Are you?" His father finally let go, took a step back. He was crying, his nose red and running, his old eyes boiling with tears.

Paul felt as though he might cry, also. Agathe opened the door, took his hand, and looked into his eyes. "Thank you," she said once, gravely, firmly. Then she gave him a radiant smile, and then he was on the other side of the closed door. Through the heavy wood, as he walked rapidly toward the top of the staircase, came his father's faint calls: "Good-bye, Boris! Thank you! Thank you!"

He got to the station early enough to have a couple of drinks, scotches. He bought an orange and a bar of chocolate, and glanced over a newspaper. All of this seemed strangely vivid. The day was over, and now he was done.

The train was empty, eerily so. Where was everybody? He sat alone, looking at his vague reflection in the black window glass as the station began to slip away. He was suddenly very tired; he hadn't slept well the night before. And the scotches were probably getting to him, too.

He'd have to think about what to tell Kurt. He could imagine what Kurt would say: *Well, that's the thing about these deathbed reconciliations—you get to forgive him and then you never have to see him again. Very convenient.*

And: *You know, you didn't have to forgive him just because he needed you to.*

He peeled his orange and ate some squares of chocolate. The wheels clicked on the tracks and lighted towns flew by, each divided from the next by a long swath of darkness. It had begun to rain. Trailing streaks of silver water flung themselves against the cold windows of the train.

He had a book with him, a spy novel he had bought the other day in Frankfurt. He opened it now and read a page. The hero was transporting some documents out of Bucharest in the lining of his mistress's sable coat.

But Paul's eyes were heavy; his head dropped to his chest, and he slept, rocking back and forth in his slippery seat. He was going over a border; he'd almost escaped to safety but there was still some worry, still a chance he'd be caught. In his dream, the gold watch was working, and he had stolen the knife. His hand slid into his pocket and he felt them with his fingers, cold, heavy, metallic, tumbling and scratching against each other. He was holding them both, the loot and the gift: something fierce and something ticking.

Suicide:
intrafamilial relationships reexamined in light of
my grandmother

HER HAND. GRACEFULLY HELD UP IN CONVERSATION, WHEN SHE is making a point. A dancer's hand, palm pressing forward, curved fingers arching back, with the pinky and thumb straighter, slightly more extended than the rest. A square scuffed old sapphire ring, the only jewelry she ever wears, loose, slipping sideways.

On Christmas Eve, we take a taxi through Central Park to the West Side, where my grandmother lives. Her apartment is full of candles. I am told about the Christmas trees in Germany, lit by candles, with always a bucket of water standing nearby in case there's a fire. The food she serves is strange, and awful: herring salad, with beets and hard-boiled eggs; damp black bread; German wursts bulging with gristly bits of bone and blood. But then for dessert there are cookies my grandmother has baked. Weightless chocolate meringues. Buttery hazelnut circles. Spicy cinnamon stars that shatter when you bite them.

My grandfather is there sometimes. He and my grandmother are divorced. He's completely bald; his Russian accent is hard to understand; and he has a fierce face and a way of speaking that is too much. He is so happy to see me! He hopes I will like the present he got for me, because it was very difficult for him to find something he thought I might like! He hopes I will remember to send him a thank-you letter, because it would be rude not to! He hopes I understand that even though he doesn't get to see me as often as he would like, he does love me very much!

The grownups sit at the dinner table for a long time. I wander around the apartment. There are things that frighten and disgust me: brown stains in the bathroom sink and tub, beneath faucets that never stop dripping. My grandmother's roommate, Renee, who lives in the other bedroom, has white hair and dead-white skin and gigantic floppy breasts under a stained man's cardigan, and is constantly smoking and coughing, a wet retchy cough that sounds like she's throwing up.

But there are also things I love. An old Easter egg that sits on my grandmother's desk, pale yellow, painted with intricate interlocking flowers and vines. A bronze statue of a dancer in a corner by the sofa. A chipped-gilt mirror, so old that the glass is smoky and everything reflected in it is rippled and distorted. A set of tiny plastic barnyard animals, with a farmer carrying a bucket that actually swings on an infinitesimal handle. A little plastic garden with dark flat beds the size of graham crackers, with holes poked in them, and flowers whose stems stand upright when pushed into the holes.

I take off my shoes and run around on my grandmother's bare floors in my white tights. The bottoms of my feet turn black. Sometimes my grandmother takes off her shoes, and I see that her feet are black, too.

———

Her feet are long and narrow, with high curved arches. Red, mangled-looking toes. Dancer's feet.

Dance is what she does, her profession. Not ballet, which she says distorts the body's natural alignment. She does modern dance. She takes me sometimes to a studio to watch while she is teaching or choreographing. There is a lot of crouching, leaping, slithering, creeping, rolling around on the floor. The other dancers' bodies are like hers: lean and muscled. When they stand and gesture, everything juts: hips, elbows, chins. They're all very serious. Sometimes one will come over to talk to me, bending gracefully in her leotard near where I'm sitting in a corner on the floor. She asks me a question—Do I like school?—imbuing it with enormous gravity, tragedy almost, and then listens too carefully to my answer, which makes me feel that I have not given enough consideration to the matter of school.

The three my grandmother is closest to have amazing names: Eleonora, Faustina, Vashti. They collaborate with her not just on the dance, but on the other work she does: movement therapy. She works with polio patients, and with mental patients. She goes all over the world to study how people move in different countries. She writes articles, gives lectures.

"Your grandmother is a very great woman," Vashti says, staring at me with sad dark eyes.

"Vashti. I bet her real name is something like Mildred, or Ethel," my mother says.

My mother doesn't like my grandmother, and I don't understand why. I try asking.

"What do you mean, I don't like her? Of course I like her! Don't you ever say anything like that ever again!" she screams at me. "Don't talk about things you don't understand!"

When other people are around, my father and my grandmother speak English. But sometimes, when the two of them are alone in a room, they have long quiet talks in German. It always sounds like they're whispering—lots of hissing "s" sounds—but I'm never sure whether that's the kind of conversation they have or the sound of the language itself.

"Mostly about business," my father says when I ask him what they're talking about. "She's not good with money, so sometimes she asks for my advice."

My grandmother has a lot of money, but not as much as there once was. This, I know, is one of the things my mother is furious about.

Some of it got lost when my grandmother left her first husband to run off with my grandfather, who was her dance teacher. I never understood how this loss happened. Did her first husband get the money in the divorce? Did her parents take it away from her?

Some got lost when my grandparents fled Germany just before the war. ("Other people," my mother says firmly, "were smart enough to get out and get their money out, too.")

Some got lost when she invested it with her brother-in-law, who ran a chemical company in Dusseldorf. Though he managed to hang on to his own money (we visit him, one summer; he has a castle on the Rhine), he either stole or lost hers.

The details of how she lost bits of her money are so vague that I imagine vagueness itself as the culprit, implicated in the losses. I imagine my grandmother sitting down with her money on a park bench, and then getting up and wandering off, abandoning it like an empty lunch bag or an umbrella.

Abandoned. That's the word my mother uses, over and over again, when she asks my father about his childhood. "Didn't you feel *abandoned,* when they left you alone in Germany?"

"I wasn't alone," my father says. "Kurt was with me, and we liked the school in the Alps. And in the vacations I stayed with the aunts, whom I loved."

"What kind of parents go off like that and abandon their children for three years?" my mother wants to know.

"They didn't want to bring us to the States before they had a home and a livelihood. They wanted to get a little bit established."

"Three years?" my mother persists.

"That's how long it took," my father tells her coolly.

I don't understand why she keeps trying to make him upset about something that apparently doesn't upset him.

"They abandoned you," she says again.

And my father gives her that cool, closed look. "I was happy," he says.

My grandmother is doing something called a movement choir, in a church in Greenwich Village. My family drives into the city—we've moved to Connecticut—and we take her out to dinner first, but she eats only a bowl of broth. Then she leaves. We sit at the table and eat a rich meal and dessert; it's all delicious, but I feel gluttonish, slothful.

The church is packed when we get there. Vashti has saved us seats up front. "An important evening," she says, grave and excited. I see my mother and father look at each other when she says it; they don't roll their eyes, but that's the feeling.

Kurt and his wife are there, sitting on the other side of my father, but beyond saying hello my parents don't talk much to them. There's a coolness there, another of those family things I don't understand. It has something to do with Kurt and his wife being actors, and my father being in business.

My grandmother stands up at the front and talks about movement, and people in groups, and the ways in which we circle and observe and imitate each other without even being aware of it. "A contagion!" she says in her brisk German accent, and people laugh. She's wearing a black leotard with a purple scarf wrapped around her waist like a skirt. The lights on the ceiling behind the altar shine through her hair, making a cloud-white halo.

She starts to move, to dance, lifting her arms and swaying. Then, almost immediately, people from the audience stand up and begin moving too, swaying out of the pews and up the aisles to where my grandmother is. They start to make loose circles around her; I can see her white hair glowing at the center. There is no music, just a low murmuring humming buzz coming from people's lips. I am horrified, embarrassed, frightened. All these grownups, with half-closed eyes and wild hair and raised arms, dancing, stamping, swaying, buzzing. No one is in control. Or maybe my grandmother is: she started this, caused it, presumably condones it, is turning slowly in its center.

Kurt and his wife are up and dancing. So is Vashti, who grabbed my hand and tugged and then, when I wouldn't go with her, smiled sadly and slid away into the aisle. My parents are still in their seats, looking straight ahead, their faces stiff and expressionless. We are not the only ones not dancing; a few other people, mostly very old, are still scattered around, seated, in the pews. But their faces are animated, interested. My parents are the only ones with that look of stiff disapproval. Even though I think I disapprove also—the dancing feels so unsafe—I can't ally myself with them. Their coldness is prudish, disloyal. The dancing goes on and on. My father leans down and whispers something in my ear, which I can't hear. He whispers it again, louder. "Not your cup of tea either?" I'm too frozen even to shrug.

Finally, finally, it's over. We have to wait a long time to get to my grandmother, who is still standing at the center of a crush of people. When we reach her, she puts her thin strong arms around me, and I kiss her damp cheek.

"What did you think?" she asks, and I nod my head up and down many times and say, "I liked it."

"Wonderful, Mother," my father says, in a big, false voice.

There is going to be a party afterward, in the church basement, but my father says we need to get home. I kiss my grandmother again. As we're making our way up the aisle to the door, I see Vashti, and we smile at each other apologetically.

It's Vashti on the phone. She sounds upset and asks if my grandmother is with us. I say yes, she's visiting for the weekend.

"Well, can I speak to her?" Vashti's voice is high and vibrating.

"Just a minute, I'll get her," I say.

She is in the living room, alone, working out some dance steps. "It's Vashti," I tell her, and she stops abruptly, with one foot lifted and an arm curved above her head. "Oh," she says. "Yes."

Later that day my mother tells me, in a low voice, what happened. Vashti was getting married that day, expecting my grandmother to be her attendant. My grandmother had promised, months ago. And then she had come to Connecticut for the weekend instead. She told Vashti over the phone that she was very sorry, she'd forgotten.

"Can you believe that?" my mother asks me. "Forgetting the wedding of your closest friend—a wedding you're supposed to take part in? So here's Vashti, on her wedding day, having to call around, trying to locate her. Trying to see if there's some explanation. Which, really, there isn't."

"Maybe she did just forget," I said. "Maybe she's starting to get old." This had never occurred to me before, that my strong grandmother might start to weaken.

"She's not *that* old," my mother said. "And you know what? This is typical. This not showing up for the people you're closest to. She abandons people. All she really cares about is her work."

The book she has been writing for as long as I can remember, a summation of her work, is published. My mother is furious when it comes out, because of the dedication. It reads "To my two sons, Boris and Kurt."

No one has called my father Boris in years. He had always hated the name, and changed it to Paul when I was a baby. Even my grandmother calls him that. So why did she use the name "Boris" in the dedication?

"To embarrass him," my mother says. "There's no other explanation."

But then she keeps coming up with more. "To rebuke him, for throwing away the name she gave him. To put him in his place, for daring to reject her sloppy bohemian lifestyle, unlike Kurt. Or," my mother says, getting even angrier and more excited, "maybe she just forgot. Maybe Daddy means so little to her that she can't even remember his name. I mean, he's only her *son*. I mean, that's nothing, when you're busy writing a book and founding an *institute*."

I come home from college and drive into New York with my parents to the opening of the institute for movement studies. White loft space, with photos on the walls of people moving: dancing, walking, running. You can tell from their bodies how they were feeling when the pictures were taken: happy, frightened, tired, angry, depressed.

The rooms are crowded, festive. I recognize Faustina from a distance, though I haven't seen her since I was a child; she's as erect and beautiful as ever. Vashti comes over to talk to me, and I think: So, that friendship did survive. She isn't wearing a wedding ring, and I wonder whether or not she's still married.

"Isn't this just breathtaking?" Vashti asks me, sweeping an eloquent arm at the crowd.

"Yes," I say, meaning it.

My father and I stand together looking at the photographs. A young woman standing near us introduces herself and says she's a student here. "And what's your connection to the institute?" she asks. When my father tells her, she begins to breathe very fast, and to flap her arched dancer's hand in front of her face. "Oh, my God—you're her *son*?" she says. "And her *granddaughter*? Oh, my God."

"I half expected her to genuflect," my father says in the car going home. "Didn't you?"

My mother says, "It's ridiculous, the way they idolize her."

"Really, it was as if I'd said, 'Hi, I'm John the Baptist, and this is Mary Magdalene,'" my father says.

Forgetting. It's happening more and more. My grandmother forgets birthdays. Forgets where she put her glasses, or her checkbook, or her scarf. Writes to me and leaves out letters in the middle of words, words in the middle of sentences. Comes for Christmas and forgets one of her bags on the train. Forgets the recipes for the Christmas cookies she's been baking for years.

She is getting older. I realize this one day when I walk by the living room doorway and see her moving, working out steps with the same dreamy grace and energy she's always had—and there's a long piece of toilet paper trailing behind her, hanging from the waistband of her loose black trousers.

But then suddenly she leaps, flying across our living room in a dance step, like an arrow shooting through space. And I also see that she's managed to push all the furniture against the walls, to get it out of her way.

Her foot is gone. There's a structure beneath the bedclothes, a kind of tent, so that nothing will touch the site of the amputation.

She's been fleeing this operation for six months, ever since she got out of the hospital the last time, with a not-quite-healed infection on her toe. She went to Hawaii and taught, but the damage kept creeping upward. A toe, then two toes, then all the toes. No amputation, she said, and she tried other treatments—biofeedback, chelation therapy. Finally they told her she would die without the surgery, and it was scheduled. That's when her students found her lying on the floor. Maybe she took something, an overdose, they are saying now. Maybe she couldn't face living without her foot.

"No," my father says, when I ask him about the rumor. "Mother would never do that. She would find the idea of suicide completely unacceptable."

Is she aware that the foot is gone? No one knows if she's conscious or not. Her eyes are open, but she's frozen. She can't move or speak. She's like some character out of a terrifying fairy tale—fleeing, but then frozen and helpless and captured.

My father is sitting next to her, holding her hand. He doesn't turn around when I come into the room; he thinks he's alone with her. He is saying, "Mother, it's me. Paul. It's Paul, Mother." His voice is quiet but desperate. He leans in, and I hear him say, "Mother, it's Boris."

He's crying.

Her memorial service is held on a sweltering day, in the auditorium of the Ethical Culture Society. Kurt gets up and speaks. So do I. So do Faustina and several of the students and colleagues from the institute. A musicologist talks about going with my grandmother to Africa and Australia in the 1950s, to study indigenous songs and dances. Vashti does an eighteenth-century dance that my grandmother reconstructed and performed in Berlin in the late 1920s. My father doesn't get up to speak. He keeps his sunglasses on, and stays silent. Tears are running down his face. He ignores the movement choir. I get up to join it, though, and I look back at him. He and my mother are marooned sitting there, alone in the midst of everyone else who knew her.

The movement choir loops down the aisles, up onto the stage, and back down again. We're all swaying, sweating, crying. Nobody is in the center.

After it's over, people linger. They stand in the aisles, in the vestibule, on the front steps, outside on the baking sidewalk, all reluctant to break away.

Breaking up her apartment is hard. Everything looks like her, and it all belongs together, in a jumble. Dividing it diminishes everything.

There is no sign of the farm, or of the plastic garden.

We throw out her clothes, which are old and worn; in the last few years she'd got to the point of not caring.

"Oh, my God," my mother says. She is holding a piece of paper which she's just pulled out of the bottom drawer of my grandmother's dresser.

"What?" I ask.

She keeps looking at it, but moves close to me so that I can see it too. At first it doesn't make any sense. A big drawing of concentric circles, dated a couple of months ago, with "Circle of Love and Healing" at the top in my grandmother's handwriting.

The circle at the center is very small, with my grandmother's name written in the middle of it.

It's surrounded by a slightly larger circle, in which my grandmother wrote the names of Kurt and his wife, along with Faustina and Vashti.

My family is in the next circle outward. "Boris," she wrote, and my mother's name, my sister's, and mine. Along with ours are several other names I don't recognize.

There are more circles surrounding ours, radiating outward, filled with names.

My mother's hands, holding the paper, are shaking. "Now do you see?" she says. "Now do you see why I never liked her? She never protected him, not from anything. What kind of person does something like this? What kind of mother loves one child more than the other and then writes it down? What kind of mother has to map it all out in *circles*?"

She's upset but triumphant: at last my grandmother's villainy has been documented. Here it is, laid out clearly, for the record.

My father comes in, from the living room. "What's all the commotion?"

I look at my mother. No. Don't show it to him, I think.

But she's already giving him the piece of paper, the evidence, all mapped out in circles—something irrevocable and permanent, the last word he'll ever have from his mother, written in her graceful hard-to-read hand.

Suicide:
items found in my husband's closet and

A SATURDAY MORNING, A YEAR OR SO AFTER MY FATHER'S DEATH. I was in my house, sitting on the floor of my husband's closet. I was rummaging around in the stuff on the floor.

I'd been doing this—these aimless, restless searches—ever since my father died. In closets and basements and chests of drawers, in my parents' house and in my own. I was looking for clues. Also, I kept hoping I'd find a note—that maybe my father, with his ornately circuitous ideas of honor and secrecy, might have written a note and hidden it, for reasons we wouldn't understand until we found it.

My husband's closet floor was a jumble of shoes and boxes of old papers and shopping bags full of old clothes to be donated to charity. I moved one of the bags, and behind it was a large manila envelope. When I opened it, another envelope slid out. I read the writing on it: my father's name, and the date of his death, and the words CONTENTS OF POCKETS.

Inside was a collection of smaller envelopes. I tipped them into my lap.

RIGHT REAR POCKET, one said. I opened it. My father's wallet. His face looked up at me from his driver's license: a tiny, law-abiding citizen.

RIGHT FRONT POCKET. A white handkerchief. A roll of peppermint Certs, half gone, with the gold foil folded over to protect the top one. A prescription bottle of Lomotil. His key chain.

LEFT REAR POCKET. A green plastic compact filled with Tucks hemorrhoid wipes.

I sat there. After a moment, I screamed for my husband. He came running up the stairs and saw me sitting there with all the little envelopes in my lap.

I said: "I think he was murdered."

"Why do you say that?"

"Because look." I held up the thing of hemorrhoid wipes. "There's no way he would have put these in his pocket if he'd been planning to kill himself. Or here—" I held up the prescription bottle "—this is diarrhea medicine. You know how private he was. He would never have wanted this stuff to be found on his body."

My husband sat down on the floor near me. "He wasn't murdered."

"Yes!" I said. "My mother was asleep. Someone could have come into the house without being heard, and gone into his study, and shot him."

"Why would anyone have wanted to murder him?"

"Maybe he borrowed money from someone and couldn't pay it back. You know the business was failing. Or maybe he was involved in something we didn't know about. He spoke all those languages; he was always traveling. Maybe he was a spy."

I looked at my husband's face. "I'm serious—why couldn't he have been a spy?"

"Because he wasn't sharp enough. Not in the last few years." My husband's voice was gentle.

"Well, maybe that's why they killed him. Maybe he'd started fucking up, so it was too dangerous to let him live. Have you checked the telephone records? Have you gone through all his file drawers?" I was shouting. I knew that what I was saying sounded crazy, impossible—but so was the idea that he'd killed himself. After all these months, after all the moments when I'd thought I'd known it was the truth, I still didn't know; I still didn't believe it.

My husband said: "They know it was suicide."

He said it in a clear, deliberate way. He was telling me something new.

"What do you mean?"

"They know because of the way he was shot."

"In the heart?"

"In the head," my husband said.

I turned my body to face him.

He said, "The police told me, one of those times I went to the station. I wasn't going to tell you."

"But the blood was on his chest. There wasn't a head wound."

"Yes there was."

"How could my mother not have seen it?"

"It was inside."

There was a silence, a new abyss slowly opening. "You're saying he put the gun in his mouth." We were sitting cross-legged on the floor. The sun was gilding the window glass; the morning was passing. The house smelled of bacon and eggs. I was still in my nightgown. "So the blood on his chest must have come out of his mouth and his nose." We sat there some more.

I thought: So that was the bulge.

I said, "But why wasn't his head blown apart? Isn't that why people shoot themselves like that, so their heads will blow apart?"

"The police didn't understand that either. They said they'd never seen this happen before. They said it might've been because the gun was so old. A malfunction of some kind."

"A malfunction," I said. "So it could have not worked. It could have just wounded him, not killed him. He was lucky."

"In a sense."

I said, "So all my mother's stuff about how he shot himself in the heart to be considerate of us, to not make a mess—that was all bullshit. For all he knew, he was going to blow his head apart. And she would have found him like that, and he didn't care."

I kept sitting on the floor in my nightgown, with the contents of my father's pockets lying in my lap.

In that moment, I knew he was dead.

I knew that he'd killed himself, and I knew how violently he'd wanted to wipe himself out.

I knew that everything we thought we'd known about him—his gentleness, his love for us—was open to question.

And I knew I would never understand how he'd gotten from putting hemorrhoid wipes in his pocket to shooting himself in the head forty-five minutes later.

———

I forgot it all again, afterward. Those moments of knowing are sharp and merciless, but then they fade out, like stars when the sky gets light in the morning. You know, and then you don't know. And then comes another moment when you're learning—something new, or the same things over and over again.

Suicide:
life summarized in an attempt to illuminate

LET'S SAY I AM A BIOGRAPHER. I AM HIS DAUGHTER, BUT I ONLY happen to be his daughter. Say I am also scholarly and earnest. I intend to write slowly, to think carefully. I want to look at the bigger picture, to examine his suicide in the context of his whole life.

I read somewhere that every year in America, there are twice as many suicides as murders. I want to write about it because it's important.

Let's say I'm impartial.

Let's also say that I've been given a grant to pursue this biographical piece of work. A residency at an artists' colony. I've been given a studio to work in, a quiet cabin that overlooks both a patch of woods and a sloping, grassy field. It's only the beginning of November, but it snowed last night; and this morning the field, which was green and rippling, looks hard and flattened and faded.

The room I sleep in is in a house in another part of the colony. I hike over here, around seven each morning. I come in and make tea, in a red teapot I brought from home. I brought other things as well. Old papers and photographs. A draft of the failed novel I tried to write about my father. Music that reminds me of him.

1.

Start with a thesis, or a statement of purpose: I am going to try to reconstruct who he was, because I'm not sure anymore.

Suicide destroys memory.

It undercuts one of our most romantic, and most comforting, notions: that we don't really die when we die, because we live on in the memories of those who love us.

When you kill yourself, you're killing every memory everyone has of you. You're taking yourself away permanently and removing all traces that you were ever here in the first place, wiping away every fingerprint you ever left on anything.

You're saying, "I'm gone, and you can't even be sure who it is that's gone, because you never knew me."

So what did I know about my father, really?

He was tall.

He was tired.

He liked desserts made with berries. Shortcake. Sundaes. A German pudding called *rote grütze:* whipped raspberries, or maybe it was red currants. His mother used to make it sometimes.

He liked Purcell, Vivaldi, Telemann, Mozart—anybody composing before 1800. After that things got too overblown for him, too overtly emotional.

He liked Shakespeare and Oscar Wilde, and could quote long passages. Once he got going at the dinner table, it was hard to stop him.

He spoke German, French, Spanish, and Portuguese.

He was fascinated by Japan, at least until he had a bad experience doing business with a Japanese company, and then he decided, abruptly and irrevocably, that "you can't trust them." Them. Suddenly these colleagues whom he'd liked and respected became Them.

What he meant was: they had hurt him and betrayed him by having seemed so trustworthy. They'd been polite and thoughtful and *then* screwed him, whipped out a knife that he hadn't even imagined they could be carrying.

(Oh, but that last paragraph is fiction—my moving away from the cautious, measured, responsible tone of biography into the kind of wildness I now believe was churning behind his calm face. Slipping from what I know is true to what I think must have been true.)

(And of course that betrayed bitter wildness is true for me, too. He was so polite and considerate, and wound up using a weapon I never knew he had.)

He liked to read books that prophesied disaster—economic or political—and that suggested that if you were prescient and canny enough, you could not only avoid being harmed by the impending catastrophe, you could actually profit from it. He liked novels about conspiracies and espionage. I think he believed that there was a different, dark world operating beneath the bland cover of ordinary life. You'd be crazy and naïve to deny that it was there. It was cleverly hidden, but sometimes it gave itself away; if you stayed alert you could sometimes glimpse it. Its forces, if seen and understood, would explain everything.

Maybe, for him, such an explanation felt necessary. He had experienced those two worlds—the safe one and the terrifying, merciless one—in his childhood. Life was a war between civilization and brutality. Civilization was a deliberate construction;

it was very much to be desired, but not to be trusted. He wanted to trust it. He believed he could choose it. So his father had hit him years ago, so what? So his childhood had been rough. Was he going to let that determine the tone of his whole life? Of course not.

Bad stuff happens. You can wallow in it and feel sorry for yourself, or you can get on with things. Be a grownup, be a man, be reliable and dependable. Love your wife and daughters. Succeed. Forget about brutality. It's old, it's over. It can't hurt you anymore.

Ah, but brutality was real. You could wish it gone, you could try to geld it, but you knew it was there. It was what lurked underneath. If you fell down into it there was no point in screaming for help, because no one would come.

2.

Okay. We've learned something: a formal biographical essay won't work. In this case, with this writer, it gets too emotional, too easily out of hand. It may act like a well-schooled horse, but then the minute it gets out of sight of the stable, into the open countryside, it gallops away, with its rider clinging desperately to mane and saddle.

Let's try something different.

Let's look at the photographs. Spread them out, put them in chronological order, use them to organize and anchor the narrative.

The first one isn't a single photograph; it's a whole album, from my grandmother's childhood. She came from a rich family that made all the pins and needles in Germany. The album is bound in heavy maroon leather, with an ornate brass clasp. The words

UNSER LIEBLING are stamped in gold on the front cover. *OUR DAR-LING.* Chunky, gilt-edged leaves: photographs of posed children with big, soft, timid eyes, their hair in ringlets, wearing starched white dresses. My grandmother was the oldest. When she was twelve, they all got rheumatic fever. The brother died, the sister was left with a heart condition, and my grandmother's joints were affected. She started dancing as a kind of physical therapy. She married a university professor, who disappointed her by turning out not to want children.

Then she met my grandfather.

The next picture is of the two of them, dancing, presumably with the touring troupe they formed. They're wearing ragged vagabond costumes, facing away from each other. Her elbows are looped through his; he's leaning forward, lifting her off the ground so that she's lying on her back against his back; her feet are kicking in the air. They're both laughing, big free open-mouthed laughs. Sex cackles and shivers off the old photographic paper.

My grandfather was a childlike, charismatic, self-dramatizing man, a Russian who'd grown up rootless and parentless, wandering through eastern Europe until he eventually found his way to Berlin. Before he met my grandmother he survived as a dancing teacher, and a gigolo. He sneered at my grandmother's smug, sheltered, bourgeois life; yanked her out of it by her thrilled arm; assumed, of course, that her money would come with her. But it didn't. Running away with him (and away from her marriage) made her the black sheep of her family.

But her family must not have broken with her completely, because here is my father, at the age of four, sitting next to a tall jar of flowers on the floor of my great-grandmother's apartment in Berlin. His hair is a mass of blond curls, and he is wearing a dress. They got hold of him for a while, while his parents were touring with their dance troupe, and raised him in the *Unser Liebling* mold.

He remembered that life as organized and formal. Safe, but stuffy and restrictive. They thought he ate too slowly, so they put an alarm clock next to his plate and when it rang, the food was taken away. This was how it was done: *so*.

Another piece of my father's childhood needs to be in here, but there's no photograph of it. The times when his parents took him along on their tours, which he hated. No bedtime, no set mealtimes. Being left alone in a dark hotel room with his baby brother while his parents were out performing, the baby smearing shit on the walls and my father not knowing what to do about it.

All his life he believed that artists were irresponsible.

Now he's a little older, six or seven, away at boarding school in the Alps. Standing in a group of children, all of them in costume for a play or pageant: elves in tights and doublets and peaked caps; my father, unmistakable because of his wild hair, in a white gown, wearing a crown and carrying a lantern. He told me once that in the winter, at that school, they all got around on skis, casual and skilled enough not even to need poles. It wasn't a sport, he said; it was transportation. He told me about climbing mountains, walking up through clouds and emerging above them.

He was happy there.

———

Something else that couldn't be documented photographically: his parents' absence. They left Germany and went to America in 1936, when my father was seven, with the intention of sending for their children once they were settled. They'd been staying in Munich one night, and a Jewish man was beaten to death beneath their window. My father told me, "They knew they didn't want to stay in a country where things like that could happen."

I didn't learn until after my father's death that my grandfather was Jewish; my father made it sound like the issue was one of ideology, not survival.

When I said that to my mother, she got angry. "Oh, that didn't matter. Your grandmother's family was very powerful and could have protected everybody." Well, maybe—or very possibly not. My mother's Jewish family in France was decimated. Does she think it's because they weren't powerful and had no one to protect them?

Now we come to the greatest happiness of his childhood, the place that would always haunt him as a lost paradise. Here we have another album: a big one, covered in linen that must once have been cream-colored but is now brownish-gray. *HAUS MERBERICH*, it says on the cover. *KINDER UND BLUMEN*. Children and flowers. Merberich was the country house near Aachen that belonged to his two unmarried great-aunts. Leaf slowly through these heavy pages, the life there recorded in muted shades of dove and fawn. A long row of French doors opening out onto terraced gardens and a lake with swans. Fields, barns, goats. Nine cousins stepping across the lawn holding hands, with a great-aunt in a white dress smiling at either end of the line. A big Christmas tree blurry with candles. A close-up of my father in the garden, laughing, his hair whitened and cloudlike, its ends radiating and disappearing in the sunlight.

My father went back there once, on a trip he made to Germany in the early 1950s. Four or five families were living in the house, and the land was being strip-mined.

1939. He and his younger brother, Kurt, are standing by the ship's railing, watched over by some starchy-looking woman in a uniform who must have been a nurse hired for the voyage. They're on their way to New York.

It was summertime, and theirs was the last boat to get out of Germany before the war started.

I don't want to write this next part. And there aren't any photographs.

When he got to America, to his parents' cold little apartment in the Bronx, his father started beating him. His mother watched. Kurt lay in bed in the next room, hearing the screams.

No photographs. School in the Bronx. He got teased for not knowing any English; he learned English very fast. He got teased for his foreign-sounding name. Early on someone pulled a knife on him; the next day he brought in his own knife, and after that they left him alone.

A boarding school in the Berkshires. No photos here, either. But I have a diary he kept. Full of rage and swearing and bad grades and how unfair the bad grades were. On almost every page, hoping for a letter from Mother or hoping she'd come to visit. And then, "No letter, God damn it," or "Shit, she didn't come."

Kurt told me about this school, after my father's death. Sadistic teachers, maggoty food. No heat in the winter. For a while some of the boys kept a pet rabbit, but the headmaster wouldn't let them have food for it, and it starved to death.

Kurt also told me that my father ran away from the school once, to New York. They made him go back.

The biographer isn't supposed to cry, or shiver, or feel like she's about to throw up. She moves away from the computer and looks out at the sky. It's a dull, luminous gray through the bare branches in the woods; but above the field it's blue, streaked with clouds that look like shredded tissue paper. The clouds are moving very slowly. Or maybe what she sees is the world turning.

In the distance, at the top of the hill, is another small building, red-shingled, with big windows. She doesn't know who is using that studio, but she knows it's being used by someone: lights go on in the evening. It must be a painting studio, with those windows. Maybe the painter is looking out at the sky now, too. Maybe trying to paint it.

His old college yearbooks. Four volumes, four different photographs. He is a member of a club: the Future Business Leaders. In his freshman year, he is a thin impassive face, half hidden in the back row. By the next year, he's moved up to the middle of the group. As a junior, he's in the foreground, club secretary. And by the time he's a senior, he's the president, sitting in the middle of the front row, relaxed and keen, grinning. If brains and patience and quiet confidence are the necessary ingredients, then he can't possibly miss.

3.

I can go forward chronologically or thematically: look at what happened next, or think about how and why he did, after all, miss.

The word "miss" is so wistful. As is the word "wistful," for that matter. They both have sighs embedded in them, that "iss" sound. Which also sounds like "if."

Biographers don't usually play with words—they leave that to the poets. But when I think of the word "miss" in connection with my father, I'm instantly drawn to leap further, all the way to the even more wistful, sighing word "missing."

He had something missing. By the end it was something big.

Was it missing all his life? Or did it start small and grow?

So: a tentative choice to proceed thematically brings me right back to chronology.

He was young and poor when he met my mother, on the train coming back from Tanglewood.

"Young" and "poor" sounded so promising, the way my mother always told me the story. Temporary conditions: poignant "befores" that existed only to contrast with triumphant "afters."

He was tall and skinny and confident. In the train he smoked all her cigarettes and then told her he would need to see her again in order to replace the pack.

Their first date. A hot summer night. She waited for him in a brown sleeveless dress, with her arms raised over her head so she wouldn't sweat on the dress and ruin it. He brought her champagne, and then took her to ride on the Staten Island ferry. She found it dashing, the way he was so wittily forthright about being poor. They stood at the railing and he told her his plan for himself. One day I'm going to be the president of a company, he said.

She was twenty-nine, four years older than he, working in public relations with the men who invented the Diners Club card. She was sleek, intelligent, voluptuous. A sophisticated New York career woman, living with a roommate in a Sutton Place apartment.

He saw her that way. He saw what she hoped was true.

Here's what else was true. She had only recently broken away from living with her big, close, poor family in Brooklyn. Her mother had always said that something terrible would happen to her if she moved to the city, and her mother said dark things with such conviction that they seemed to contain some truth. And dark things had already happened in the family. The oldest daughter dead at thirty of cancer. One son with all his hair gone, and his scalp pitted with brown and white burn scars—there had been a little spot, when he was a child, and the doctor had said, "No problem, we'll just use x-rays to get rid of it." Another son, who had gone to Korea to cover the war as a reporter for the *Times:* his plane had crashed, and he'd lost a leg and nearly died.

You're my baby, her mother told her. Stay with me; don't leave me.

Maybe this is part of what drew my parents together: they both knew bad things could and did happen. They were confident and attractive and on their way up—they firmly believed this, but they also deeply doubted it. They shared, in nearly identical proportions, an idiosyncratic mix of jauntiness and pessimism, of hope and catastrophe.

4.

If my parents were to read this, they would say, "You're getting it wrong."

And of course I am. I'm not my father or my mother. I don't know what it was like to be either one of them.

I remember some things. Other things were told to me; I either believed them or felt uneasy with them. Or I believed them once, but don't anymore. Or I was too young to understand, but now I can see better what might have been going on.

About some things—but not others—I could ask my mother. She might fill in details for me. Or she might insist, her voice rising in annoyance or panic, that the thing I'm asking about never happened, I am making it up.

There's no way to check out what's true. The kind of truth I'm looking for is slippery.

The biographer listens to anecdotes, looks at diaries and letters. But people remember things wrong when they tell anecdotes; they slant things. And people lie in diaries and letters. Or they write in moments of passion, and then they put down the pen and go make a sandwich. A biography may highlight a certain pivotal letter—but maybe the writer sent it off and then forgot all about it, and the recipient read it once, shrugged, and tossed it into a drawer.

Lives are made up of days, and days are made up of hours—good ones, bad ones, so-so ones. Biographers try to organize the mess, which inevitably changes its nature.

I don't believe there's any subject of a biography who would say to the biographer, "You got it right." How could biographees not be disgruntled? They'd point out oversimplifications, wrong emphases, big lapses, and an infuriating tendency to link spurious causes to dubious effects.

On the other hand, I suppose a really nervy biographer might say to the subject, "No, you're the one who's getting it wrong." And go on to point to instances of self-delusion, glossing over of embarrassing or painful memories, self-justification in retrospect, and a general inability to see the forest for the trees.

You can't possibly understand my life, the subject would tell the biographer, because you didn't live it.

And the biographer would retort: *You* can't possibly understand it, because you did.

5.

Before I show up they are two people, sharp and distinct. Once they become my parents, they start to blur.

They were mysterious to me when I was little. I wanted to get closer, to get inside, to know.

I kept asking questions. Why were my father's parents divorced? Why did my mother seem to dislike my father's mother? Were we rich or poor?

The answers came back like slaps: never mind. None of your business. That's private.

I wanted to know why my father had changed his name. When I was very young, he'd had first and last names that sounded Russian, but then our last name suddenly changed to something shorter and American-sounding; and then his first name wasn't Boris anymore, it was Paul.

"Because," my father said when I asked.

My mother said, "Because it sounded like a Russian spy, that's why. No one would give him a job with a name like that."

"But it's a secret," my father added, "it's nobody's business. If anyone asks you why your last name is different now, you just tell them to mind their own business."

In the morning, when they were still asleep, I would prowl the apartment. They'd had people over the night before. Coffee cups with lipstick-smudged rims, smelly ashtrays, little bowls flecked with salt and a few brown shreds of peanut skins. The bridge scores lying on the card table, radiating a kind of Cold War paranoia that I felt in my stomach but was too young to understand. We–They. We–They.

My father read to me at night. The *Madeline* books, setting up each couplet and then pausing so I could crow out the final rhymes. *Curious George* and *Babar*. Edward Lear and A. A. Milne, which he read with patient silliness and an assumed English accent.

We got up early and made pancakes together on Saturday mornings. He had a special way of making the batter, with extra milk and eggs; his pancakes were thin and weightless. Every week he would pop the first one into my mouth and wait, eyebrows raised: "My hand has not lost its touch?"

He took me out to buy a Christmas tree. To see a parade. To pick up Chinese takeout. To see the snakes in the zoo on Staten Island. To buy a fish tank, on my fifth birthday. He painted the outside of the aquarium's rear wall a deep blue-green, filled the bottom with pebbles, packed the plastic filter with charcoal and white cotton wool, and filled the tank with water he'd shaken up in an old milk bottle to remove the air bubbles. I was impressed that he knew to do all this. When he got home from work at the end of the day, he would come with me into my room and ask after each fish by name.

When he was here, he was here. But when he was gone, he was emphatically, horribly gone. He went away a lot, for business, on airplanes, which I was always sure would crash. He was gone for weeks, sometimes months. Europe, South America, India, Egypt, Australia. We had a framed map, with pins stuck in the places he'd been. I counted the pins over and over: all those places where something bad could happen to him. Even when a postcard came saying he had arrived safely, I worried. He could die there, or the plane could crash on the way home.

Other times he was gone because he was in the hospital. Kidney stones. Gallstones. Pneumonia. Appendicitis. Pericarditis. Diverticulitis. Ulcerative colitis. I didn't know what all these words meant, only that miserably painful things were always going wrong with him. My mother would shake me awake in the middle of the night: "I'm taking Daddy to the hospital." Bad sounds of him groaning in the bathroom; my younger sister's frightened face.

When he finally came home he would be thin, white, hunched, quiet. Himself but not. No jumping on him. No bothering him. He needed to rest. In the summer, when he wore his bathing suit, there would be a new purple shiny ragged scar somewhere.

Did I imagine it, am I exaggerating it, this air of imperiled fragility that seemed to hang over my father? Did he get sick more often than other fathers? Was I more of a worrier than other kids?

Some of the atmosphere of crisis came from my mother's grim panic: her dire whispers in the night, her big frightened eyes, her absences when he was in the hospital, her inability to deliver reassurances that she wouldn't have found convincing herself. ("But is Daddy going to be all right?" And she would scream, "Leave me alone, I don't *know*.")

As time went on, he hid discomforts and minor symptoms from her. She watched him suspiciously, on the lookout for winces and grimaces. "What?" she would demand, if he looked uncomfortable. "What's wrong?"

And if he did admit that something was wrong, then it must be bad. "Where's the aspirin?" he might ask, and my mother's mouth would tighten: "Shit! Shit!"

I grew up believing that he was doomed. It wasn't that he got sick and got better; it was that he almost died and then didn't. Each episode closed with a sense of nervous temporary reprieve. Not this time? The next time, then.

Depression, the condition that would actually kill him, was never diagnosed or even mentioned. Doctors didn't look for it back then. And he didn't have it all the time, not yet. If he did have some glimmering that it was there, it wouldn't have occurred to him not to conceal it.

We worried about his heart, his liver, his stomach, his lungs. It was like Brueghel's painting of the fall of Icarus—we were looking the wrong way; the focus was on the big events in the middle of the canvas. Nobody noticed the terrible small thing that was starting to happen in one corner.

6.

When did it begin to form, the plan that he might take over the American branch of the family business, the German pins-and-needles company?

Let's invite my mother to tell this part. She is bursting to tell it.

"It was my idea," she says. "I was the one who saw it so clearly. I knew that this was what he should do. I was the one who said, 'Start by getting a seat on the board of the company in Germany. Get your mother to give you her proxy votes—she's never been interested in the business anyway. Get on the board, and cultivate your cousin Franz Axel. He's the president of the American branch; he's the one you should get to know. Start going up to Connecticut, and have lunch with him a few times. Let him know about all your import-export experience. Let him know you're interested in becoming more involved with the business. He's getting old, he's probably getting ready to retire, and you're the only family member in America with the right kind of experience to take over from him.' I saw it so clearly, how it could all happen for Daddy."

Her tone as she says all this is miffed, hurt, baffled. How could this intelligent, logical plan have failed to work out?

Or rather, how, after it had started to work out exactly as she'd imagined it, could my father have screwed it up?

Her plan didn't kill him. He was the one who had the desire, after all, to be a company president. She was only the strategist. But the way he died makes any plan she might have had for him seem dangerous, Lady Macbeth-ish.

And the part that I do think may have been lethal was her contempt (which she hid from herself, though not from him) for his inability to pull it off.

(After he died, when we learned that the gun had malfunctioned slightly—it put a bullet into his brain but did not fire with enough force to blow his head apart as might have been expected—my mother said, "Jesus Christ, he couldn't even do *that* right.")

But I'm jumping ahead. Stay with the pins and needles, the family sewing business.

I will, I'll get back to that in a minute. But that last paragraph about the gun is bugging me. It's angry. It's true, but it's only part of the truth. And that feels like an unfair use of the power that I'm grabbing by writing.

This is my version. I get to say what happened. I get to leave out whatever I want to. You can't interrupt me. You can't say, "But."

I want that power, but I hate the nagging feeling of needing to be responsible with it. Any stark, violent truth makes me want to equivocate, to disclaim, to soften. To write a next sentence that begins, "On the other hand. . . ."

On the other hand, they used to stand in the kitchen kissing.

On the other hand, he gave her a string of pearls for Christmas.

(Ah, but on the *other* other hand, he gave them to her because she made him feel he was supposed to. He couldn't really quite afford them. And she raged to me later, in her bedroom, because the pearls were a single strand and she had told him, *told* him, that she wanted a double strand. What did I think it meant that when he gave her a present it was never the thing that she really wanted?)

These stark violent truths are true. That's the problem.

7.

The studio where I'm working is ordinarily used for photography. When I get stuck or bored or scared, writing this, I stand up and wander into the darkroom at the back.

It's full of warnings. PHOTO FIXER SILVER SOLUTION— HAZARDOUS WASTE. EMERGENCY EYE WASH STATION. 28% ACETIC ACID—POISON. Some of these items actually have little skulls and crossbones printed on them.

Dangerous work has been done here.

The people who have used the place before me—photographers, writers, filmmakers, sculptors, painters, architects—all signed their names on the wooden plaques hanging on the wall just inside the door. The earliest signatures, some so faded as to be almost invisible, date from 1969. There are twelve plaques, with twenty-eight signatures on each.

That's 336 people who have spent time in here, making something.

The wall behind my desk is a long one, made entirely of tackboard. I've hung up some of the family photographs, and I tack up my pages at the end of the day. The wall is pockmarked with pinholes, made by the 336 people over the years.

I'm alone here all day; those 336 people, with their signatures and their pinholes, are my company. I think about them tacking up their work, along with other words and images that meant something to them. The pinholes are many and tiny and oddly clustered, like stars—constellations of pinholes, galaxies, an entire universe.

Okay, pins and needles. The family business.

1969. We moved to Connecticut. A big old white farmhouse, on a shady corner. A tumbledown carriage house which we might fix up one day. Cats, dogs, an old horse. A garden: huge forsythias, then peonies, then tomatoes and corn. Summer evenings, my father's car coming noiselessly into the circular driveway. He would change into his bathing suit; there was an old swimming pool, out beyond the giant spruce trees that cast soft dark shadows on the lawn. The smell of smoke from the stone barbecue on the terrace. The phone always ringing for my mother, who was involved in everything: the League of Women Voters, the opera board, the school building committee.

My father drove me to school in the morning and then went on to work. He was being groomed to be president of the company, but Franz Axel wanted to stay on for a year or two before retiring, and so for now my father was the number-two man. He was great at this. Quick, alert, good at anticipating problems. Good at generating ideas, good at listening to other people's ideas, good at explaining ideas to Franz Axel, and good at carrying out any ideas that Franz Axel approved of.

He was the sure-footed fellow from the old Future Business Leaders Club, filled out now, starting to live up to all that promise. The future, which used to seem so far away, was very close. He was almost there.

And then, suddenly, he was there. Franz Axel stepped aside. My father was a company president.

And this, I think, is the moment when something starts to be missing. Or the moment when the thing that was missing all along starts to matter.

He was a better heir to the throne than he was a king.

He, of course, didn't see this. And my mother was thrilled. Adored and admired him. Picked out sweet-smelling grass-cloth wallpaper for his new office. Accompanied him to business conventions at various resorts. Borrowed Franz Axel's chauffeur on weekends to run errands, and later, to pick me up at boarding school in New Hampshire. (My mother wanted the chauffeur to wear his uniform on these occasions. I said that if he did, I would lock myself in my dorm room and refuse to come down to the car.)

Franz Axel had not retired after all. When he had made my father president, he'd made himself chairman. He was having trouble letting go. "Which is understandable," my father said.

"He's run the company for a long time. It's hard for him to turn it over to another man."

Things went along. As far as I knew, everything was fine. My parents were my parents, big and secure in their lives. I was away.

One Sunday afternoon my father was driving me back up to school after a weekend at home. Suddenly the car swerved toward the edge of the highway. I said, "Dad!" and looked over at him and saw that he was asleep, and his eyes flew open and the car straightened out.

There was a long silence. "Sorry," he said.

He kept getting sick. I kept getting called to the narrow phone booth on the second floor of the dorm: "Daddy's in the hospital." I kept taking buses home and visiting him, bringing him the most vivid-bloomed plants I could find in the hospital gift shop. Cinerarias, begonias, azaleas. He looked white and exhausted in all those beds, just lying there in the middle of the day, smiling at me and saying quietly, "I'm so glad you're here." I knew he was glad, but I also knew he'd be glad when I left; he was too tired to have anyone in the room with him. They thought he'd had a heart attack, but it turned out to be an infection. They thought he might have cirrhosis, even though he wasn't a drinker. They took out his appendix. He got pneumonia.

"And of course the pressure is terrible, with the business," my mother would tell me on the car ride home. "He's under terrible pressure to get up and take control of things again. He needs to rest, but he needs to get well fast."

I kept going back to school. He'd get better, but then sick again. Things went along.

That summer I had a job working in the town drugstore. One night when he came to pick me up, I got into the car and he told me he'd quit his job that day.

I asked him why, trying to match his calm tone.

He said it was a lot of things. Basically, he said, every time I make a decision, Franz Axel undoes it the minute my back is turned. Basically, he said, Franz Axel will never let go. I can either fight him, which will ultimately undo me, or I can turn into a yes-man, which will ultimately undo the company. Basically, he said, it was a no-win situation.

I told him I thought he was brave. A lot of men, I said, stay in jobs they hate; they never have the guts to leave. I'm so proud that you had the guts.

Well, he said.

When we got home, my mother was upstairs in her room with the door shut. My father stood at the foot of the stairs in his raincoat, looking up at the shut door.

She's pretty upset about this, he told me. You go up. Go in and see her. She needs you to be nice to her right now.

I knew that he was sending me up to her because he was afraid to go himself.

All that summer, and then after that for months and years, my mother's fury went on.

"I probably shouldn't be telling you this," she'd say, and then she would go on to tell me.

He hadn't really quit; he'd been forced out. If he hadn't resigned, Franz Axel would have fired him.

He was too passive. When they'd gone to all those business conferences at the fancy resorts, when all the other men were downstairs having drinks and mingling, my father was sitting in the hotel room, reading. He thought that once he'd attended the seminars, his day was over. She would think: skip the seminars, for God's sake—but go downstairs in the evenings and mingle! But when she tried to tell him that, he'd tell her to stop nagging. You couldn't tell him anything; he never wanted to listen.

He was too soft. There had been a vice president maneuvering him out, angling for Franz Axel's ear, planting doubts. Daddy saw this, but he never knew what to do about it. It had gotten worse all those times he was in the hospital—the other guy had used those absences to bolster his own position. And now that guy was president of the company. Could I imagine how she felt, how Daddy felt, to know every day that that guy was sitting in the chair that used to be Daddy's?

He was too stubborn. He wouldn't compromise. She knew I thought that absolute integrity was a virtue—but it wasn't, not in business. She knew I thought he was so noble—but he wasn't, he was naïve. It was his *job* to compromise; it was *smart* to compromise; he was *supposed* to compromise.

And how could he have done this to her? She couldn't hold her head up. She was resigning from all her committees. Did I understand what it was like, to be on the planning committee for the Lions' Club Ball knowing that she was going to have to sit at the head table up on the stage with Daddy, knowing that everyone there would know he'd been forced out of his job? Did I understand the humiliation?

I feel like I'm humiliating her a second time, telling this. I should be able to temper and shade these memories. Give her some more dimension, make her less extreme. Sympathize.

Sometimes she would catch herself—hear herself. Come up with her own "on the other hand."

"Do you know how much I love Daddy? Do you have any *idea* how much?" she would ask me, out of nowhere.

She was scared. I understand that now, looking back. She'd grown up poor, and she was afraid of being poor again. The plan, which had been hatched and refined and counted on for years, had failed, and there was no plan B.

And she was starting to be scared about my father. If he couldn't do this, what could he do? And why hadn't he been able to do it?

He had lost his job. Something was wrong. He was a failure.

That's what she thought, and that's what he thought.

That event, his leaving the job, or losing the job, was the turning point in our family; before it we were rising, and after it we just kept going down.

Whoa. Too bald a statement for a biographical essay, or even a memoir. This kind of writing is never really objective—though it sometimes pretends to be—but the writer doesn't usually come right out and tell you what she thinks.

Still, it's impossible to look closely at lives and not begin to discern, and to impose upon them, some kind of shape. Even the physical structure of a volume of biography has an implied shape and arc to it, a concept.

Take a biography down from the shelf and look at it—it doesn't matter who wrote it, or whom it's about. There is a big clump of pages occupied with the subject's birth, background, education, and initial tottering steps toward success, or notoriety, or whatever achievement or quality led to the biographer's interest. The ascent, one might call this part.

Then comes the arrival—or, as old popular biographies used to title these chapters, The Years of Triumph. Elections won. Movies starred in. Plays written and produced. A love affair with a king. Continents explored, territories claimed. A long streak of bank robberies or murders, gotten away with.

At some point, right around here, there's a section of photographs. A glossy, captioned interlude. If the subject's face is well known, the childhood and youth photos look unformed—intriguing because whatever it became, it isn't there yet. Then come the pictures from the Years of Triumph: familiar, the famous face we know. And then there are the last few images: my God, look what happened.

And what did happen? Sometimes it's tame or ordinary—aging, retirement. (Still: how much smaller, more faded, less themselves they look.) But often it's sensationally bad, gripping. Political scandals. Hollywood scandals. Plays that flop. Syphilis. An avalanche. Hanging.

Once you get past the pictures, the going generally gets tough. Life is harder and sadder on the other side of the photographs.

8.

I am walking in the woods near the edge of the artists' colony, and I hear a gunshot.

Maybe there's a ceremony going on in town, some kind of military thing. Today is November 11: Veterans' Day.

Or maybe someone is hunting deer.

My feet keep moving forward on the path. I keep listening, wondering if there will be a second shot. But no: just one.

He started sending out letters and résumés, looking for another job. His old secretary came over sometimes on Saturday afternoons to help him. Once I saw that she was crying as she got ready to leave. "Your father is such a good man," she whispered to me fiercely.

In the fall, my parents drove me to college. We unloaded my stuff and then my father went to park the car. I was outside on the sidewalk, and he came walking toward me, smoking a cigarette. He hadn't smoked in years. When he saw me he threw the cigarette into the street. He didn't mention it, and neither did I.

He was going into the gold business. Gold was about to be put on the market as a commodity. My father didn't know anything about commodities trading, but his new partner did. My father had valuable knowledge about international business, and also he was investing money in the company. For Christmas he had miniature gold bars mounted as cuff links for my mother's three brothers.

At college I got the *Times*. I never had a chance to read it; it piled up in my room and I used it to make fires in my fireplace. But I did start checking the price of gold every day. It just sat there. This gave me a sense of dull unease. Wasn't my father's business predicated on the idea that gold was sure to go up?

After a while he wasn't in the gold business anymore. It was partly that gold hadn't performed, and partly that his partner had been rotten. Somehow the partner had gotten away without losing any money, while my father had lost his entire investment.

"I won't tell you how much," my mother said over the phone, "but it was a lot. A *lot*."

He was going into the machinery business. His partner invented machines that cut shapes out of wood, and plastic, and

Lucite. Manufacturers used them to make tabletops, or the mats that went under office chairs to protect the carpeting. There were also machines that made carving boards with depressed channels in which meat juices could collect.

His partner knew about machines, but nothing about business: that was where my father came in. Once again, his title was "president." They rented space, two long rooms in a corrugated metal building in the woods near his partner's house. They made up a corporate-sounding name, to which they appended the word "International." My mother rolled her eyes.

The business was diagonally across the state from where my parents lived, almost three hours away. My mother didn't want to sell their house and move if things weren't going to work out, so my father rented a small apartment to live in during the week. He would drive down there on Sunday nights, and on Friday he would drive home again. The town where I went to college was on his way, and he began stopping there on Fridays, to take me out to dinner.

We ate and ate: that's what I remember about those dinners with him. Mostly we went to a restaurant that faced out onto the town green. It was a hybrid of elegance and gluttony: thick white tablecloths, a platter of tiny potato pancakes with sour cream that would appear on the table before you'd even had a chance to order. We ate tenderloin with béarnaise sauce. Lobster tails. Coq au vin. The lighting was warm and dim. I don't remember what we talked about. We smiled at each other a lot, and ordered coffee, which neither of us wanted, to make the meal last a little longer. "Everything all right?" we both kept asking.

———

I met my husband in college, and after that my parents started slowly to recede. I was twenty-one when I got married. During the wedding ceremony, when the judge read the part about "forsaking all others" I started to cry; the idea of forsaking my parents, even for the man I was marrying, seemed unbearably disloyal. But as time went on my allegiance, and all my attention, shifted.

My parents moved. The machinery business seemed to be solid, so they bought a house nearby and started living together again. But my mother had changed. She told me she wanted her own business and her own bank account. She didn't trust my father anymore to take care of her.

I thought this was great—not that she didn't trust him, but that she wanted to have something of her own. I had always thought she'd been born too early, that if she had come of age among feminists she would have gone out and become president of her own company, instead of being my father's frustrated backseat driver.

She decided to open an art gallery. She rented an empty H&R Block store in the next town over. She went into New York and bought a lot of prints and lithographs from a friend who dealt in modern art. She had a sign painted, and cards printed, and an opening show and reception with wine and cheese. But between May and December (after that the H&R Block people would need their space back), she sold virtually nothing. It was the wrong town: people went there to buy hardware and shampoo and snowblowers and groceries, not art. When the lease was up, the gallery was dismantled. The pictures leaned in stacks against the walls of her basement, and the sign sat in her garage until she sold the house eight years after my father's death.

So her business failed. But it didn't seem to smolder and sear between my parents, the way my father's failures always did. It had happened to her, not to him. Less was at stake.

9.

Aren't lives apples and stories oranges? What really goes on when you try to change one into the other?

At dinner last night I sat next to a sculptor who had spent the day trying to make something out of welding rods, silk, and invisible thread. To me that kind of project sounds magical, alchemical—an unfettered curiosity about whether these unlikely materials can be transformed into something else—but the sculptor's eyes were tired, and she sounded daunted by the prospect of going back into the studio to try to get the piece to work.

I'm writing about my parents. I can ruminate coolly about professional biographers and their limitations and responsibilities and scruples, but I'm not a professional biographer. I'm their child.

I'm writing because I need to understand the story of my family. But I'm also appropriating it, trying to transform it into something I *can* understand.

Biography, in the case of someone who commits suicide, is particularly dangerous, misleading. It looks at a life through the lens of a death. Every time a bad thing happens, the temptation is to say, "Aha!"

I have to be careful not to make it too orderly.

Sitting in my quiet studio, I know that other people have struggled here, too. Today when I open my lunch basket and unscrew the plastic cup on top of the thermos, I see that someone has bitten a piece of its rim clean off. A whole crescent-shaped piece of the edge is missing, and there are jagged outlines of tooth marks.

Another convention from the arc of biography: the modest comeback. The second eruption can never hope to reproduce the impressive glory of the first—the spewing lava, the boiling smoke, the noise—but the volcano isn't dead yet. Steam and fire can still spit from the crater. If you once starred in movies, and have been drinking since then, you're cast in a sitcom. If a sitcom was your pinnacle, you land some commercials. You'll always have the memory of your long-ago idyll with the king, but you've since fallen on hard times, and now suddenly a California cattle baron wants to marry you.

My parents had a period like this, for a little while. An almost-return to almost-grace.

She became a real estate agent.

He met some Japanese businessmen at a trade show. They were there representing their own machines, which were similar to his, but much bigger, and priced ten times as high. They wanted a foothold in the American market, but they didn't have any experience doing business here. Maybe I can help you, my father said.

And for a while he did. From their corrugated little office in the woods, he and his partner demonstrated the Japanese machines to interested buyers. In the evenings, he sat in his study with language books and tapes. He still had his old talent for languages, but Japanese was much harder than anything he'd ever tried to learn in the past, with its several alphabets and its complex code of nuance. He went to Japan several times, came home and developed roll after roll of photographs.

I found the prints when I was cleaning his study after he died. Endless pictures of gardens and temples. No one knew anymore what or where they were.

Let's be merciful and cut this part short; we already know it ends badly. My father sold some machines, but not enough. The Japanese signed a deal with his big competitor.

My father felt betrayed. He thought of getting out of the business and doing something else. His mother had recently died, and though her estate was tangled, there was still some money left in the end. Maybe he should quit business altogether.

(Another classic biographical moment, close to the end. You consider canceling the duel, or wonder if instead of the *Titanic* in April you should sail on the *Oceanic* in May. But you decide that no, it makes more sense to proceed with your original plan.)

My father and his partner decided to build their own big machine. My father would need to put more money into the business, but with the contacts they'd built up and the fact that they could deliver the same kind of product at a lower price, the investment was sure to pay off. Not right away, but eventually, and hugely. The hell with the Japanese.

What was more, they were going to diversify. Never again would they risk putting all their eggs into one basket. They'd start another business, a door company. My father met someone at a trade show who was importing wooden doors from Korea and wanted to expand. With the way new-home starts were rising in America, my father reasoned, this was another great investment opportunity.

———

Some historical context here: it was the 1980s. There was money everywhere; people were just plucking it out of the air. My husband's stepfather got together with a group of guys and did a leveraged buyout. They picked up a company, broke it up, and sold it. My husband's stepfather got sixteen million dollars.

Look at any biography of a businessman, the part where he's quoted reflecting on his own success. You'll find the words "Don't be afraid to take risks."

And also: "Never give up."

10.

This is what it was like to talk to him on the phone.

"How's everything with you, Dad?"

"Not too good right now. How's your job?"

"Fine. What do you mean, not good? Do you mean your business?"

"Well, that and a lot of other things. So, have you been listening to Mozart lately?"

Finally he admitted to me that he was close to bankruptcy. "But don't tell Mom," he said.

I called my sister, and she agreed with me that my mother needed to know. But we thought my father needed support, in order to tell her. The next weekend, I drove down to my parents' house from Boston, and my sister flew in from the Midwest. We sat my parents down in the living room and said, "Mom, Daddy has something to tell you, and it's going to upset you, but you just need to listen and try to understand."

My father, who had seemed relieved that my sister and I wanted to come, took a breath and said, "Okay. All this may turn out fine if I can just sell two machines at the Louisville trade show next week. But if the machines don't sell, then I need to tell you: I'm bankrupt."

My mother started screaming and ran out of the room and up the stairs. The bedroom door slammed.

My father looked at me and my sister. "Well," he said. "That certainly didn't go the way we'd hoped."

A couple of days later, he called to tell me that he and my mother had talked, really talked. "Thank you so much for coming, for doing that."

My mother called and said the same things. "Daddy and I are feeling much closer. It was so good that you girls came. I don't know what comes next—our life is obviously going to have to be different—but we'll be okay somehow, no matter what happens."

My father went to Louisville, and sold the two machines.

11.

He got sick again, a couple of years before he died. Assorted vague symptoms. Headaches. A cough. Stomach troubles, which he'd had since a trip to India thirty years ago, but now suddenly they were worse. His color was bad. He went to his doctor for tests.

The doctor saw a thickening in the wall of the intestine, and thought there might also be a problem with the lungs. More tests were scheduled.

I drove down from Boston to spend the weekend with my parents. My father had a doctor's appointment on Friday afternoon. When he and my mother got back, she told him to talk to me. She left us in the living room and went upstairs. My father sat down, motioning to me to sit, too.

"All right," he said. "The things in my lungs are pretty big, and the odds are excellent that they're malignant. What they have to find out now is whether the lungs are the primary site, or whether it might have spread there from somewhere else."

I tried to match his factual tone. "How would they treat it?"

"Chemotherapy."

So it's inoperable, I thought.

He went on: "Apparently it's in too many places to operate. But I want you to know I'm not giving up. I think there's a chance it may be tied up with this sinus infection I've had."

We talked some more, about second opinions, various hospitals; me questioning, him answering. Then there was a silence. "How was *your* day?" he asked, and I said, "Better than yours."

He threw back his head and laughed.

We all made dinner together, red-eyed, jabbering. We kept asking him questions. Daddy, how do you grow such sweet tomatoes? Paul, where's the round steel platter? Can you taste this salad dressing? I feel like it needs something, but I can't figure out what.

It was as though we were enumerating his skills, his value, arguing with some higher-up: you see? This person has too much specialized knowledge for his job to be eliminated.

For the next few weeks he went from doctor to doctor, test to test. I kept a journal, chronicling all of it: the colonoscopy, the debate about whether to do a bronchoscopy or proceed straight to a needle biopsy, whether to keep it all in Connecticut or go to New York.

Now when I look at that journal I see things that in hindsight mean more, and pierce deeper, than all the medical blow-by-blow.

This, from another weekend I spent with them:

The illness is barely discussed; my father talks briefly to me about business problems. I am telling him about my day: a tough train ride with the baby, the upstairs toilet overflowing, the light above the stove falling down when I touched it. It's the opposite of the Midas touch, I say. That's been my problem lately, too, says my father. Does he mean the illness? But no: it turns out they've been having quality control problems with the doors. The first sample sent to the biggest U.S. distributor, who was set to take on the line, was defective. Fine, they said, that can happen; send us another one. The second one arrived from Korea, defective also. The distributor canceled the order.

Or this, from the same weekend. He had begun, suddenly, to tell me family stories about his German cousins. "Did I ever tell you that I have a monocle?" he asked me, and went on to say that it had belonged to his grandmother. His cousin Marian had given it to him one night when he was visiting Germany in the 1950s; they were going to dinner with a particularly stuffy aunt, and Marian thought it would be funny if my father wore the monocle and bowed and kissed the aunt's hand.

My father says it's so disappointing now, that Marian herself has become so stodgy. She wasn't like that. She had spirit. But now, he says, to hear her talk you'd think her life was over. I think that's really sad, he says. She's resigned to the end of her life.

Or this:

Later, we all get into a discussion of lawsuits. A guy was operating one of my father's machines, standing in the wrong place, and his leg was crushed and had to be amputated. There was no concept of contributory negligence, my father says. The suit was settled out of court. But you were insured, weren't you? I ask. No, he says, we can't afford it. Why don't you just close the doors of that damned business? my mother says. What kind of a business is that, where you can't even afford to carry liability insurance? My father turns away.

Here's my last journal entry from that episode.

The red light on the answering machine, flashing. My father's voice: "I'm back from the hospital, and I just wanted to let you know: it's benign." I grab the phone, call, get him. He sounds subdued. Says he's relieved, but doesn't sound relieved. In pain? Still absorbing? Still frightened? Angry at the false alarm? Who cares. If it's not cancer, it's okay. Anything else is beatable.

I think, now, that he was sorry when the whole cancer thing turned out to be a false alarm. It would have been a good, sad death. He would have fought hard against the cancer and suffered a valiant defeat. He would have died in our arms.

Something else would have killed him. He wouldn't have had to pick up the gun and do it himself.

12.

Sometimes, when I'm in the studio and really desperate for some distraction, I leaf through the only book in here, which is a dictionary. This afternoon I look up the word "suicide." The first definition is "The act or an instance of intentionally killing oneself."

An instance? Doesn't that sound a little casual? As if it were a momentary lapse, a goof, a dopey one-time mishap the lesson of which was: well, I guess I won't be doing *that* again. How would one use it in a sentence—"On Friday he had an instance of intentionally killing himself"?

The second definition of suicide is "The destruction or ruin of one's own interests."

Yeah, to put it mildly.

But it's the third definition that sobers me. "One who commits suicide."

It's the only cause of death that can be used as a noun to describe the dead person. If you die of cancer you are not called "a cancer." If someone else shoots you, you are not referred to as "a murder."

But if you shoot yourself, you are labeled as a suicide.

Your death becomes your definition.

In fiction, or in a play, you can let a big thing happen between the lines, or offstage.

In biography, though, you have to state the facts.

He died on Friday, February 8, 1991, at around 6:30 in the

morning. He shot himself at home, sitting in the blue armchair in his study, with his feet crossed at the ankles, resting on a footstool.

13.

I have one of his shirts. It's red, with a small green-and-tan windowpane plaid. He used to wear it on weekends. When I brought it home with me, ten days after he died, my memory of him in it was still vivid. I put the shirt way in the back of my closet, because I couldn't stand to look at it. But sometimes I would burrow back there, behind my own clothes, and put my face against his shirt, searching for the smell of him.

Now that he's been dead fifteen years, I can't really remember him in the shirt. The fact that it belonged to him is just that: a fact. I can't picture him in it, any more than I could have pictured, on one of the many days when I was with him and he was alive and wearing it, that one day it would become a talisman, one of the few tangible things I have that belonged to him.

The writer stands up again and moves away from the computer. She walks around the studio, looks at the old photographs and the pages tacked to the wall.

She keeps trying to tell his story, all the different pieces of it. She wrestles with form, with genre. A novel? Memoir, biographical essay? First person or third? My father shot himself, or her father shot himself? So many things bore down on him, for so many years—should the story be told year by year, or thing by thing? It's obsessive, it's gone on for years.

She believes that someday she might be able to tell it in a way that's definitive, that makes it stay told, like a picture that finally stops falling off the wall once the right hook or adhesive is found. Sometimes she almost gets it, she thinks; but then, restlessly, she starts needing to look at it again. Does it have to do with trying to let him go, or trying to keep him?

She flips through the dictionary again. Someone has cut something out of one of the pages, very neatly, with an X-Acto knife; a long skinny rectangle is missing, in the middle of the definition of the word "look." Why would someone have cut out only part of a definition?

Then she looks at the flip side of the page. On this side, the excision makes more sense: an entire word and its definition are gone, between "longicorn" and "longish." (A longicorn, she reads, is a long-horned beetle.) What's missing? Tonight when she leaves the studio to go to dinner, she can find another dictionary and check.

But she doesn't have to. Suddenly it occurs to her that the missing word is "longing."

In a novel that detail would be too much. But I can take refuge behind the voluminous skirts of nonfiction and tell you that this is the truth. Someone cut the word "longing" out of the dictionary in here.

I wonder what became of it, that narrow flapping rectangle sliced away with surgical precision, along with whatever brief words defined it.

But more than that, I find that I am wondering about its meaning and its purpose: why it beckoned, and what use it was put to.

Suicide:
numbness and
Bullwinkle

AFTER YOUR FATHER'S DEATH, YOU STAY WITH YOUR MOTHER for ten days. Then you drive back to Cambridge, to resume your own life.

You are numb.

Every morning you drop your son off at nursery school. Then you go home and sit in your living room, in the big flowered chair. Your husband calls from work, to check on you. Friends call to ask if you'd like to have lunch. You thank them, and say you'd like to have lunch another time. You try to get some work done. Mostly you just sit in the flowered chair.

You pick your son up at noon, bring him home, and make him a peanut-butter sandwich. Then he naps, and you sit in the flowered chair.

When he wakes up, the two of you lie on the bed and watch Rocky and Bullwinkle videos. *The Treasure of Monte Zoom. The Ruby Yacht of Omar Khayyam.*

Your son laughs. He doesn't understand the puns or most of the jokes, but he gets that it's supposed to be funny. He goes along with the spirit of the thing. This kind of time with him has always thrilled you—watching him leap fearlessly forward into something he's not quite ready for. It's one of the best parts of having a child, you've thought. One day, a couple of months ago, your son was watching TV and you'd left the room for a few moments, when suddenly you heard a shriek. You ran back to see what was wrong. But nothing was: he was shrieking with laughter.

"What's so funny?" you asked, smiling with relief that he wasn't hurt.

He pointed to the TV screen, where some old comedy was unreeling itself in jumpy black and white. He could hardly tell you what was so funny, he was still laughing so hard.

"Mommy," he gasped, "that man just threw a pie in the other man's face!"

You called your father that night, and told him the story. He laughed. He said: "See? The oldest joke in the world is suddenly new again."

Now, watching Rocky and Bullwinkle scheme and bumble their way through whatever the plot requires of them—you don't know what's going on most of the time—you see your son laughing, and you know this is the sort of thing that has always delighted you. But it doesn't, now. You'd like it to, but it doesn't. Now you're just glad that there's something you and your son have found to do together that amuses him and doesn't demand much of you. In a dull way, you're angry: you worry that the numbness, if it goes on too long, will cheat you and your son of something you would have had if your father hadn't done this.

You're not angry at your father. Just dully angry at "this." At "what happened." At "it," whatever "it" is.

There's a part where Rocky and Bullwinkle go to a place called Submervia. It's a city under a glass dome at the bottom of the sea. If the dome cracks and water gets in, the city will be destroyed.

You lie there watching the tapes over and over. Your son laughs and leans against you, resting his chin on your hip.

Suicide:
numbness and
chicken pox

CHICKEN POX SWEEPS THROUGH THE NURSERY SCHOOL. YOUR
son gets it. You give him oatmeal baths, watch a lot more Rocky
and Bullwinkle, tell him not to scratch.

After a week, when he's almost completely better, you notice a red spot on your chest.

The next day you wake up and there are more spots, and
your legs ache. You smile at your husband. You're sick; you can
lie in bed all day without feeling you should be doing something else. Too bad you can't read. You haven't been able to pick
up a book for two months, since your father's death. You can't
remember sentences after you've read them.

You can feel yourself getting sicker. It's sucking you down.
Wool is all over your skin, hot and itchy; someone is rubbing
it into your skin, someone is igniting it. It's in your mouth,
under your breasts, between your legs, on the soles of your feet.
You are festering, you're wet and sticky, all the little spots of
fire are leaking. You take a sip of hot tea and feel it igniting all
the spots inside you, down your throat and inside your chest
and belly. You lie in bed with your head thrown back against
the pillows, shivering, letting the air ignite you. You scratch

and it hurts; you scratch more. Your eyeballs are molten. You fill the tub with cool water and oatmeal and lie down flat, put your whole head under and feel all the little fires on your scalp go hissing out; you laugh and imagine cartoon steam curling up out of the water.

"Is there anything I can do?" your husband asks, sitting down gently on the edge of the bed.

You shake your head. You have everything you need. He's intruding. The bed is full of sweat and oatmeal, filthy and wet and sweet. Your bones are hurting and shaking. Your skeleton is dancing, thudding inside of you.

Finally the burning recedes. You get up, shower, change the sheets, put on clothes instead of a nightgown. You are numb again, smooth, bereft.

The spots take a long time to fade. Every day you look in the mirror and see that they're fainter. You miss the feeling of them, alive and blazing.

Suicide:
numbness and
duration

YEARS.

Suicide:
numbness and
food

YOU EAT. GOD, HOW YOU EAT.

Brownies. Dark, sweet, rich ones that you bake yourself, adding chocolate syrup and chocolate chips as well as the chocolate called for in the recipe. Deliberately undercooked, these brownies have the texture of very thick frosting. You can slice them, sort of, into squares, stopping after each cut to rub the chocolatey blade of the knife and then sucking your fingers. These brownies are gritty black sugary warm mush in your mouth. You bake them all the time.

But if none are handy you'll eat brownies from the rack at the gas station, the dry bland ones wrapped in plastic.

You eat Ring-Dings and Yodels, with their sweet smothery white centers.

Kit-Kats, whose layers you flake apart with your tongue.

Potato chips, the not-too-salty kind, thick, golden, translucently oily.

Croissants—plain, chocolate, and apricot.

Lasagne, especially the crisp brittle browned parts at the edges of the pan.

Pistachios.

Grilled-cheese-and-bacon sandwiches.

Hot chocolate with whipped cream.

That's the pleasure in each day, the lust and the delight, waking up and figuring out what to eat. You read cookbooks while you eat your lunch. You make your family homemade guacamole, soufflés, Sacher torte. You learn to bake Portuguese sweet bread.

You get fat.

The food is, literally, sensational. Sweet, hot, spicy, creamy—your mouth is always a lively place.

There's something self-pitying about this kind of eating, of course. You know this and don't care. Or, rather, you know it's self-destructive and you do it anyway. You can't stop. You enjoy it and hate yourself for it. It comforts you and makes you miserable.

You feel you deserve it.

Suicide:
numbness and
husband

HE SEES THAT YOU ARE NUMB. IT WORRIES HIM. HE DOESN'T try, in any big heroic way, to do something about it. He accepts it. He knows you hate it, that it feels clogged and unnatural. You call it "the ice." Sometimes you are able to cry for a minute or two, and then you say hopefully to him, "I think maybe the ice is starting to break apart."

But nothing really changes; the ice stays frozen.

He holds you at night, if you want to be held. Most nights you don't. It has nothing to do with sex—which oddly has continued to be great, after the first month or two, when you didn't think you'd ever feel like having sex again. The numbness isn't about sex, or about him, or about loving him, you say.

He says he knows that.

It's years, more than a decade, before you know how angry he is.

One night the two of you are fighting in the kitchen, and he says, "Your father really fucked this family over."

You're shocked, furious, betrayed. Your husband loved your father. He's always understood your father's goodness and sadness. He has understood that suicidal depression is an illness, not a moral failing. But suddenly here is your kind, compassionate husband, his face red and twisted, yelling about how your father's suicide fucked everyone over.

"It did not," you say—fat, numb you.

"Look at you, look what it did to you," your husband says. He is not referring to the fatness, which he claims loyally and almost believably not to care about.

"What did it do to me?" you say, your voice ominously low and even. You're like a snake uncoiling, rattling its tail.

Your husband sees it, hears it, starts to back away. "Nothing," he says. This is something you hate about your marriage: that your husband is afraid of you when you're angry.

"No. Tell me. What?"

He doesn't back away farther, but his eyes are wary. He holds his ground, but only just. "I'm thinking about what it did to all of us. How much space it takes up." He looks at you. Then, as you continue to watch him, to glare at him, he startles you. He makes a decision. He takes a breath, steps forward, and grabs the snake. He says, "I resent having to protect you all the time." He says, "I feel like this terrible thing happened to you, and so my job is to shield you from any more bad things that might happen."

"What do you mean, your job? Who the hell hired you?" But even as you spit out these questions, your rage is only about half of what it was before he told you this. You know what he means. It's a relief to hear him say it. It's also horrifying; you see instantly that it's true. "I'm sorry," you say.

The sudden capitulation rattles him. "No, no, it's not your fault," he mumbles.

You look at each other for a while. Then he says he's scared about your son.

"I know," you say. Your son is sixteen now, depressed, seeing a psychiatrist, taking medication. Some days he can't get out of bed. You and your husband have talked a lot about how hard it is to gauge the seriousness of all this. Certainly it's something more than just ordinary adolescent misery. But you don't know how much more. Because of what your father did, it's hard not to be engulfed by the most drastic fears about where your son's sadness might lead.

You know that this is what your husband is thinking about now as he says, suddenly, savagely, "I hate your father."

Those words are taboo in this house. No one is permitted to even think them. But hearing them, tonight, you're not outraged. You're even a little glad your husband has said them. You, yourself, can't, but you're glad someone did.

You stand there in your kitchen wondering if perhaps the ice really is, finally, starting to break up.

Then your husband says, still furious, "And I hate that I always have to be scared about what you might do."

It takes you a minute to understand what he means.

And another minute for the numbness to envelop you so that you can shrug and answer him, in a flat voice that makes it clear the conversation is over, "Well, don't be."

Suicide:
numbness and
psychiatric response

YOU START SEEING THE FIRST PSYCHIATRIST FIVE MONTHS AFTER your father's death. The words that come to mind when you think of her are "perky" and "glue." She tilts her head sideways after each thing you say, looking startled and interested. Her interest is like balm to you: you can't cry about your father, but her frank interest makes you want to weep with gratitude. No matter what you say, she says she understands.

You picked her because you thought she might get it about the money. You'd been given a couple of names, and you picked one after driving by her enormous house, in one of Cambridge's fanciest neighborhoods. Money seemed to play such an important part in your father's death: growing up rich, growing up poor, being close to family money all his life but never having any of his own, being close to people who were making money but never making it himself. And the mess of Neil asking for his money back, and your husband's father selling the Boudin—it could all sound so bizarre, and spoiled, if told to a shrink who didn't understand. You thought this one might. And she does. She tries. She's nice. You're nice. The two of you sit there being nice ladies together.

Her view is that the suicide doesn't invalidate what you thought you'd known about your family. It is a sad, new thing to add into the mix. She sets about helping you remember the good things: how much your father loved you, how much you loved him. She gets very excited at one point when you mention that among your father's medical problems was a dramatically elevated level of alkaline phosphatase, a liver enzyme. She hypothesizes, her eyes flashing behind her large glasses, that since the liver's function is to filter out toxins to the brain, and since your father's liver wasn't functioning properly, then maybe unfiltered toxins to the brain were a chemical factor in his suicidal depression. Hmmm, you say. It is sort of comforting to you, the idea that there is medical detective work possible here. A clear, clinical, causative explanation of what he did. In the months after his death, you are still hoping that a single culprit might be apprehended and brought to justice.

You relish the chance to create him, fresh, for a new audience. Someone who didn't know him, and who wasn't personally hurt or angered by his suicide. Someone to whom you can tell the story of his life, and the catalog of his attributes—his tenderness, his tolerance, his subtlety, his love for you—who will listen gravely and come up with a judgment that you can accept as objective and fair: "He sounds like a wonderful man."

A not-guilty verdict is what you are after, and what you get.

And it is balm, because in different ways almost everyone who knew him seems to be saying that he was guilty of something. Your mother: of abandoning her. Your sister: of weakness, or a kind of hollowness at the core. His partner: of bailing out. Your husband's stepfather: of leaving him holding the bag. Even your friends, most of whom hadn't even known him, seem to be convicting him, at a sad distance, of having been a crazy man, since anyone who had committed suicide could not have been fundamentally sane.

You hate that he is dead and everyone is angry at him. He needs someone to stand by him.

The psychiatrist seems to understand this, and agree with it.

You stop seeing her after a year or so. Her optimism has glued you back together—not perfectly, but a kind of imperfect gluing is what you need at this point. You probably couldn't have stood anything else. You are like a nearsighted person who can see the cracks in the bowl when she's wearing glasses—and so chooses not to wear glasses while looking at the bowl.

You are fine. Numb, but fine.

You start with the other psychiatrist nine years after your father's death. You are not fine. The cracks are opening; sharp edges are protruding. This doctor is your father's height, and only a few years younger than your father at the time of his death. (When your husband meets him, at one point, you are taken aback that he can't see any resemblance, physical or otherwise, to your father.) You feel safe and comfortable with this doctor right away. Balm again.

You tell him everything you've figured out. How your father was a gentle, kind, sensitive man. How he was much harder on himself than anyone had realized. You tell him all the contributory factors in your father's death: his brutal childhood, his business failures, his health problems, the fact that your mother was angry at him and flirting seriously with someone else. "None of those things, by itself, would have killed him," you say, wisely, to the psychiatrist. "It was the combination. And the loneliness. The sense that he'd let people down. He didn't know how to tell anyone how bad things had gotten."

"What did his death do to you?" the psychiatrist keeps asking.

You sit there. You shrug. You're blank. Whenever he asks what it did to you, you see a blank white room, brightly lit, with no windows and nothing on the walls. You see yourself sitting on a stool in the middle. It's a waiting room, you say.

"What are you waiting for?" he asks.

"Duh," you say.

You spend a long time with him, waiting. The two of you sit across from each other and wait together, like fishermen trailing lines in a still, opaque pool of water that is reportedly teeming with ravenous fish.

He watches you. He's waiting with you, for the feelings to hit hard or to trickle out. But he's also watching you wait.

You've gotten good at explaining to him what the feelings would be, if you had them. You can locate and analyze the places where the wires are crossed. The numbness feels unnatural. Not credible. You tell your shrink that you're suspicious of it. Come on—nothing? You feel *nothing*? You're not even mad at him for sticking a gun in his mouth?

Nope. No anger. You can see that the anger ought to be there. You can plot it out with exclamation points. Your father shot himself! In the house! He knew your mother would be the one to find him and he didn't care! He abandoned everybody!

But: nope. Nada.

You have some theories. You posit that you can't get angry because your father already turned such appalling anger on himself; he'd done a terrible thing, but in doing it he'd also given himself the worst possible punishment. One day you say, "I hate the way things keep canceling each other out. I can't just miss him, because of what he did. But I can't hate him for what he did, because I miss him so much."

"So what are you feeling, right now?" your doctor asks.

You sit for a moment. "Nothing," you say.

"Nothing? Or too much?"

"Maybe too much," you agree, though it feels like nothing.

Occasionally you do cry in his office, talking about your father. It's something of a relief, but it also feels a bit circumscribed and fake: even when it's going on, a part of you is thinking, "Wow—how therapeutic." The crying is brief and soundless. What you'd really like to do is roll around on his floor howling and clutching your stomach.

"You'd like to do that now?" he asks, when you mention it.

You shake your head. You almost say politely, No thank you. You say, "I wish I had to restrain myself from doing it." Then you ask him if people ever scream in his office.

"Sometimes," he says. He watches you. You wonder if he's waiting for you to scream, now that he's given you permission. No thank you, you almost say again.

Then one day you're talking about how for you, men are divided into two categories: the nice ones and the killers. "My father was one of the nice ones," you say, with a dreamy mixture of adoration and pity.

"Until he became a killer," your doctor says.

Ah. Now he has your attention.

Suicide:
numbness and
various reprieves

IT'S NOT LIKE YOU'RE A ZOMBIE. THE NUMBNESS IS SPECIFIC TO your father.

You can actually remember the moment, seven months after his death, when you first realized that happiness was still a card in the deck. You were apple-picking with your husband and son, and you all sat down on the ground to rest. Your son got up again after a moment and ran into the next row of trees, and your husband went after him. You could hear them, though not what they said—your son laughing, your husband's low voice answering. You lay on your back in the orchard grass, looking up. It was a clear deep-blue September day, almost cloudless. You thought, with sudden wonder and gratitude, "I'm happy."

Since then you've had a lot of happiness.

The birth of your second son, good times with friends, love for your husband.

Health scares turning out to be nothing.

An Easter morning in Venice, with the windows wide open and all the bells of the city ringing.

A *St. Matthew Passion* sung by a Japanese music group in a candlelit old church in Boston.

Reading Turgenev, and thinking, Yes you're right—that's *exactly* where Lavretsky would have gone after dinner.

Asking your kids what they're making with the clay they got for Christmas, and having them tell you, "A nightclub."

Being with your husband in a city where you've traveled to see the architecture, and having him say, "The hell with the architecture" and taking you into the hotel bar instead, and drinking Campari and eating peanuts and then going upstairs to bed and spending the next day in bed too and leaving the city without ever looking at a single building.

But.

Suicide:
opposing versions of

"I CAME HOME FROM WORK, AND IT WAS COLD, AND I REALIZED I didn't know how to make a fire," my mother told me over the phone. "He always did that, made the fires. How could he leave me alone, with no one to make the fire? How could he abandon me?"

I said, "I know."

My sister said, "Our family was rotten from the beginning. We came from rot."

I said, "You think?"

My mother said, "Poor Daddy. Poor man. I have nothing but compassion for him."

I said, "Mmm."

My sister said, "I think it was in him for a long time. I don't understand how he held on for as long as he did, why he didn't do it sooner."

I said, "Well."

———

My mother said, "Do you think it was my fault?"

I said, "Of course not."

My sister said, "You know what? I'm not sure I'm even all that sad. He had a right to do what he did. If life had gotten that painful for him, then maybe he made the right choice."

I said, "I don't know."

My mother said, "Do you remember Valerie Smith? Well, guess what: her husband left her. She came home the other day and he was gone. Can you believe it? She had absolutely no inkling that he was thinking of leaving. How can a woman live with a man and not pick up the slightest signal that he's planning to leave?"

I said, "It does seem strange."

My mother said, "Today's the anniversary." Of his death, she meant.

I said, "I know. That's why I called, to see how you're doing."

"It's a very hard day for me," my mother said.

I said, "I know. For me too."

"Yes, but it's *very* very hard for me," said my mother.

I didn't know what to say.

My mother said, "I had a mole removed on my back, and I can't reach the spot to change the dressing. He promised to take care of me in our old age. Where the hell is he? What kind of man promises that and then just disappears?"

There was a silence.

"Why don't you answer me? Are you there?" she asked.

"Yes," I said.

Suicide:
other people's stories concerning

IT TURNED OUT THERE WAS ANOTHER MOTHER AT MY SON'S nursery school whose father had killed himself. I learned this when I came back to Boston, ten days after my father died. I dropped my son off at the school and watched as he darted off, quick as a released minnow, into the space that was so familiar to him. One of the teachers came over and asked how I was doing.

I nodded.

"You should talk to Kate," she said.

I barely knew Kate.

"Look," said the teacher. "I haven't told anyone what your father did. I just said he died. But if you want me to, I'll tell Kate. Her father did the same thing."

"Okay," I said.

The next morning when I brought my son to school, Kate came up to me. "What are you doing right now?" she asked. "Do you have some time?"

We went to my house. For some reason we decided to sit in the backyard. It was a warm day for February, but it was still February. We had mugs of tea, and we kept our gloved hands wrapped around them. I remember Kate blowing on hers, the steam rising in front of her cold face. She sat with her long legs up on the table. She was seven months pregnant, wearing overalls and a red down jacket.

She asked me what my father had done, and listened while I told her.

"Mine used a gun, too," she said, "but other than that it was pretty different."

"Different how?" I asked.

"First of all, he kept threatening to do it. For years. He had this whole big Hemingway thing going on. The drinking, the guns. He kept telling us he was going to shoot himself. We didn't believe him anymore. Nobody wanted to listen. We were all exhausted."

"Did you feel guilty, then, when he did it?"

"No," Kate said. Her voice was cool; she made it sound convincing. "I wasn't relieved, either. Just: okay, yup, now I know the ending."

She told me that her father had been staying alone in their house in Florida. "My brother and I flew down that night, as soon as we heard. He wasn't there anymore. They'd taken him away."

Her cool, soft voice got even quieter. "The room was a mess. He would have liked that; it would have pleased him, knowing what a mess he'd made. My brother and I cleaned it ourselves. I guess we couldn't figure out how else to get it done. I picked this big thing off the floor and I didn't know what it was. Then I turned it around and I realized it was his jawbone."

My mother-in-law's friend Doris, whom I'd met only once, years ago at a cocktail party, sent me a note in shaky handwriting, from the nursing home where she lived now.

"I know how you feel," the note said. "I remember what it was like for me, when my father did what yours did."

I told my mother these stories. She shook her head. "They keep crawling out of the woodwork," she said.

She had an old friend named Gloria, who was so beautiful that my father had nicknamed her "Glorious." That's what our family had called her for the past thirty years.

Glorious had come to visit my mother some time after my father died. They'd sat up late, talking, not about anything much, according to my mother.

Then, out of nowhere, Glorious had suddenly said that her mother had committed suicide. She'd been in and out of institutions for years, Glorious said. She was a beautiful, beautiful woman—she was always being painted, and photographed.

"And she shot herself in the face, in front of my father. In their bedroom—she'd kept the gun in her glove box. A tiny pistol. He didn't even know she had it."

My mother had been stunned. "All these years we've been friends, and you've never told me this."

"I've never told anyone," Glorious said. Then she leaned forward and took hold of my mother's wrist. "Promise me you won't tell. I don't want Dan to know about this."

Dan was Glorious's son. He was forty.

At prep school, my husband had been close to a boy named Thad. Thad's mother died during their tenth-grade year from an overdose of pills and alcohol. Thad had been furious at his father, who kept insisting that the death was accidental, and who married his secretary seven months later. My husband spent hours listening to Thad talk about how miserable his mother had been (she'd known about the secretary), how desperately sad, how lonely.

After my father died, my husband called Thad. They'd kept in touch over the years, but sporadically, not in any deep way. My husband told Thad what my father had done, and said, "I need to talk to someone who's been through this. And I'm remembering what it was like for you, some of the things you were feeling, after your mother's suicide."

There was silence on the other end of the line. Then Thad said, "I'm not sure what it is you're remembering, but my mother's death was an accident."

One of the men I worked with was married to a woman named Jane. They invited us to dinner one night, and when everyone was settled with drinks in the living room and Jane disappeared into the kitchen, I followed and asked her if I could help.

She smiled at me—thanks—and then the smile dropped off her face. "I hope you don't mind, but Rob told me about your father."

"I don't mind," I said.

"It's hard," Jane said.

She put down the salad spoons and sat on a stool, and motioned me to sit down, too. She said, "My sister did it when she was on the phone with me. She told me what she wanted to do, and I spent about forty-five minutes trying to talk her out of it. I kept trying to think of a way to call someone else to go to her house, to just *get there,* but I also wanted to keep her talking. Finally she put down the phone, but she didn't hang up. She cut her throat. I could hear—"

Jane and I looked at each other.

Then Jane said, "I don't think she was trying to torture me. I think maybe she was afraid, and she didn't want to be alone."

Claire was someone I liked from a distance. I'd been to her Christmas party; she'd been to my house for dinner a couple of times. Then her brother cut his wrists and jumped from the roof of his apartment building.

When Claire reappeared a few weeks later, I asked if she wanted to get together. Yes, she said. I brought her sandwiches. We sat in her kitchen. She told me that the saddest thing was the stacks of Help Wanted sections in her brother's apartment, so many ads neatly circled in red marker.

"He was so smart," she told me. "You should have seen his bookshelves—history, political theory, economics, musicology, anthropology. He was one of those people who could have done anything, but nothing ever quite worked out. And then all those careful red circles: copy editor. Public relations assistant. Hotel management training. He had a Ph.D. in *astronomy.*"

She said, "I hope you don't mind if I ask you this." She asked me if there had been a lot of blood in the room, when my father died. I told her that I didn't think so. The gun had malfunctioned, so that even though he'd put it into his mouth and it had killed him, there had just been a little bit of blood on the baseboard. My husband cleaned it up late that night. He told me it had been just a small amount, and I believed him.

I told Claire that I'd been the one to ask my husband to clean it, but afterward I was sorry. "Or not sorry, exactly," I said. "I don't know what it was. But I kept going into that room. Not just that week, but for months after that, years. I still go in there. And I kneel, and I look at the woodwork. Like I just want there to be some trace of him, or of this thing that happened."

She said that was why she had asked: she felt the same way. She had stayed away from her brother's apartment for weeks, because she was afraid of seeing the blood. But then when she finally went there, and saw that there wasn't any blood, she was disappointed.

I went to visit a friend who was teaching English at a small college in upstate New York. She told me that a man in her department, a writer who had been there on a one-year fellowship, had hanged himself the month before.

That night we went to a department picnic, and she pointed out the man's wife to me. I watched her for a while, from a distance. She was a little younger than I was, maybe in her late twenties, pretty, with long black hair. She was standing alone, with her arms crossed. I went over and introduced myself. Then I blurted out—quietly, but it was still a blurt—that I was sorry to hear about her husband and that my father had killed himself, too.

She looked blank for a moment, and I was appalled at what I'd said to her. I started to apologize, but she said sharply, "No. No. Tell me. Did you have any idea? Did you know he was going to do it?"

I shook my head. "I'm not sure he even knew he was going to do it. And he certainly wouldn't have given any warning. He was a very gentle, considerate man—"

"That's just like Johnny!" she said. "That's just how he was. He never told anyone he was unhappy—everyone else came to him with their problems." Her face was white, pinched, excited. Her thin fingers were opening and closing like bird claws.

The outing was being held on an asphalt basketball court. We moved over and stood next to the chain-link fence. We talked for a while about these exceptionally kind men. How they could be so accepting of other people, and so secretly intolerant of themselves. How they could listen, but not talk. How they were like radiators that lack the little valves to let the steam off, and it just builds and builds and eventually explodes. How they couldn't see that there wasn't a lot of territory between keeping everything private, and dying. It got dark while we were standing there.

She turned to face the fence, and threaded her fingers through the metal links. "It's so weird for me here," she said. "I'm only here for the rest of the year, and then I have to figure out what to do next. I only came here because of Johnny's fellowship."

She said, "I'm so glad you came over to talk to me. None of them talk to me." She jerked her head sideways, at the milling-around people from the English department. "Not that they ever did, before. Then I was just Johnny's wife."

She flashed me a smile, a mix of irony and panic. "But now they *really* don't know what to say to me."

My friend Claire went to a wedding in Australia, where she stayed in a guest cottage with three other women. One night they sat up late talking, and they found that all four of them had brothers who'd committed suicide.

We find each other. We're referred by friends. Or we happen to sit next to each other on an airplane. We end up standing together in a hallway, during a party. We stop noticing who is coming and going around us. We talk. It's urgent. We have nothing new to tell each other. Even when the stories are different, they're the same.

A friend's sister dies: pills. The friend disappears; she's gone home, to be with her parents.

I drive by her house and leave a note. "Call me," I write, and I give her my love. I leave the note in the space between the front door and the screen door.

I drive away. I am thinking that a day ago my friend didn't know any of this; now she will never not know it. I'm sorry for the freshness of her knowledge. I'm sorry that she's just at the beginning of it.

I'm thinking about all the things that have happened, or that will happen but haven't yet. All the things that are teeming, unseen, behind the walls of all these houses.

Suicide:
other shoe and

THE WEEK AFTER MY FATHER DIED, SOMEONE CALLED AND ASKED to speak to him. I was still staying in my mother's house, and I answered the phone. The woman asked for my father, in a crisp, confident voice.

It was the first time since his death that this had happened, and for a moment I couldn't answer her.

"Hello?" she said.

"I'm sorry," I said, "but he's dead. He died last Friday."

"Oh, my God," she said.

There was a long silence.

I thought, She's his mistress.

She's the daughter of a mistress he had a long time ago.

She's his blackmailer.

She's the person he was working for at the CIA.

She's a banker, and there's an even bigger loan that we didn't know about.

She's a reporter, and there's a crime he got away with years ago, but she recently uncovered it and has been hounding him.

I thought all these things, and didn't believe them. I thought them all without explicitly thinking any of them. They didn't crop up sequentially in the moment, as newly formulated ideas; rather they were items on a list that had been building in my head since his death. A list that built itself in response to the question *What else was going on that we didn't know about?*

Here it is, I thought, during that silence on the phone.

Finally I said, "I'm his daughter. Can I help you?"

The woman explained, her voice uncertain now, that she wasn't sure how to proceed. She was calling from an insurance company. "Your father was in a car accident two months ago, down in Virginia."

Here it is, I thought again. "What happened?"

"Well—" she began.

"Was someone killed? Or hurt?"

"Oh, no," she cried, flustered, sorry to have alarmed me.

"Did he leave the scene? Fail to report it?" I went on. Shut up, I told myself.

"Oh, no, no, no, no, nothing like that."

"Then why do you need to talk to him?"

"Maybe I don't. I was calling to go over some of the details with him, to clarify a few things. I need some more information for one of the forms—but listen, maybe I can just talk to my supervisor and see if we can just, you know, proceed with what we already—"

"Was someone else in the car with him?"

"No, no, he was alone. It was nothing. A fender bender, really. Really nothing."

"Are you sure?"

She was sure. She was sorry. She would call back if she needed anything else; meanwhile she was very very sorry to have bothered us.

She never called back.

Someone told me about a man who had killed himself without leaving a note behind. But the following year, at Christmas, his family found a note, tucked into a box of ornaments. He was hiding it, he wrote, because he knew that reading it would be painful for his family, and he didn't want them to find it until some time had elapsed.

Whoever this guy was, he sounded self-indulgent and manipulative. Hey, buddy, if you're killing yourself, then you are exiting permanently. You can't stage-manage your family's reactions. You can't resurrect yourself months later as a considerate guy.

It was a lot easier for me to get angry at this stranger than at my father.

But much as I thought I disapproved of the stranger, I was envious of his family. The story made me wistful. I went from thinking, "My father didn't leave a note" to "Maybe we just haven't found it yet."

I ransacked my parents' house whenever I went to visit my mother.

I went up to the attic and looked through the Christmas ornaments, and boxes filled with wedding presents that my husband and I hadn't liked but had never bothered to exchange, and boxes full of the dirndls that my father's cousins used to mail from Germany when my sister and I were little, and boxes of family papers and photographs.

I went down to the basement and looked in my father's toolbox, and under the lids of old, mildew-smelling Monopoly and Clue and Risk games—any of which, if my father had been feeling clever and bursting with ironic significance when he hid his suicide note, might have seemed like a suitable cache.

I knew even as I was looking that my father wouldn't, by that point, have felt clever or sought a witty hiding place. I knew he hadn't written a note. I knew that he'd felt definite about wanting to die, and about letting his death be as stark and mysterious as it in fact was. But every time I got one of those brilliant tiny ideas—I wonder if he slipped it between the pages of *The Sorrows of Young Werther*!—it seemed, for a moment, possible that he'd been waiting patiently all this time for me to join my thinking with his, to follow his footprints down the path he'd taken in those final days and arrive at the big clue or answer or apology or *something* he'd left behind.

I went through his bureau drawers and found a broken gold pocket watch in an old jeweler's box from Wiesbaden, and packets of pins and needles from when he'd been president of the family business, and foreign coins, and breath mints, and, beneath a pile of boxer shorts, a couple of issues of *Penthouse*.

I went through the pockets of the clothes hanging in his closet and found business cards from competitors and suppliers, and empty cases that had once held traveler's checks, and a small calculator that still worked, and a crumpled Kleenex, and more foreign coins and breath mints.

I looked in all his shoes, which were empty.

Eventually my mother gave away his clothes, but I kept looking. In the backs of closets. On the shelves of the garage. Again and again in the attic and basement.

One day I climbed up on a chair to look at the top of the canopy that hung over my parents' four-poster bed. In that moment, it suddenly seemed likely, even certain, that my father had stuck the note up there, not wanting it to be found until the day came when the bed was dismantled because my mother was moving out of the house. The day when this part of our lives, the whole big part that had included him, and his death and our sorrow or rage or bewilderment or whatever it was that we were feeling, was over.

I never told anyone that I was looking. I never found anything.

Suicide:
philosophical conundrums stemming
from
first

DID HE HAVE A CHOICE?
  If so, then he did something unforgivable.
  If not, then how can we blame him?

Suicide:
philosophical conundrums stemming from
second

DID HE KNOW WHAT IT WOULD DO TO US—MY MOTHER, MY
sister, and me?

If so, then he did something unforgivable.

If not, then I wish he had known. But only if he really did
have a choice, and only if knowing would have stopped him.

Suicide:
possible ways to talk to a child about family tree

"WHEN DO YOU THINK I SHOULD TELL MY SON ABOUT ALL THIS?" I asked the first psychiatrist.

We were sitting in her office, an upstairs room in her house that looked out into the flickering leaves of an old maple tree. I saw her in the morning. The room was cool and fresh, with chairs covered in rough oatmeal linen. There was a red-and-black batik cloth hanging on the wall behind her chair, and a small blond wooden shelf filled with reference books. It was all very organized and soothing.

When I asked her the question about my son, she nodded and pressed her forefinger hard against the nosepiece of her glasses. "Well," she said, "that's a tough one."

My father had been dead for six months. My son was three and a half.

"How much does he already know?" the psychiatrist asked.

I looked through the window at the shuffling leaves of the maple tree. "I'm not sure. We told him that his grandfather got very sick and then died."

She nodded again, and said that this was probably about as much as a three-year-old could understand. She cautioned me that the next time one of us got sick, we might need to reassure our son that sickness didn't always mean death, that in fact most people who got sick went on to get well. She said, "The tough thing about reassuring kids is that you don't always know what it is they're worrying about."

I told her that my son had said one thing that made me wonder how much he knew. It had been the day of my father's memorial service, in the evening, and my son had come over to the couch and stood facing me, with a hand on each of my knees. He had looked at me and asked, "Why did Pa want to die?"

The psychiatrist blinked. "How did you answer him?"

"I asked him what made him think that Pa had wanted to die."

"And?"

"He didn't say anything else. He sort of wandered away. I think he started playing with his Lego. The rest of us just sat there staring at each other."

After a moment, the psychiatrist said, "Well, you did the right thing. You gave him a chance to talk more, without pushing him at all."

I asked if she thought my son had overheard the grownups talking—if it sounded to her as if he were trying to grapple with a fragment of conversation that had bewildered and scared him. She said it was possible, but that he might also have made an uncannily apt accidental remark. We agreed that I shouldn't quiz him, that all I could do was stay alert in case he alluded to it again.

"But what if he doesn't allude to it again? At what point should I tell him what my father did?" I asked her.

She blinked and considered for a moment. Then, as briskly as she might have pulled out a prescription pad, she applied herself to the problem. She glanced at the photographs of her own three children, ranged in plain wooden frames along the windowsill near her desk. "Listen," she said. "This is what you do. When he's in—let me think—around fourth grade, he'll probably get an assignment to do a family tree. And he'll come to you, and he'll ask a bunch of questions about your parents, grandparents, et cetera. Where and when were they born, when did your father die. Et cetera. It will all be very factual. He'll be nine or ten, which is about the right age for him to begin to understand this. That's when you tell him. Wait for the family tree project."

Suicide:
possible ways to talk to a child about full disclosure

"OH, HE KNOWS," KATE SAID OF HER SON. WE WERE SITTING outside, in her backyard this time. It was a late summer afternoon, and our little boys were running through her sprinkler, wearing sagging bathing trunks.

"You think he knows?" I asked. Her son was flinging himself through the spray of water, chest out, with a kind of fearless glamour; my son followed, admiring, imitating.

Kate was nursing her daughter, who had been born in the spring: a small oval head, wisps of soft dark hair curling in the damp heat. "Oh, I know he knows. I told him."

"Really? All of it?" I remembered her telling me about picking her father's jawbone up off the floor.

"He knows his grandfather shot himself." Kate held the baby upright, between her breasts, slowly rubbing one tanned hand up and down along the baby's bare heat-mottled back. The baby, her head slumped against Kate's shoulder, gave me a lazy, sated, milky, sideways smile. I smiled back. The baby looked away, then looked at me and smiled again.

We went on flirting like this for a while, while Kate kept talking in her cool, even voice.

"He knows it happened in Florida, when he was a baby." She glanced down at her daughter. "He knows it made everyone in the family sad and angry."

I wanted to ask her, Don't you feel the need to protect your son? What can he possibly make of this knowledge, at the age of four?

"He asks about it a lot," she went on. "More often than I would have thought. I tell him what he wants to know, and I say, 'Granddad was a very sick man.' Which he was." Her voice hardened. "And a very selfish one."

"Do you worry about—?" I stopped.

"About what?" She lifted the other side of her T-shirt, swiftly but gently laying the baby in a horizontal position and helping her to find the nipple. I suddenly remembered, rather than heard, the sound a nursing baby makes, that soft, rhythmic, squeaky, clicking hum.

"About—" I looked over at my son.

Kate said, "I didn't want it to be this big secret. I think it's better for him to grow up knowing than to suddenly find out one day."

I nodded. I could see the logic and the sanity of this, and I admired Kate's clearness.

But I said, "I guess I worry about him growing up knowing that people actually do this. Kill themselves, I mean. I worry that if he knows too early, he'll just take for granted that it's part of the normal range of human actions."

"It is," Kate said.

Suicide:
possible ways to talk to a child about not yet

I WAS LISTENING TO THE CAR RADIO, DRIVING HOME FROM THE shoe store, when a story came on about Vince Foster's suicide, which had happened the week before. "Apparent suicide," the announcer called it.

I glanced in the rearview mirror at my son, who was almost six; he was calmly buckled into his seat, looking at a Berenstain Bears book.

"Questions remain about the death of the presidential aide," the announcer went on. "Although a lengthy note was found near the body, some close to the investigation are speculating that Foster's death may have been—" I reached over and turned off the radio, knocking the bag containing my son's new sneakers off the passenger seat.

He was still turning the pages of his book.

"Do you know what that word means, 'suicide'?" I asked suddenly.

His eyes found mine in the mirror for a wary instant, then slid away. "I'm not sure," he said.

"It's when a person kills himself," I informed him.

He didn't say anything. I checked the mirror again; he was looking out the window.

"Did you know that that's something which happens sometimes?" I asked.

After a moment, still looking out the window, he said, "Yes."

I stopped for a red light. I turned around, gripping the back of my seat. "It's awful when it happens," I said. "Nobody should ever do it. It's wrong."

My son looked at me.

I turned around again. The light was red for a little bit, then green.

"But it doesn't happen very often," I finished.

"I know," my son said.

I drove, and turned on the radio again. The news was over and they were playing music.

Suicide:
possible ways to talk to a child about rational approach

MY SON WAS SEVEN. WE WERE STILL A COUPLE OF YEARS AWAY from the prophesied family-tree assignment. Sometimes I wondered if he already knew how my father had died. My husband and I never talked about it in front of him, but the house we lived in was small—wasn't it likely that he'd overheard things over the years?

What I did talk about in front of him was what a wonderful man his grandfather had been. "You know how much you like history?" I would say. "My father did, too. He would have found all your castle books really interesting." Or: "You know those soldiers you play with, the Japanese warriors? Your grandfather gave you those, when you were little."

He would listen and nod, not terribly interested. He never asked me any questions.

I didn't mention my father too often—that would have seemed unnatural, even to me—but when I did, it was always in that doggedly upbeat, almost hagiographic way. One night I sat on the floor of his room and read him the chapter from *Winnie the Pooh* where Kanga gives Piglet a bath. My son lay on his back in bed, smiling at the ceiling. "She knew it wasn't Roo," he said when I finished.

"She knew," I said.

"Did she know it was Piglet, or just that it wasn't Roo?"

"I think she knew it was Piglet."

"So do I," he said.

I sat there on his rug for a little while, and then I said, "My father used to read me this book when I was your age. He always did it in an English accent. I wish I could do that voice, but I can't."

There was a silence. "Good night," my son said.

"Why did that seem to wreck the moment?" I asked my friend Liz over the phone. She was a psychologist, which had intimidated me at first—but by now, two years into the friendship, we'd developed an easy, sometimes very funny frankness with each other, which often came out around the ways in which we'd blown it with our children. "Call me," we would say into each other's answering machines, without even needing to identify ourselves, "I've got a bad-mother incident to tell you about."

"Because he was picking up on the fact that you were uncomfortable," Liz said now. "And you are. You're very uncomfortable mentioning your father around him." She pronounced the word differently from the way I said it. I said "uncomfterble." Liz always gave it its due, all its syllables: she put the word "comfort" in the middle of it. Hearing "uncomfortable" said that way now made me suddenly, newly aware that its original meaning must have been "incapable of being comforted."

"Here's the problem," I said. "He doesn't remember my father. All he knows is what I tell him. I want him to know that my father was wonderful, so that when I do eventually tell him about the suicide, he'll have something to balance it against. He won't just think, 'Oh, my grandfather was a crazy man who killed himself.'"

"So he still doesn't know how your father died?"

"No," I said. I told her about the supposedly upcoming family-tree project.

Liz said, "I'd just tell him."

"You would? Now?"

"I'd probably look for the right moment. But yeah. He knows there's something there, he just doesn't know what it is. I think I'd tell him."

I was surprised. I loved Liz's directness: it usually dictated a policy of candor, but sometimes not. Once I'd asked her what she would say if her son, when he got to be twelve or thirteen, were to ask her if she'd ever smoked marijuana. "I'd lie," she had said instantly. That had surprised me, also. But I admired the way she was so definite: here's where you lie, and here's where you tell the truth. I was always dithering, always unsure.

"What stops you from telling him?" Liz asked now.

"I'm afraid he'll ask me questions I can't answer," I said.

"Like what?"

"Like, 'why?'"

There was a silence. "Maybe you'll just say, 'I don't know,'" Liz said.

That had never occurred to me.

After Liz and I finished talking I got my one-year-old out of his crib, where he'd been napping, and let him play on the kitchen floor with some brightly colored plastic shapes he liked to throw around. I moved restlessly, assembling things I would need to cook dinner. The baby loved it when I made a big point of stepping over him as I went back and forth: I would lift each leg high and grimace, as if he were a much bigger obstacle than he actually was, and he would sit there laughing. After a while this escalated into another game we had, where he would stand at one end of the kitchen and I'd stand at the other, and when I said "Go" we'd charge toward each other, and when we met I'd swing one leg up and he'd pass under it, as if it were a bridge.

Once my other son came down the back stairs to ask what we were having for dinner.

"Noodles," I said.

"Soon?"

"Pretty soon."

He took a handful of goldfish crackers and went back upstairs.

When my husband got home, the baby was in the high chair, making his usual happy mess of dinner. I kissed my husband and handed him the jar of carrots. "Can you keep an eye on the spaghetti?" I said. "I'll be down in a minute."

I went slowly up the stairs and stood in the doorway of my son's room. He was squatting on the floor, like a baseball catcher, carefully positioning plastic dinosaurs inside a block structure that looked like a labyrinth. "Hey," I said.

"Hi," he said, without looking up from the stegosaurus he was holding.

"Listen," I said.

I had a brief, violent spasm of anger at my father. You fucking coward, I thought.

"Can I talk to you for a second?" I said.

My son nodded, his hand hovering over first one part, then another part of the block structure, comparing possible situations for the stegosaurus.

It was the wrong moment and the wrong way to tell him. But there'd never be a right moment, or a right way. It wasn't going to come up in conversation. He wasn't a child who wanted to talk about life or death or why the sky was blue.

I sat down on his floor and told him. I kept it short. I kept it calm, and gentle, and rational. My son sat down, too, with his legs sticking straight out in front of him, still holding his dinosaur. He didn't look at me; he looked at his feet. I said, "He was a good man and I loved him, but he was sick in a way that no one really understood. I don't know why he did it, or even if something like that can have a reason. I wish he hadn't done it."

We sat there. I was looking at my son, and he was looking at his feet. I said, "Do you have any questions about all that, about what I told you?"

He said, very quietly, without looking at me, "How did he do it?"

I would have liked not to tell him. But I thought of the psychiatrist, and Kate, and Liz, and their unanimous aversion to secrets, and of my own growing aversion to secrets, and I said, "He had a gun."

I waited. "Is there anything else you want to know?"

He shook his head.

"Because if there is, you can always ask me."

He didn't say anything else.

After a little while, I said, "Dinner should be ready any minute," and he nodded.

I asked him what he was building. "It looks like a maze. Is it a maze?"

He did look at me then, swiftly, a glance that was private and proud, and shaded, I thought, with a sadness at my failure to recognize this thing he'd been making. "It's a museum," he said.

Suicide:
possible ways to talk to a child about weapons god

IN FOURTH GRADE, IN MY SON'S SCHOOL, THEY STUDIED ANCIENT Greece. In the spring they got an assignment to create a god.

My son had always been private and self-reliant about his homework. He didn't want any help; he didn't want anyone looking over his shoulder; he didn't even tell me what the assignments were or when they were due. I heard about the god project from Liz. She laughed about it over the phone. Her son was passionate about music, and he was ordering her to drive him around to various arts-and-crafts stores, gathering materials for his poster. "He's got this three-dimensional guy with an acoustic guitar on top of Mount Olympus," she said. "And the clouds have to be cotton, he says. And of course they can't be cotton *balls,* which we happen to already have in our bathroom; they have to be cotton batting from the fabric store so he can tear them into wisps. That's what he said: he doesn't want cumulus clouds, they have to be *cirrus.* Or maybe it's the other way around. I'm ready to kill him."

I had to go into the classroom one morning, to deliver my son's lunchbox, which he'd forgotten at home. The kids weren't there when I came—they must have been at gym, or at music—so I took a few minutes to look around at the god posters that were hanging all over the classroom walls. There were gods and goddesses of rainbows, and pets, and flowers, and sports. Some of the sports gods seemed to reign over athletics in general, but others patronized individual games: soccer, baseball. There was a god of laughter, with scraps of Sunday comics pasted around his head in concentric circles, like a giant halo. There was Liz's son's music god, astride his mountaintop in sunglasses, with sixteenth and eighth notes raining out of the wispy silver-tinged clouds.

And there was my son's name on a poster. He had drawn a large figure with many arms and hands, and each hand was holding a gun: handguns and rifles and machine guns and others I didn't recognize, complex big ones used in warfare, all drawn with careful attention to detail. Across the top of the poster, my son had printed in large capital letters, black ink shadowed with red, THE GOD OF WEAPONS.

After looking at this for a minute or two, I continued my tour of the room. A couple of other boys, I saw, had done gods of war: one dropping bombs out of a plane, and one sticking up out of a tank and holding a machine gun.

This is what they do at this age, I thought. This is what fascinates them.

But all through the day—while I was working, while I picked up my younger son at nursery school, while we were in the supermarket—I kept thinking about that poster, and how secretive he'd been about it, and how explicit and stark his drawings of the various guns were.

When he got home from school, he sat at the kitchen counter drinking milk and eating a piece of banana bread. I said,

"I saw your poster today, when I came in to drop off your lunch."

He gave me a look that was—what? Furtive and annoyed? I wasn't sure. I was rarely sure, these days, what he was thinking.

I said, "I'm curious. What made you think of doing a weapons god?"

He shrugged, and started to slip down off his stool.

"No, wait," I said. "I really want to know."

"I just wanted to," he said, frozen half on and half off his seat, with his feet on the rungs of the stool.

"Was it because you're interested in military history?" I asked, and he shrugged again.

"Because you know, don't you, that guns hurt people," I said. "They *kill* people."

A sly, exasperated smile crossed his face. He looked at me and said, coldly, "Well, I think they're interesting."

I took a breath, and felt words rising and ripping out of me. "What do you mean, *interesting*? Don't you get it? Don't you get what guns do? They blow people apart, that's what. Your grandfather picked up a gun and blew a hole in his brain. *That's* what guns do."

My son's face was stiff, terrified. "I'm sorry," he whispered.

I was looking at his face, and knowing that I'd always remember it. "No, no—I'm sorry. I should never have said that. It's okay, it's okay. You didn't do anything wrong." I was moving toward him with my arms out. "I am so sorry." He let me hug him, his stiff little body.

"I'm sorry," he whispered again, in the same tone as before, as if my apologies hadn't made any difference, which of course they hadn't.

I let him go up the stairs, his backpack sagging off one thin shoulder. I stood in the kitchen looking out the window.

After a while I went up and knocked on his door. "Come in," he said.

He was lying on his back, in bed, on top of the quilt I'd made for him years before.

"Listen," I said. "You didn't do anything wrong."

"I want to take a nap," he said.

"Okay," I said. "But I just wanted to tell you again that I'm sorry. You know that sometimes people do or say things they don't mean. Parents. You know that, don't you?" He didn't say anything. Then I said, "Would you like your door shut?" and at the same instant, so that I couldn't tell which question he was answering, he said, softly, "Yes."

Suicide:
psychiatry as an indirect means
of addressing

I'VE TOLD YOUR FATHER THAT I LOVE HIM.

I've cried in front of him.

I could describe his shirts and ties to you.

I wonder if you gave him some of the ties.

Your son has been coming to this day camp. So has mine. Today is parents' day. I knew you might be here; I saw your name on the phone list that was mailed to us before camp started.

I've never met you, but when I scan the crowd I recognize you instantly. You look like your father.

I watch you sitting on a folding chair, in the hot July afternoon. The children's skits are interminable, and inaudible. You sit patiently through all of them, and clap when each is over. You're a woman who looks strong and thoughtful, someone who could be my friend. This is the kind of thought I tend to have about your father, and then feel ashamed of having. What a waste, that he's my psychiatrist. I'd rather have him for a friend, a lover, a husband. This thinking feels both clichéd and deranged (though he keeps telling me I'm okay). It would creep you out, if you knew I was watching you.

I don't know what happened to your mother. Did she marry again? I imagine her still living around here, your two parents circling each other over the grandchildren, on holidays. They are cordial, but not quite friendly. You can have them to Thanksgiving together, with her husband and your father's partner, but you'd rather not. It's too determinedly civilized; it exhausts you.

Your mother forgave him a long time ago, but the only way she could do it was to sort of dismiss him. She doesn't think of what he did as betrayal anymore. It's been distilled down to disappointment. He was a good man who used her to try to prove something to himself. He used her in an experiment that failed.

In some ways, it doesn't matter anymore. They've both long since been happy with other people. She understands the sociology of what he did; a lot of men in his situation did the same thing in those years. He wouldn't be capable of doing such a damaging thing now. But he was once, and they both remember that she was the one he did it to.

This is all conjecture. He never mentions your mother.

He does talk about you, though. He told me you hated the intense little private school they sent you to in ninth grade. He told me this because I sent my older son to the same school, and my son was miserable, too. Your father said you got less miserable as it went along, and by twelfth grade you actually liked it. My son never liked it. He had days when he couldn't get out of bed, and other days when he'd come home at ten in the morning because he couldn't figure out how to make himself walk in through the school's front door. Your father helped me find a psychiatrist for my son. He used you to try to normalize this for me, telling me he'd pushed you to see someone when you were a teenager, and you'd finally agreed to go.

(I don't think you were depressed when you went to see that shrink. My guess is that you were angry—at your parents for splitting up, and especially at him for coming out.)

(I don't know when your father came out; that's another thing he never talks about. I'm just guessing.)

I didn't like my son's psychiatrist; he seemed chilly and arrogant. He was hard to talk to—for my husband and me, that is. Our son liked him. When they were together in the doctor's office, behind the closed door, and my husband and I were in the waiting room, it sounded like a party in there. Murmur, murmur, laugh, laugh, laugh. We raised our eyebrows hopefully at each other after every laugh. Maybe, we whispered, he's starting to be okay? The doctor walked our son back to the waiting room after each appointment; they seemed borne on a wave of goodwill together, which crested and fizzled out when they saw us. They never said a word to each other in front of us. Our son would duck his head and start down the stairs, and the doctor would stretch his arms over his head and nod at us and say, "Well, good-bye."

I was furious with this doctor, for being so opaque. "Serious depression" was pretty much all he told us. After our son had been on an antidepressant for a few months, we asked the doctor, "Do you think it's working?"

"What do *you* think?"

"Fuck him," I said to your father. "He's like a cartoon version of a psychiatrist."

"Do you think the antidepressant is working?" your father asked me.

"No," I said.

I talked to your father a lot about how scared I was. He kept reminding me that depression and suicide are two separate things. He knew that this was the hole I was falling into. Was my son having suicidal thoughts? I said I didn't know.

"Have you asked him?"

"I'm afraid to ask him."

"Why?"

"I'm afraid of putting ideas into his head."

"It's not a bad thing to let him know how concerned you are."

So one rainy afternoon when my son came home from school, we sat in the living room and I asked him if he ever thought about hurting himself. He said no. I said it was really important to tell people if he ever did have those thoughts. The doctor. Us. He said he would. I said that to stay alone with those thoughts was the worst and most dangerous kind of loneliness possible.

Your father has told me the names and ages of your kids, that the older one has been having night terrors and that the younger had hearing problems as a baby and you all still worry about her. He's told me the name and profession of the man he lives with; he talks about what play or movie they saw over the weekend and what restaurant they went to and what they ate there. He says "we" and "us" sometimes, and I always feel lonely when he says it.

Sometimes my curiosity about him feels normal, the sort of curiosity I might have about anyone I liked and wished to know better. But sometimes it feels ravenous, driven. He turns back questions; a door shuts in my face. Once I asked if he had brothers and sisters. He said, "If I begin to answer questions like that, it will change things in here. You may end up with information that makes you less free with me; you'll start worrying about my feelings too much." We talked about the delicacy of this for the next forty minutes.

At the end of the session, he said, "So, do you still want to know if I have brothers and sisters?"

"Not today," I said. I felt that this was what I was required to say. Then there was a silence, and when I spoke again I said, "I don't know what it is, but sometimes I'm tormented with curiosity about you."

"Tormented? That's a strong word," he said, and I cursed (also a strong word) myself for having said it.

I want to know more, but at the same time I worry that I know too much. When your father tells me personal stuff, I feel like he's going off the rails. I'm afraid I'm making him do his job wrong.

When I tell him this, he says he can take care of himself. "What makes you think I can't?" he asks.

He and I both know why I think he can't.

Once I brought in some earrings to show your father. A pair of gold half-hoop earrings. My mother had given them to me for Christmas the year after my father died. When I started to thank her, she interrupted me: "It's Daddy's wedding ring." She had taken it to a jeweler and had it chopped in half to make earrings for me, and she'd had her own wedding ring chopped in half to make earrings for my sister. She was smiling and tilting her head at me, with tears in her eyes, so I told her that I found the gesture touching and the earrings beautiful. I shoved the box in my bottom drawer and managed to forget about it, pretty much. But sometimes, rummaging for stockings or a scarf, I would see the square red leather jeweler's box and feel sick.

One day—and this was years afterward; I'd been seeing your father for quite a while by then and I didn't start with him until nine years after my father's death—I put the box into my purse and brought the earrings in to your father's office. I said, "Is this as awful as I think it is?"

He said, "Yes."

I told him I wouldn't have minded so much if she'd just given me the ring. But she'd hacked it in half and had it made into accessories and expected me to wear them.

"You could get it made back into a ring again," your father said. "There's a jeweler right around the corner."

When I left his office that day, I walked around the corner and stood outside the jewelry store. I opened the red leather box and looked at the gold half-circles lying there, and I remembered what the ring used to look like on my father's finger. I actually had the ring for a little while; the police gave it back to me after my father died, and when I asked my mother if she wanted it she'd said, "Not yet. I don't think I could bear it yet." Then a few months later she asked me for it, I guess because she'd gotten the idea of making the earrings. I stood outside the jewelry store that day after seeing your father, and even though I knew he was right—I could have the earrings made back into my father's ring—I didn't want to do it. It wasn't the kind of erasure that would comfort me.

Sometime after that I was doing one of my restless Internet searches—old boyfriends, old enemies, Googling my father (I'd never found any results for him, but I kept hoping and fearing that he'd suddenly appear)—and I started following your trail. I learned something about your husband: he works in the jewelry store around the corner from your father's office.

I told your father recently that I'd decided to hang on to the earrings. I also told him I'd since figured out that your husband worked in the store. There was a silence. Then your father said, "Did you think I was trying to draw you into my family?"

Once he said it, I couldn't get it out of my head. Maybe he was making some kind of covert declaration of feeling; maybe that was why he'd volunteered it as a possibility.

Still, it felt awfully convenient—embarrassingly, suspiciously convenient—to imagine that he might have wishes of his own that would so exactly mirror mine.

My husband and I took our son out of the fancy little private school and let him go to the public high school. His medication was changed, and he started to get better. Your father said he felt bad because he'd encouraged me to send my son to the little private school in the first place. He asked if I was angry at him.

"You didn't encourage me," I said. "All you did was to tell me what your daughter's experience there was like, fifteen years ago."

He nodded. I didn't know if he was giving me permission to be angry, or if he needed to be reassured that I wasn't.

Your father is always asking, "Why do you think you have to take care of me?"

———

In trying to picture your life, your father's life, I'm hampered by the limits of imagination. My father used to drop clues like bread crumbs, and then would turn evasive when I tried to follow the trail. So does yours. I need to make a story, on inadequate evidence.

There's a wall of impenetrable privacy. Things go on behind it. I stand on the other side and assemble clues, furnish houses.

I know from something your father says what book is on his bedside table. I know from what you're wearing today, from your son's Popsicle-smeared T-shirt, which things will be tossed into your laundry hamper tonight. Of your family I think: "They're just like us." And equally, or perhaps more, intensely, "They're nothing like us." I imagine you have found that mess can be survivable. I imagine you all safe, loved, understanding, understood. The grass on your side is verdantly, screamingly, blindingly green.

You are thirty-one now, maybe thirty-two. When I was your age, my father was still alive. I thought he was okay. Nobody in my family had ever seen a psychiatrist.

If I were to put it that way to your father, I'd probably frame it as self-pity. I'd say, "I've been feeling sorry for myself, remembering a time when I had no idea that my father was going to commit suicide."

Your father would say, "Sorry for yourself? Do you mean you're feeling sad?"

I would leave out the fact that I'm comparing myself to you, or even thinking of you at all.

If I did tell him that, if I did mention you, he'd shrug and tell me it was okay.

I'd say, "I was afraid you'd find it disturbing."

"What, that you feel wistful when you think about my daughter?" He'd lift his eyebrows, and look puzzled and curious, and ask me to talk about my feelings about you.

I wouldn't want to do it, but I would do it. I wouldn't tell him all about it, but I'd tell him part. I'd watch his eyes, which would try to hold steady behind his glasses, but they would move a little. And I would try, and fail, to figure out what that little movement meant.

Suicide:
psychological impact of

"'Psychologically impacted' means the effect of certain circum-
stances surrounding real estate which includes . . . 1) The fact
that an occupant of real property is, or was at any time sus-
pected to be, infected or has been infected with the human im-
munodeficiency syndrome . . . , or (2) the fact that the property
was at any time suspected to have been the site of a homicide,
other felony or a suicide."

FROM A CONNECTICUT STATUTE ENACTED IN 1990,
AND REPEALED IN 2004

1. He Haunts the House

"It really doesn't bother me," my mother said of the room
where my father had shot himself. "I go in there all the time,
to fold the laundry, or to get something out of the filing cabinet. It's just another room in my house."

Then she lowered her voice: "But once in a while the cleaning people shut the door of that room when they've finished,
and that does bother me. Walking up the stairs, and seeing that
closed door."

2. He Makes a Museum

The bulging black trash bag, from when my husband had
sorted through my father's papers the week after he died, still
sat on the floor of the study. Every time we visited for the weekend, we noticed that the bag was still there. We asked my

mother if we could throw it out. She flapped her hand at us, irritated. "Leave me alone. I'll deal with it."

She had bought a little paper shredder, which sat in its box on the floor next to the trash bag.

"Mom," I said. "You don't have to shred his papers. There's nothing all that personal. Nobody cares."

"People go through those bags at the dump," she said. "I don't want anybody finding things. It's nobody's business."

"Then how about if I take the bag to Kinko's," I said. "They have giant shredders. They could do the whole bag in about five minutes."

"Someone working there might open the bag, and get interested in what's inside."

"I'll stand there. I'll stand and watch while they do the shredding."

My mother gave me a look of combined annoyance and exhaustion. "I don't want the shreds in Kinko's garbage," she said.

I asked my husband if he remembered what he'd put into the bag. "Cancelled checks from twenty years ago," he said. "File folders full of newsletters your father subscribed to, about successful investing."

The book my father had been reading was still in the room, on top of the filing cabinet. It was a fat history of oil and the oil business. I'd given him the book for Christmas, six weeks before he died. He'd filled up some of the silences in our last few phone calls by telling me how much he was enjoying it.

The film he'd shot at Christmas was still in the camera.

The last batch of spaghetti sauce he'd made was in the freezer, in neatly stacked square plastic containers.

The last CDs he'd listened to were piled up on top of one of the living-room stereo speakers.

The wood he'd carried into the house a couple of weeks before he died was still stacked next to the fireplace. The thick suede work gloves he'd worn lay nearby on the hearth, palms and fingers still curved in the shapes of his hands.

All this stuff stayed there, petrified. An eerie accidental museum of him.

3. He Haunts the Boat

The man who bought his little sailboat, who of course had no idea how my father had died, asked my mother if it was okay if he kept the boat's name. He said he could feel my father's presence on the boat, a benign spirit wishing him well. He said, "Your husband was happy sailing. And he was a nice person. I can tell."

My mother said that of course he could keep the name, and she gave him my father's insulated picnic cooler.

4. My Mother Converses with His Picture

On her desk, my mother had a photograph of my father. One night she and I sat up late talking, and there was a silence. We were both tired, but we didn't want to go to bed. My mother picked up the photograph and held it in both hands.

"What," she said to it, "what? Didn't you know how much I loved you? Didn't I tell you often enough? Didn't I tell you how much I loved our life together, this house, our daughters?" She shook the picture.

"Mom," I said.

She was still addressing the photograph. "Did I make you feel like you were worthless? Was that it? Was it all my fault?"

"Ma," I said sharply. "Cut it out."

She put down the photograph and covered her face with

her hands. I put my arm around her shoulders. "Come on," I said. I walked her down the hallway to her bedroom and stayed there while she changed into her nightgown and brushed her teeth and got into bed. I kissed her good night.

Back in the room where I was staying—my mother's study—I picked up my father's photograph from the desk. He was sitting on the living room sofa, with his chin resting on his hand. His face was aloof, elaborately blank—not an absent expression, but like he was trying hard to look absent, to appear to be thinking of nothing. It was a look he would get sometimes, especially toward the end: a blankness that seemed assumed in order to conceal something, though I never knew what. If he'd been alive, and I'd walked into the room and found him sitting on the sofa, looking like that, his expression would have segued instantly into something else: happiness to see me, an alert realization that he needed to pull himself together. He and I might have smiled and rolled our eyes at each other, about some over-the-top emotional thing my mother had said.

But in the photograph he just sat there, closed and mysterious. When he was alive, he'd met my mother's hysterical questions with silence, and it was the same now.

Maybe my mother had questioned the photograph in front of me in order to make a point, to enlist me as an ally. "You see?" she seemed to be asking me. "See how he never answers me?"

"Jesus Christ," I said to the picture of my father sitting on the sofa. "Who *wrote* this script?"

5. He Appears in the Cheese Shop
I was in the little fancy-food store in my neighborhood, buying cheese.

My father and I used to shop here together when he was visiting me. He liked the store because it sold the smoky meats he'd had as a little boy in Germany: wursts and Westphalian ham, blood sausage, *Lachsschinken*. There were expensive tins of English tea, smartly packaged foreign crackers, jams and chocolates, glistening fresh strawberry tarts. My father would point into the display cases, his eyebrows raised in sneaky, childish pleasure. "What do you think?" he would ask me. "Shall we, just this once?" Amassing a pile of white-wrapped parcels and buttery-smelling baker's boxes tied with string. Standing in the checkout line smiling down at me, never letting me pay.

And that's where I saw him, on a cool October afternoon when he was eight months dead. He was standing two places ahead of me in line, waiting to pay.

His height. His posture. The back of his head, tall and domed, speckled with years of sunburn, the fringe of gray hair—the whole of it giving off an air of careful grooming and unwitting vulnerability. All the details that I'd forgotten and could not have conjured up, but which, suddenly appearing in the cheese shop, were so piercingly familiar, so right.

The sight of him was shocking. But it also had a kind of inevitability. I realized that I'd been imagining he might reappear in just this way: arriving in my neighborhood to surprise me, stopping first at this store to buy a few treats to bring to my house. It was as if some lost object had taken longer to turn up than expected, but then had suddenly, quietly, appeared, in a place where I thought I'd already looked.

There were two women standing between me and my father in the line. They were chatting and shifting their weight, so my father was visible and then invisible. I pushed myself forward to get closer to him, and one of the women turned around in annoyance.

"Sorry," I said loudly. I was testing. Would the sound of my voice make him turn around?

He was at the register now, pulling out his money. I strained to see his hands: his long palms and fingers. He did not turn to look at me. And his hand, when it flashed out sideways holding the money, was wrong. Small and white. The big brown wallet that he'd pulled out of his pocket was wrong, too, though the way he lifted his suede shoulder and stood very straight, with his head tilted, was right enough to hold me, mesmerized and confused.

But then he turned enough so that I could see the full soft mouth, wrong; and the small pink fleshy nose, wrong; and I saw him lift his forefinger to his lips and quickly lick it and then bring it down to peel some bills from the stack he was holding in his other hand, wrong wrong wrong.

Yet when this man walked by me, holding his shopping bag, and I saw that he in fact looked nothing like my father, I still said the word "Dad?" aloud.

I didn't look at him when I said it; I was looking straight ahead. I said it quietly, but he was only inches away from me when I spoke. He kept walking. The two women in the line ahead of me turned and looked at me.

6. Another House Is Haunted

People were always asking my mother if she planned to move out of the house. She would shrug and say, "I like it here."

To me she said, "I don't even know if this house would sell, because of psychological impact."

"The impact it would have on you, you mean?"

"No," she said, impatiently. "Psychological impact. It's a *thing*. An actual thing, in real estate. If the buyers ask whether or not a house has psychological impact, you have to tell them."

"I still don't understand what you mean."

"Like if someone in the house has had AIDS, or if a murder or suicide has happened there—"

"That's ridiculous. And the AIDS thing is probably illegal."

My mother, who was a real estate agent, shook her head. "Under Connecticut law, the buyer has the right to ask the question."

"What, you're saying that Daddy's death is supposed to have some kind of psychological impact on the house itself? That oooh, now it's a suicide house?"

"There are houses like that, where bad things keep happening," my mother said. "I had a listing that I couldn't sell. That beautiful old brick house over on Pickwilder Road. Some man murdered his wife there, back in the 'twenties. And then maybe fifteen years ago a girl, a teenager, killed herself. It's a gorgeous house, I should have been able to sell it in five minutes. But there's something about it. You bring customers there and they don't even want to go inside. Even when they don't *know*, they know."

I was furious. "So the law puts the buyer's right to be superstitious and ignorant above the seller's right to privacy?"

My mother, confused by the question, suddenly swerved. "That's why Daddy did it in the house, instead of driving off and doing it in the woods somewhere," she said. "He knew. He knew it would have psychological impact."

I clicked my tongue against my teeth.

"No," she said, "really. He knew. I told him. He knew what

a tough time I had with that Pickwilder Road listing. I remember specifically telling him: this is what happens when there's a murder or suicide."

"Why would he think it out to that extent?" I said. "Why would he say, 'Aha, I think I'll turn this into a haunted house that will be difficult for her to sell'?"

She shrugged. "He was very angry with me," she said.

7. A Friend Who Should Know Better Insists on the Supernatural

"Can you believe it?" I asked my friend Jill over the phone. This psychological impact thing was making me wild. "Why limit it to AIDS, murder, and suicide? Why not just let the buyer quiz you about your marriage? Did you and your husband fight in the house? How often? How bad were the fights? How was the sex? Maybe you should set up a hidden camera when you move in, and then when you're ready to sell, just hand the buyer the footage."

"Mmm," Jill said. The kind of murmur that let me know she thought I was ranting.

"No, but really," I said. "What the hell difference could it possibly make to anyone else that my father killed himself in the house? He was a nice man. But now just because he did this one thing, he's—"

"I know," Jill said.

"Not only is he beyond the pale, but he puts our whole house beyond the pale. He's tainted. I mean, what—is he buried outside the city gates with a stake through his heart?"

"I know."

"And what about the houses where other kinds of terrible

things have happened?" I went on. "Rapes, or incest. Or husbands beating wives. Or parents beating children. Why should they be exempt from psychological impact laws?"

Jill was silent for a moment. Then she said, "There is a house like that, down the road from where I live. Nobody knew what was happening to the kids in that house. It was a nightmare. Social services finally got a tip from someone, and came in and took the kids away."

"That's awful," I said.

"But what I'm thinking of," Jill said, "is that the people who bought the house after that just always had this weird creepy feeling there. Like there was this *aura.* They finally hired someone to do some kind of ceremony. Like a blessing, or maybe it was an exorcism—"

"Well," I said.

8. His Museum Exerts Its Power

My mother had thrown out the spaghetti sauce. But the garbage bag was still there. So were the CDs, and the firewood, and the gloves curved in the supplicating shapes of his hands.

He'd been dead for two years, three years, five.

"Mom," I said, my hand on the trash bag.

"What," she said. "Leave me alone."

9. My Mother Confesses to Murder

At the beginning, right after his death, my mother spoke about my father in big, sweeping statements. "I have nothing but compassion for him," she would announce.

Or: "I have such anger. Such anger. How could he have abandoned me like this?"

After he'd been dead awhile—three years, five—she started

to tell me stories, rather than just headlines. She was still trying to enlist my sympathy, but she also seemed to be puzzling something out.

"Did I ever tell you what happened with Troilus?" she asked me one day. We had each driven an hour and a half to meet for lunch at a deli halfway between our houses.

"Troilus the cat?"

"Did I tell you about his death?"

"I knew he died," I said, spreading cream cheese on my bagel.

"He kept getting sick. Every day there'd be this little mess of cat vomit somewhere, that I'd have to clean up. I kept telling Daddy, 'Something's wrong, we've got to take Troilus to the vet.' But Daddy would just give me this angry look. He'd get that look and you couldn't talk to him. So finally I just took Troilus to the vet by myself, and they found a tumor. They said he'd be dead within a couple of months. So I had him put to sleep."

"That's sad."

"But the point is, Daddy never asked what happened to him. The cat was there, and then suddenly the cat wasn't there. And Daddy never asked."

I stopped laying smoked salmon on top of the cream cheese. "Why didn't you just tell him?"

"I kept waiting for him to ask. It was his cat. Wouldn't you think he would have asked me, 'Hey, where's Troilus?' Then I would have told him."

I drank some coffee and tried to keep my face neutral.

My mother said into the silence: "You are so hard on me, you know that? You're always judging me."

"I am not," I lied.

"I feel guilty, all right? I go over it in my head. Why didn't I tell him that Troilus was dead? I don't understand it myself anymore. I have to keep reminding myself what it was really like to live with a man like that, who wouldn't talk. A man who wouldn't just say, 'What have you done with my cat?'"

I nodded, and drank more coffee. Part of me wanted to laugh. But also I was imagining the silences at my parents' dinner table, my father determined not to ask and my mother not to tell.

10. He Haunts Someone Else's House

I was visiting my cousin Sarah in Ohio, and she said, "Did I ever tell you about the time your father came to see me?"

"I don't think so," I said.

It was late at night. We were sitting at Sarah's kitchen table, drinking wine. Rain was slapping against the windows, and we could hear the tree branches heaving around in sudden gusts of wind.

"It was the week we moved in here," Sarah said. "We moved, and I hated it. This little dark ugly house. I couldn't stop crying. Your father came to town on business. I opened the door, and the first thing he said was, 'You have some beautiful old lilacs here.'

"I just looked at him. 'Really?' It was winter, I didn't know what the hell a lilac looked like. He took me out into the garden, and he just kept pointing stuff out to me. These were hydrangeas, these were wild roses, this was a dogwood. He pointed to a brown glob on a twig and told me it was a praying mantis egg case, and how good they'd be for the garden. Then we went inside, and he did the same thing with the house. Look at this great south-facing window. Did I know how lucky I was to have fir floorboards? What a wonderful deep bathtub.

"So that's what he did," Sarah said. "He showed me my house, which I really hadn't seen before. He sort of blessed it."

We sat there. It was a moment when it would have felt good to cry, but I waited and nothing happened.

Sarah looked toward the dark kitchen window. "I always think of him, when the lilacs bloom, or when I spot a praying mantis in the summer. I hear his voice, telling me how wonderful it's all going to be."

11. The Neighbors Vanish

My mother decided to sell her house and buy a condo. My father had been dead for seven years.

"That's great!" I said. "I think it'll make you feel so much better to get out of this house."

"Yes, well, George and CeCe Oliver just sold their house. They're moving to Arizona," my mother said. I knew that the Olivers were her next-door neighbors; their house was hidden in the woods about a quarter of a mile away.

"And the Giffords are gone, too," my mother went on. "Ed died last year, and Daisy bought something smaller."

"Uh-huh," I said into the telephone. I wasn't sure why she was telling me about the Olivers and the Giffords leaving; my parents had never been close to any of the neighbors.

"And then those other people in the yellow house—what was their name, the woman with the weird hair, and they used a clothesline instead of a dryer. Anyway," my mother said, "they've been gone for ages."

"So you feel like the old neighborhood is breaking up?" I said doubtfully. I knew that wasn't it, but I didn't know what it was.

"No, the point is," my mother said impatiently, "that this is what I've been waiting for. Now there won't be anybody left to *talk*. To start a rumor that might put off a buyer. The point is that when George and CeCe go, there won't be anyone left who remembers how Daddy died."

12. My Mother's House Is Cursed with His Presence and Inadequate Closet Space

My mother put her house on the market.

We went down to help her get it ready. We cleaned, and we persuaded her to get rid of stuff. We put away the CDs. We threw out the bag of trash from my father's study, opening it briefly to stuff in the curved supplicating suede work gloves.

The next time we went to visit, we saw that the house had begun trumpeting its own virtues. Little signs, embellished with the logo of my mother's real estate firm, were taped up everywhere. ESTABLISHED PERENNIAL GARDEN! announced one hanging next to a living room window. BUILT-IN BOOKSHELVES! crowed another, in my father's study.

The house sat on the market.

My mother called me and said, "Apparently my house is unacceptable, and I'm unacceptable too."

She called again. "Maybe I should burn it down. Would that make people happy?"

———

Finally a buyer materialized. The offer, according to my mother, was insulting. But she made a counter-offer, which was accepted. She began happily debating the pros and cons of various condominium complexes, and talking about which furniture she would take with her.

Then one afternoon my phone rang, and when I picked it up she said, in a flat drained rasp that was so quiet I could barely hear her: "It's happened."

"What has?"

"Psychological impact. The buyer. I knew it. I knew this would happen."

The buyers had heard a rumor about my father's death, and they had submitted a question to her, in writing. She read me the sentence from their letter: "We heard that your husband died in the house, and that a gun was involved."

She was sobbing; she could hardly talk. "I'll never get out of here, I'll never get away from this."

"Mom," I said. "Mom." I started asking her a lot of crisp questions about what exactly the law allowed and required. She, choking and crying, told me that the buyers were allowed to ask the question, and that she could choose whether or not to answer it. "But not answering *is* an answer," she cried, "not answering is like saying, yes, you're right, my husband did blow his brains out in the house."

"Are you sure the law allows this? Are you sure this isn't discriminatory?" I said, still in my crisp efficient problem-solving voice. "What does your lawyer say?"

"I haven't talked to him! It doesn't matter what he says! The point is that people are always going to be asking this question!"

She was like the person in the horror movie who sees the

ghost and can't stop screaming. I was the one who doesn't believe in the ghost, and then goes numb when it appears.

She screamed, "Daddy did this to me. This terrible thing. It was his job to take care of me, and he didn't! How could he have done this to me?"

I said, "I know how you feel, I know you're upset, but I don't want to listen to this."

"Every time I try to talk to you, you tell me what I say is wrong. Everything I feel is wrong. Maybe I should commit suicide, too, and then you wouldn't have to worry about me anymore."

A silence. I hung up on her.

My mother decided to answer the buyers' question. She told them that yes, her husband had died in the house. She said it was an accident. He'd been cleaning his gun, and it went off and killed him.

The buyers withdrew their offer. They said the closets were too small.

13. He Appears in the Airport

My mother's house finally sold, to a buyer who loved the pool and the garden and the private setting, deep in the woods. She and I decided to meet in Paris, to spend a week there together. (That's how it went between us. We would have a horrible fight, which at the time would feel insurmountable. It was impossible to see how we could continue from there. And then somehow, we would continue.)

I checked in for my Paris flight at Logan, and sat in a chair drinking tea and doing a crossword puzzle. I got stuck on a clue and looked around the room. My father was sitting across the lounge, at the end of a long row of chairs.

He was wearing a suede jacket, reading the *Times,* waiting patiently for his flight to be called.

It was different from the other times when I'd spotted him—in the cheese shop, or sitting a few rows ahead of me at a concert, or climbing slowly out of a parked car as I went by, helplessly, in the passenger seat of a moving one. This time I knew it wasn't him. I was like a veteran of the desert who knows about mirages but can still be stirred by one, capable of simultaneously discounting and savoring the sight of green trees and a pool of clear water.

I sat in the departure lounge looking wistfully over at this guy. Not only did I see him, I understood him. He was living a peripatetic life, flying to and from Europe where he could travel easily, comfortable in the German of his childhood and the French, Spanish, and Portuguese he spoke so fluently. He was living this other, secret, gypsy life because he was afraid to come home.

I knew I wasn't going to get up and move closer. But I imagined what might happen if I did. I imagined that he would have looked up to stare at me with uncertain, smiling amazement. His cover would have been blown, but we would both have been relieved that I'd blown it.

I would have said to him: "It's okay. You don't have to worry anymore. It's safe. The mess you left has all been cleaned up. You can come home now."

14. I Have It Out with His Ghost

I went down to my parents' house one last time, before my mother moved. She had sold some of the furniture and pictures, given away extra dishes and the lawn mower and the pool equipment.

That night, when everyone else was asleep, I went into my father's study and shut the door. I sat on the floor in the blank space where the blue armchair had been, the one he'd sat down in to shoot himself. I took a last look at what he must have looked at that morning: the grass-cloth wallpaper, the Japanese samurai sword hanging on the wall, the photographs of the grandchildren, the shelves with their rows of optimistic-sounding business titles (*Successful Hedge Fund Investing, The Twelve Hats of a Company President*).

I wondered what the buyers would do with this room. Once it was empty, and no trace of my father lingered here, it could be anything. It could be a baby's room, or a place for exercise equipment. It could be turned into a large bathroom. It could be knocked together with the room next door to make something big, or it could be knocked down altogether as part of a major remodeling project. Or someone might use it as a study again.

It would either vanish, or survive; most likely it would survive but in some unrecognizable form.

He wasn't here, in this room. It was us, not the house, that he was haunting. He was our ghost. We were the only ones who could see him, and even we couldn't clearly recognize him. Other people were scared by what he'd done. We were scared that he was the one who had done it.

Sitting there for the last time on the floor of his study, with my knees drawn up to my chin, I spoke to him. I didn't talk out loud, but I was addressing him and he was listening.

I said: *You swung a huge punch at me and then ducked out of my reach.*

You did it because you felt unacceptable.

But you only became unacceptable by doing it.

But if "it"—that ending, that irresistible desperation to blow yourself apart—was encoded in you all along, secretly and inseparably part of you, then maybe you were right. If I had been able to see you clearly, maybe I would have found you unacceptable too.

But I loved you. The words "acceptable" and "unacceptable" are gibberish.

The more I sat there thinking about him, the more I felt like I was focusing on the wrong things. I was standing at the gate arguing with some pompous uniformed official, while the right things, the real things, whatever they were, were vaporizing, escaping into the air.

Suicide:
readings in the literature of

"Although Enlightenment writers had fought to establish the right to suicide as a moral, rational act, the argument in the nineteenth century was not whether suicide was moral but whether suicide could ever be rational."

—GEORGE HOWE COLT, *The Enigma of Suicide*

"Anyone who could imagine the terror—the pain—of those who survive a suicide—against whom a suicide is *committed*—could not carry it through . . . Of course, when one is at that point, imagining others becomes unimaginable. Everything seems clear, and simple, and *single;* there is only one possible thing to be done—"

—A. S. BYATT, "THE CHINESE LOBSTER"

"At Metz, each suicide was put in a barrel and floated down the Moselle away from the places he might wish to haunt. In Danzig, the corpse was not allowed to leave by the door; instead it was lowered by pulleys from the window; the window frame was subsequently burned. Even in the civilized Athens of Plato, the suicide was buried outside the city and away from other graves; his self-murdering hand was cut off and buried apart."

—A. ALVAREZ, *The Savage God*

"But even in suicide, seemingly the ultimate expression of free will, fate, over which one has no control, plays a part."

—YUKIO MISHIMA, *The Way of the Samurai*

"Each way to suicide is its own: intensely private, unknowable, and terrible. Suicide will have seemed to its perpetrator the last and best of bad possibilities, and any attempt by the living to chart this final terrain of a life can be only a sketch, maddeningly incomplete."

—KAY REDFIELD JAMISON, *Night Falls Fast*

"For every person who successfully commits suicide, it is estimated that there are seven to ten people intimately affected: parents, siblings, children, aunts, uncles, grandparents, grandchildren, close friends. If we accept the official United States Health Department suicide toll of approximately 30,000 people a year, that means that between 200,000 and 300,000 people become suicide survivors each year. If, on the other hand, we take the more likely (unofficial) figure of over 60,000 suicides a year (a percentage of automobile accidents, drug overdoses, alcohol-related deaths, suicides that are covered up by relatives and coroners), then the numbers become larger—between 350,000 and 600,000 new survivors are created each year."

—CHRISTOPHER LUKAS AND HENRY M. SEIDEN, *Silent Grief*

"For suicide is, after all, the result of a choice. However impulsive the action and confused the motives, the moment when a man finally decides to take his own life he achieves a certain temporary clarity. Suicide may be a declaration of bankruptcy which passes judgment on a life as one long history of failures. But it is a history which at least amounts to this one decision which, by its very finality, is not wholly a failure. Some kind of minimal freedom—the freedom to die in one's own way and in one's own time—has been salvaged from the wreck of all those unwanted necessities."

—A. ALVAREZ, *The Savage God*

"Living, naturally, is never easy. You continue making the gestures commanded by existence for many reasons, the first of which is habit. Dying voluntarily implies that you have recognized, even instinctively, the ridiculous character of that habit, the absence of any profound reason for living, the insane character of that daily agitation, and the uselessness of suffering."

—ALBERT CAMUS, "THE MYTH OF SISYPHUS"

"No single theory will untangle an act as ambiguous and with such complex motives as suicide."

—A. ALVAREZ, *The Savage God*

"One who chooses to go on living having failed in one's mission will be despised as a coward and a bungler. . . . If one dies after having failed, it is a fanatic's death, death in vain. It is not, however, dishonorable."

—JOCHO YAMAMOTO, *Hagakure*

"The suicide doesn't go alone, he takes everybody with him."

—WILLIAM MAXWELL, *The Folded Leaf*

"There is a doctrine whispered in secret that man is a prisoner who has no right to open the door and run away: this is a great mystery which I do not quite understand. Yet I too believe that the gods are our guardians, and that we men are a possession of theirs . . . And if one of your own possessions, an ox or an ass, for example, took the liberty of putting himself out of the way when you had given no intimation of your wish that he should die, would you not be angry with him, and would you not punish him if you could?"

—PLATO, *Phaedo*

"We want to die because we cannot cause others to die, and every suicide is perhaps a repressed assassination."

—GUSTAVE FLAUBERT, IN A LETTER TO LOUISE COLET

Suicide:
romances of mother in years following

1. Her condo
"Isn't it elegant?" she asked me.

"Yes," I said.

It was big and sunny, a brand-new townhouse in a suburban Connecticut development built to look like Georgetown or Beacon Hill, with red-brick facades and black iron lampposts. Her condo felt, to me, both grandiose and rickety, with a polished marble hearth and a banister that jiggled like a loose tooth when you put your hand on it. My mother bought herself a Steinway grand piano, which bestowed a curvaceous, odalisque glamour on her carefully pale living room. She knew how to play only one piece, a Chopin ballade she had learned as a child; but whenever I visited she sat down and played that piece over and over, with graceful wrists and a look of concentrated rapture on her face.

"I'm finally living the way I want to live," she told me.

2. Going on cruises
My father had had two modes of travel: business, and visiting family. He'd traveled with a sense of purpose and belonging.

His trips had a fundamental austerity that made my mother wistful and uncomfortable and also, frankly, angry. She wanted Caribbean vacations, romantic aimless wanderings around Paris. The way they traveled was luxurious but utilitarian and, she felt, inconsiderate of her and her wishes. They went where he needed to go. When they got there, she was often left alone, unable to speak the language and needing to fend for herself. (Once, in Germany—a country that put her back up anyway, because of all her French cousins who died in the camps—she was being driven around by my father's aunt's chauffeur, and he told her, by way of conversation, that he'd begun his career as a driver for Eva Braun.)

After my father died, she didn't go anywhere for a while. "He was the one who always figured out the money and the restaurants," she cried to me. "He was the one who always got us to and from the airport."

It was after she finally sold her house and moved into the condo, eight years after my father's death, that she began traveling on her own. She did something that she'd always wanted to do, and that my father would have sneered at: she took cruises. He would have thought them hokey, boring, and timid, a thousand passengers sharing a mass delusion that they were traveling when really they were staying in a luxury hotel that happened to troll the world's oceans, stopping briefly at various shopping streets. In my mother's cruises, and in her life, years after he died, there was a clear note of defiance of him, as maybe there always is after a marriage ends (no matter how it ends) and once the first shock has passed. A decision to listen to music that the other person would have hated. A gradual diagonal spreading out in the bed at night, arms and legs sprawled across what used to be the other person's side. A general Damn you, you're not here anymore so now I'm going to do what I want.

Still, though my father had deplored the notion of cruises, my mother's cruises weren't quite the kind he'd been deploring. Hers didn't dip into warm ports filled with Hermès boutiques; they dipped around the coastline of Alaska, or Antarctica. Her boats weren't luxury liners; they were freighters, fitted up with a few plush cabins and a small fancy dining room where the twenty or so passengers who'd paid heavily to travel alongside containers filled with frozen fish or scrap metal could eat consommé and rib roast and talk about the day's scenery. My mother liked the wildness of what they saw, and the safety of the place from which they saw it. She saw birds, and bears, and seals, and penguins, and she met men.

By this point she was in her mid-seventies. She was very large, as she had been all her life; and after years of dyeing her hair black and then a series of odd blondish shades, she'd finally let it go gray. She got short of breath when she walked even a few steps. But she still had a racy, juicy candor that switched on in social situations. She liked men, and wanted them to like her. She had a sizzle that said, "How about it?" and a comforting, matronly warmth that said, "No, of course I don't mean *really*," and a wicked self-aware twinkle that acknowledged the contradiction of these two guises—the vamp and the matron—and said, "Doesn't the ambiguity intrigue you?"

She came home from each cruise talking about a man. The purser, who still secretly dreamed of trying to make it as a painter. "I told him to do it! It's his dream—he should go for it!" my mother said. She bought sketchbooks in Tierra del Fuego, one for him and one for her, and they'd sat together at the ship's bow each morning, making drawings. Then there was a man who was married—but, said my mother, "His wife is such a cold bitch!" This man also had a secret desire to do something other than what he'd actually done with his life. They all did, according to my mother: they were bankers who'd hoped to be Shakespearean actors, or airline pilots who wanted to write poetry. My mother listened with passionate attention and asked questions and cheerled them out of their pessimistic certainty that they'd made their beds long ago and had to lie in them. (That my mother emphatically believed in this new vision of herself as a muse of thwarted dispirited men made a kind of sad and nutty sense to me, even though it also drove me crazy.)

She would talk about each man for a few months, maybe correspond with him. Then, "I don't know," she would tell me. "He sort of dropped out of the picture."

I wondered if her romantic intensity put them off. If what had seemed charming for a week at sea alarmed them when she adhered to it over time. If she took offhand, slightly drunk ship's-cocktail-party answers to her insistent, provocative (but not drunk, she never drank) questions—"Come on, if you hadn't gone into mechanical engineering, what would you have done?"—and then held them to it, writing to them for months afterward to press them to enroll in a sculpture studio, or to ask how the violin was going.

Or maybe she simply couldn't stay merry. That subversive, candid merriment of hers was enchanting, electric; but it was a social phenomenon. It was something elicited by, and dazzling to, a new acquaintance. It was like makeup: it looked good in public, but in private, sooner or later it had to come off.

There was one man, a widower from England, with whom things got more serious. Of the others, my mother had said, "I liked him"; but this man she was "seeing." The seeing happened mostly in the form of hearing; their relationship, after the cruise, was conducted in transatlantic phone calls, initiated by him, because by the time my mother's rates went down at five, he was asleep in Hertfordshire. He didn't call often enough, she felt.

The high point came when she invited him to visit her in Connecticut, and he said yes. She redid her guest room in blue-and-white stripes—"crisp and masculine" was how she described it. "Of course I'm not really sure *which* room he'll sleep in," she told me, with a delicious shiver that suggested she both feared and hoped it would not be the guest room.

"My 'friend,'" she called him, when she told people he was coming, managing to endow the word "friend" with enough burlesque innuendo that her listeners would have been incredulous to learn there was the slightest uncertainty about which room he would be sleeping in.

"He did sleep in the guest room," she told me after the visit, her voice carefully neutral. I couldn't tell if she was disappointed or relieved, and I didn't ask; the speculation about where he might sleep, and the revelation of where he had slept, was already more than I'd wanted to know.

For Christmas he sent her an early French guide to Paris, which, he said, he had found in an old bookshop in the Strand. She said to me: "A book? An old book? That's his idea of a Christmas present?" I said I thought it was a romantic gesture, an acknowledgment that he knew Paris was her favorite city; but she kept saying, "An old book?" She thought it should have been a piece of jewelry, or an alligator bag. Then she started telling me that he was under his daughter's thumb. That he spent too much money on the daughter and too much time with her. He was planning to take his next cruise with the daughter and her husband. "He said I could come if I wanted to," she told me. "But not really an invitation. Not, 'Of course you will come with me.' And besides, do I really want to tag along on their cruise? Shouldn't he and I be taking our own cruise?"

A month or two after that, she told me he'd dropped out of the picture. She said she thought he wasn't really over his wife's death. And she said again that he was under his daughter's thumb. She said, "And such a cowardly way to do it. He just stopped calling me. No explanation. Don't you think that's cowardly?"

"I do," I said, though I wondered what sort of explanation he could possibly have given her.

She said, "He abandoned me. Like Daddy did. And Ted. Why do they always abandon me?"

3. Her idea of herself as invincible

One morning, after she been living in her condo about five years, she woke up, tried to get out of bed, and fell. She had no sensation in her legs. A friend called an ambulance. It was Election Day. The whole time they were carrying her on a stretcher down the two steep staircases in her condo, my mother was yelling, "But I have to vote! How am I going to vote?" She made such a fuss that they sent a state trooper to bring a ballot into the emergency room that afternoon. An extremely handsome state trooper. When she called me that night, she was more elated by his looks than she was worried about her paralysis. "Gorgeous," she kept saying. "You know that kind of Adonis handsome—so gorgeous that it's not quite real?" She called him "My trooper," and told me several times that he'd been impressed by how eager she was to vote.

I recognized the mode she was in: spunky and invincible. It was something I'd first seen in her (and felt, sometimes, in myself) right after my father's death. A denial of feeling that was possible because the thing that had happened was too weird, too extreme, to be felt. It was as if someone said, "Okay, from now on you're going to speak only in Farsi" and there was no higher authority to whom you could say, "Excuse me but none of us know Farsi," so what could you do but be silent for a moment while considering your options—none—and then laugh nervously and keep speaking in the only language you knew?

Who would imagine that my father would die that way? Who would expect that my mother would be carried out of her condo in her nightgown one Election Day and would never go back?

"Why me?" she would ask, when spunky and invincible failed her and she was in what she referred to always as "the black place." I never knew what to say. It could only have been a rhetorical question, but I always felt that she was pressing me for an answer. Or a response, anyway; she wanted me to hold her while crooning, "I don't know, I don't know, it's not fair." But I couldn't bring myself to do this. It felt too angrily demanded, too scripted. A drama of familial love that was as fake in its way as the drama of spunk and invincibility. A wailing, a rending of garments. Wasn't there something in the middle? Something that was neither falsely brave nor grandiosely tragic? Some way she could talk without demanding and I could listen without feeling mugged? "Why can't you be real?" I might have asked, if I'd felt like voicing my own over-the-top rhetorical question.

In fact, we were real. Our reality was a bitchy, edgy, tense back-and-forth picking on each other that went on constantly, and mystified and repelled the few observers who were permitted to see it (my sister, who could only deal with my mother's histrionics by withdrawing; and my husband, who'd grown up believing that any yelling within a family meant divorce). Yet somehow, in some perversely bracing way, it was this squabbling that kept order between us.

We could do it over anything. A sandwich. "Bring me a ham and cheese."

"But Mom, doesn't cheese upset your stomach?"

"I'll be fine."

"But the last time you had it—"

"I'm lying in this bed paralyzed from the waist down. Do you know what the doctor called me yesterday? A paraplegic. Can you believe he said that word to me? And now you won't even let me have the sandwich I want?"

"I'm sorry he called you that. But it doesn't change the laws of cause and effect. Cheese disagrees with you. If you eat it now, you're going to be miserable later."

"I'm miserable all the time! Don't you understand? I'm miserable every minute of the day. And now my daughter is telling me I can't have a slice of lousy Swiss cheese?"

"Fine. I'll bring you ham and cheese."

I would bring it. She might eat the cheese, or she might ostentatiously remove it from the sandwich and lay it aside before taking a bite. Either way we wouldn't say anything; we would maintain an injured, charged silence. Neither of us would say the word "sorry."

But eventually, she would say, "This is just really hard."

And I would say, "I know."

After she'd been in the hospital a while and the paralysis hadn't gotten any better, they moved her to a rehab place. They told her she probably wouldn't walk again.

"Screw them, they don't know you," I said. Spunky and invincible. She smiled at me from her wheelchair, where she was sitting in a rumpled sweatshirt and too-short pants, feebly lifting a one-pound weight over and over again.

At the end of a hundred days, her Medicare coverage would run out. The physical therapists told her she couldn't go back to her condo, because of the stairs; and she told them she was going back anyway.

"What do they know, they're the ones who told me I'd never walk again," she said to me. By this point she was able to shuffle along a little bit with a walker, a step and then a stop and then another step.

"You're doing great," I cheered.

"So tell them I'm going back to the condo."

"You can't."

She stopped in mid-step, gripping her walker and glaring at me. "You're supposed to support me, not undermine me."

"I'm not undermining you, I'm just trying to be realistic. They won't discharge you to go back to the condo."

"So then let them keep me until I can go back there."

"They won't."

"They can't make me leave. What are they going to do, lift me bodily and deposit me on the sidewalk?"

I went out and looked at assisted living places. She said I was betraying and abandoning her. She wanted to go back to the condo. Her physical therapists drove over and looked at it, and agreed that no amount of conversion could make it habitable for her.

"Hire help!" she said to me. "Hire big strong male aides to carry me up and down the stairs."

"Mom," I said.

"What? You promised you'd never put me in one of those places."

"It's temporary," I said. The director said she could move in for a three-month trial period. My mother said she would not take any of her furniture to that place. There was no point, she said, in moving it in when she was only going to have to move it out again. "Three months," she said to me, "that's what you're promising me. Ninety days and not one day longer."

The stakes were different, but it was the same fight we'd been having since my father died. She was mad because I couldn't fix it; I was mad because she expected me to.

On the day my mother moved in, the director of the assisted living place sat her down in a conference room to sign papers and go over the new-resident's questionnaire.

"Any special stories you'd like to tell us regarding your childhood?" the director asked.

"No," my mother said.

"Religious affiliation? Favorite songs? Hobbies?"

"Drinking coffee and reading *The New York Times*," my mother said, shooting me a look of canny contempt: are you satisfied, now that you've enrolled me in this senile kindergarten?

"And your husband," the director said, pen hovering over the form, "is he still living?"

My mother shook her head. "No."

"Would you like to tell me a little about him?"

"No."

We took my mother upstairs in a wheelchair, the director chatting brightly about how the dining room was just like a fine restaurant, and about the afternoon bus that took residents to Kmart and Walgreens. Then we came to a door labeled with my mother's name, with balloons floating from a ribbon tied to the doorknob. My mother said, "Oh, Jesus," under her breath and started to cry.

The director knelt by the wheelchair. "This is hard for you, isn't it?"

"It's terrible," my mother whispered.

They talked for a few minutes, in low murmurs. I moved away. I felt the way I had when my sons were little and I'd held them in my lap while the doctor gave them a shot, as if I had to detach and float above this thing that was happening in order to be able to stay there.

After a while the director patted my mother's hand and stood up again, and we went into the room. It was large, with two windows that looked out over a garden. "And as you requested, we've put a little furniture in here for you," the director said.

There was a hospital bed, and a La-Z-Boy reclining chair; a pale veneered dresser and a couple of rickety lamps. My mother gazed at it all furiously.

"You're not happy," the director said.

"My daughter told me you were going to put in some model furniture," my mother said. "This is not what I think of when I think of *model* furniture."

"Maybe the term 'model furniture' was misleading—" the director began.

"'Model' means 'nice,'" my mother said. "Like what you have in your lobby. Not this—this depressing old—"

"I'm sorry," the director said. "We don't generally furnish the units at all, since most people prefer to bring their own things from home. But since you didn't want to bring your own things—"

"—because this is *temporary*," my mother interjected.

"—because this is temporary, we found a few things to put in here for you. I'm sorry you don't like it; it's clearly not what you're used to—"

"I'm used to antiques," my mother said. "Beautiful European pieces from my husband's family. *Museum-quality* pieces." She paused to let this sink in. Then she looked at me. "Why don't you say something? You're supposed to be my *advocate*."

"Oh, dear." The director looked at her watch. "Listen, I have to go downstairs now, but why don't I ask them to bring you up something on a tray, some tea and cookies maybe—"

I followed her out into the hall. "I'm sorry she wasn't happy with the furniture," she whispered, "but you know we don't really have furniture, these are just a few pieces that were left after someone died—"

"No, no, I understand. She's just having a hard time, she's not really like this," I said.

We both kept fluttering, apologizing to each other. I said I would arrange to have some of my mother's furniture moved from the condo the next day.

When the director left, I stood outside my mother's door. I wanted a cigarette, though I hadn't had one in years. Her accusation of betrayal (*You're supposed to be my advocate*) stung. I wanted her to be graceful. And yet if she had been, it would have been completely fake and out of character. I was glad she wasn't meek, proud of her for not going gentle—but it had never occurred to me that not going gentle might take the form of a tantrum about model furniture.

I should have gone in and crooned and held her hand. Instead I stood there and thought *Fuck you,* and fantasized about not going in at all.

As I stood there, a tiny brittle woman, bent almost double over the handlebar of her walker, came inching toward me; as she reached me she smiled slightly, vaguely, but she obviously needed all the concentration she could muster just to make her way down the hall. She was beautifully dressed, in a knit wool suit and nylon stockings, with gold earrings beneath carefully waved white hair. I thought of my mother, messy and cornered and smoldering and terrified behind the closed door of her "temporary" new home. And of how we both kept repeating the word "temporary," each of us endowing it with our own stubborn nuance. Hers was defiant, sarcastic, daring me to keep pretending that "temporary" wasn't the piece of bullshit we both knew it to be. Mine was apologetic, craven, pleading with her to pretend—or to stop pretending, to stop insisting on the word at all, to tell me frankly that she hated this but recognized there wasn't an alternative and that she didn't blame me.

I took my car key and used it to make holes in the balloons, squeezed all the air out of them, and put them into my pocket. Then I went back into my mother's room.

4. A new man
My mother met a man in her assisted living place.

"He's eighty-two," she said. "I'm not sure why he's in here"—as if it might have been for either armed robbery or murder.

He had gotten on the elevator with us the first night, when my mother and I were heading down to dinner. "Oh, you must be new," he'd said to her. "Do you play bridge?"

"I used to," she mumbled, sunk in her misery at being in that place. "But I don't remember the rules."

"Nobody does," the man said briskly, and strode off the elevator, as much as anyone can stride in a walker.

His name was Doug. A week or two later, he invited my mother to play bridge. She was nervous beforehand, but she called me afterward to tell me it had gone well. "It was me, Doug, another man, and then this woman who always wears gaucho pants. She's completely senile, but she's a fantastic bridge player. She never makes a mistake. Doug calls her 'Gaucho Girl.'"

"He's eighty-two," my mother said, "but he is such a flirt. You should see him work a room. He comes into the dining room, and he flirts with the lady with multiple sclerosis, and then he flirts with the one who has Parkinson's, and then he flirts with Gaucho Girl. It takes him forever to make it to his table."

"People do pair off here," my mother said. I was down for a visit, and we were eating together in the dining room. My mother, in an undertone, was giving me a rundown on the couples sitting at the other tables.

"Okay, at the end there, that's Norma and Frank. They met in here. I think he may have very early Alzheimer's. They sit together, but they never talk to each other. I think they just like the feeling of being a couple.

"Ah. Then we have Honey Johnson," she said.

I looked over at the table she'd jutted her chin at, where a dazzling, gently smiling woman was sitting with a tall concave man. He was in a wheelchair and had an oxygen tank at his feet. "She's gorgeous," I said.

"Can you imagine what she must have looked like at twenty? You're never quite sure, when you talk to her, if she's all there. But Amicangelo certainly seems to like her."

"Is he her husband?"

"No, that's Don Amicangelo. She's with him all the time. I hear his family doesn't approve."

"Oh—she's from the other side of the tracks?" I asked, and my mother laughed.

"Now, the next table, they did come in together, they're married. Betty Ann and Howard. She's got the loudest voice in the place. The other night Howard fell trying to get up from the table, and Betty Ann just stood there saying, in that voice of hers, 'HOWARD FELL. HOWARD FELL.' And Doug called across the dining room, 'So pick him up, Betty Ann.'"

"I was asking my physical therapist about sex," my mother told me over the phone. "Can you believe it? Can you believe your seventy-nine-year-old mother wants to talk about sex?" She was giggling. "Not that I have anything going on personally at the moment, though you never know . . ."

"What did the physical therapist say?"

"Well, that there's a lot of it. Sometimes they have to ring the call button afterwards, because they need help getting up off the floor."

I laughed at that, and she did too.

"I think he really likes me," she said of Doug once, over the phone. And then, in the next conversation: "No. Nothing is going to happen. We're just friends."

"He's a jerk," my mother said. She had called me very early one morning and asked if she could tell me something upsetting, something that had kept her up all night.

"Why?" I asked, dismayed: I'd been so happy to think of her with this sizzly little flirtation.

"There's this new woman here. Antoinette," my mother spat out the name. "She's going after Doug. And he *likes* it."

"What do you mean, going after him?" I asked.

"She stalks him. Wherever he goes, there she is. She practically knocked me down yesterday—I'm in the walker, but she uses a cane, so she's faster."

I drove down and took her out for a Sunday lunch. "It's okay," she said, in a lackluster way, when I asked her about Doug. "We're friends, I guess."

"And what about Antoinette?"

"Oh." She gave a dismissive wave with her hand. "She's not his type."

She ate a little more of the Moroccan chicken she'd ordered. She was happy to see me, and to be eating out in a restaurant, but she seemed lower than she had. I asked about some of the other people whose names I had come to know on my visits to her over the last few months.

"Norma and Frank?"

"She had to leave, because she ran out of money."

"Where did she go?"

"Somewhere cheaper," my mother said. "A Medicaid place, I guess. You don't ask, and nobody tells you."

"And what about Frank?"

"They moved him to the Alzheimer's unit." She put down

her fork. "You remember when I moved in, how it just looked like a bunch of old people? But you get to know the stories, and it's like you're all in the same boat together. Amicangelo is in the hospital," she went on. "Honey dumped him out of his wheelchair." In answer to my questioning look, she said, "It was an accident. She was taking him out for a walk, and she didn't see the curb."

I asked her if the bridge group was still meeting.

My mother toyed with her chicken. "No, that broke up. Doug insisted on playing by his own rules, which somehow always worked to his advantage. The rest of us got fed up. And then Anna Pierson died."

"Who's Anna Pierson?"

"I told you about her. She always wore—"

"Gaucho Girl?"

"Right," my mother said.

5. The possibility of contentment

But after all, things worked out with Doug. They were in love, my mother said. "It's physical," she told me, and I tried to smile in a way that would applaud this and at the same time discourage further details. They sat at a table for two in the dining room. They took naps together in the afternoon. They listened to Frank Sinatra. "Can you imagine what Daddy would say if he knew I would end up liking Frank Sinatra? 'Why are you listening to *junk*?'"

She told me Doug was no-nonsense. He'd owned a small business, which had been very successful. He knew his way around. "You promise not to get mad at me?" she said.

I nodded.

"In some things Daddy knew his way around. He could

get a taxi in the rain, he could talk to the waiter. But in some things, in some big things, he just didn't know his way around."

"I'm not mad," I said. It was the shortest, and most neutral, conversation we'd had about my father since his death.

Her ability to walk had not improved much, and she was in a wheelchair a lot of the time. A year had gone by since the morning when she'd first been paralyzed. Nobody was saying "temporary" anymore. But she said she was happy—the first time I'd ever heard her use that word about herself. "Being in love helps," she told me. "So does being on an antidepressant."

She decided to sell her condo. She was ready, she said.

My sister and I went and spent a week there, sorting out her stuff. Some of it—a few of the "museum-quality pieces"— had already been moved to her room at the assisted living place. Some of it went out on consignment to an antiques dealer, who annoyed my mother by opining that the "museum-quality pieces" were actually good nineteenth-century reproductions of seventeenth- and eighteenth-century furniture. Some of it my sister and I divided.

I took my father's small collection of wooden Buddha statues. Two of them had been in our house for as long as I could remember; he'd brought them home from India when I was little. And one had been given to him on his sixtieth birthday, a year before he died, by my aunt Irene, who said she wanted him to have it because he was the most serene person she knew.

I took my mother's cut-glass bowls, and my grandmother's chipped-gilt mirror, and a chair that my father used to sit in when he listened to music. The chair had come in a shipment from Germany years ago, after my father's grandmother had died. In my childhood it was covered in a shredded old tapestry fabric, but now it wore muted fake needlepoint; my mother had had it reupholstered when she and Ted were in their decorating phase.

I remembered when that German shipment had arrived, a sudden city of crates in our small living room. The crates were full of things that spoke, in a way both tangible and elusive, of my father's childhood, the foreignness hidden beneath his familiar making-pancakes-in-his-bathrobe-on-Saturday-morning self. There were silver hairbrushes, and linen towels, and miniature portraits of ladies with powdered hair, and medals that the Kaiser had given to my great-grandfather, who had been a cabinet undersecretary of some sort. There were seventy-two place settings of Limoges china, which my sister and I now divided.

"What am I going to do with thirty-six place settings?" my sister asked, kneeling on the living room rug wrapping plates in newspaper. I remembered watching my parents unpack the china, my mother saying, with a dismay that even then I could tell masked a giddy delight at the abundance, the richness that was emerging from the crates: "What in the world will I do with seventy-two place settings?" The memory was so clear that it seemed as though it had just happened, as though time had folded to allow that moment to immediately precede this one.

"Careful!" I could remember my mother saying, as she and my father unpacked and my sister and I threw the brown packing paper into the air. "Careful! We don't want to lose anything."

Suicide:
"things" folder and

IT TOOK ME A FEW WEEKS TO GO THROUGH THE BOXES I'D
brought back from my mother's condo. I hung pictures,
arranged furniture, fit my parents' books into my shelves. I had
the silver basket that my mother served the peanuts in, when I
was little and they had people in for bridge; and I had my
grandmother's smoky, chipped-gilt mirror. My father's Bud-
dhas smiled on a table in my living room.

Then one Saturday afternoon, kneeling on my living room
floor going through a box, I pulled out a manila folder, on the
tab of which my mother had printed the words PAUL—"THINGS."

What were "things"? I wondered, sitting down and opening the folder; but I think in some way I already knew.

autopsy

First there was an envelope from the chief medical examiner of
Connecticut: the postmortem report on my father. Someone
named Ira J. Alpert cut him up, the day after he died, beginning at 8:00 A.M. and ending at 8:30.

"The body," I read, "is that of a well-developed, well-
nourished white male appearing the stated age of 61 years. The

upper and lower extremities are symmetrical. The back is straight. The external genitalia are those of a normal male. The deceased is balding in a normal pattern of male baldness with sparse white hair. The teeth are natural. The eyes are gray. The deceased has a wedding ring on the left fourth finger. The deceased is clad in a blue and white shirt, tan sweater, brown shoes and socks, brown pants, and belt."

Their matter-of-factness, your vulnerability. Here are the clothes you were wearing, and here's what your body looked like underneath them. Your back, your penis, your balding head.

bullet

Under EVIDENCE OF INJURY, the typed copy read: "There is an entry-type gunshot wound located on the upper right maxilla with several avulsed teeth associated with the entrance wound. Associated with the wound is a recovered bullet in the vertex slightly to the left of midline. It is a medium caliber, lead alloy bullet labeled with a 'K.' In addition two small fragments are recovered from the brain. The brain is markedly disrupted and hemorrhagic due to the gunshot wound."

Your teeth were smashed. Your brain was "disrupted."

drugs

They screened your blood for cocaine, opiates, and benzodiazepines. You were clean.

fee

A letter from the chief medical examiner's office, dated two weeks after you shot yourself, stating that sufficient data were not yet available to certify the cause and manner of your death.

But then, a week later, they were ready to commit. The cause of death had been determined: "Gunshot wound of head." The manner of your death had been classified as "Suicide."

Official records of these findings could be had for a fee of $6.00.

guns

A photocopy of a document certifying that my husband went to the police station five days after your death and, "for safety reasons," turned in some guns and ammo—a Winchester rifle, a Marlin, two gun-cleaning kits, and five boxes of cartridges. I found them in the back of your closet.

If I'd found them a week before, when you were still alive, they'd have seemed silly to me. "Um, Dad, what are all these rifles doing here? We haven't shot targets in years." And you would have reassured me that they were perfectly safe, no one even knew they were there. Or you might have looked at me coldly and said, "None of your business." Or I might have assumed you would say that, and so if I'd happened to find the guns, I would have said nothing.

search warrant

There it was again, the document that was lying on top of the washing machine the day after you died. MURDER, it said on the first page.

The second page granted the police the warrant, citing "personal knowledge based upon their experience and training that crimes of violence involve a struggle, a break-in, a use of weapons or other instrumentalities, and/or the element of unpredictability. That the person or persons participating in the commission of a violent crime is in contact with the physical surroundings in a forcible or otherwise detectable manner. That there is often an attempt to alter, destroy, remove, clean up, or cover up evidence of a crime. That traces may be left in the form of blood, semen, saliva, physiological fluids and secretions, hair, fiber, fingerprints, palm prints, footprints, shoe prints, weapons and firearms including pistols, rifles, revolvers, shotguns, hatchets, axes, cutting instruments, cutting tools, blunt force instruments, projectiles, ammunition, bullet casing and fragments, dirt, dust and soil, paint samples, glass and plastic fragments, marks of tools used to gain access to locked premises or containers and items containing traces of any of the above-mentioned articles."

seized property

A receipt of items taken from the house by the police the morning you died:

1. White envelope containing ledger sheets
2. Colt Police Positive special .38 cal. handgun
3. .38 cal. shell casing
4. Four live bullets
5. Gunshot residue kit
6. Yellow tissue

Yellow tissue? Did you keep the bullets, or the gun, wrapped in yellow tissue paper? Was there a crumpled sheet of it lying on your lap, or the floor, or the footstool?

Or was "yellow tissue" a piece of your brain?

———

By the time I'd gone through the whole "things" folder, I was crying. I cried for a long time.

It had never occurred to me that the other shoe might turn out to be, after all, the original shoe, dropping again, years later, when I was awake and available to feel it.

Suicide:
thoughts on method of

IT'S CLASSIC.

It's what military officers do, after they've disappointed themselves, or their superiors, or their men. It has a dry, noble, tragic, Prussian precision. You're dealing with yourself coldly and fairly. The punishment for disgrace is execution.

Your sense of honor, of impassive justice, leaves no room for mercy here. No whimpering, no pleading, no mitigation. No consultation necessary: the case is quite clear. You do what needs to be done. It's stylishly understated, almost quiet.

A bullet to the head.

It's violent.

You imagine it deafening, red, boiling-hot. It's like a comic book: the bright colors, the crude outlines, the words in capital letters: BANG! SMASH! CRUNCH! You think "smithereens."

You crave the explosion.

It works.

Put it in your mouth and pull the trigger. *Voilà*.

None of this botched, messy, angry, pathetic waking up in

the hospital. "Do you know why you're here? You're here because you tried to kill yourself." And you're stuck with that. Your secret hanging out there, white and naked, like your ass in the not-quite-closed hospital gown. Not dead, but everyone knowing you wanted to be. A new failure for you to add to all your others.

A decision you now have to make all over again.

It's irrevocable.

Once you've pulled the trigger, it's done. You can't change your mind.

Not like swimming out from the shore, or taking pills, or wrapping your head in a dry-cleaning bag, or sitting in the car with an exhaust hose threaded through the window, or using a knife or a razor—all those methods that allow for second thoughts: what am I doing? In the midst of killing yourself, you might begin to consider emergency rescue plans. Swimming back. Throwing up. Unwrapping the bag. Opening the car door and getting out. A tourniquet, a call to 911.

Even jumping allows for vacillation (no rescue possible there, but all that awful time to regret it on the way down).

With the gun lying on your tongue, the deed and the result are pretty much simultaneous.

There's no separation between action and oblivion.

It's available.

You already own it. It's right there on the top shelf of the closet.

You bought it years ago, to protect your family.

It's emphatic.

If you want to say "fuck you," there's no louder way.

It'll be swift. It'll be clean (well, not for whoever finds you—your wife, you assume).

But for you it'll be fast and clean: you won't have to watch the gory draining away of your own life.

All you have to do is flex your knuckles, and move your finger a total distance of an inch and a half. Maybe less.

Suicide:
where I am now

bed

I am in bed with my husband. Maybe we are reading. Or maybe we have turned out the light and are lying side by side in the dark. Somehow we find ourselves talking about my father.

This isn't one specific night; it could be any night. We've been talking about something else, or we've been silent.

We don't talk about him too much anymore.

We sort of try to figure it out, but not really, not anymore. The subject is like a fish that's probably dead, but every now and then thrashes briefly, startlingly, convulsively on the dock.

Maybe we've been talking about my husband's law partner, who is in his early sixties and who, after several years of widowhood, is about to make a passionately happy second marriage.

"He can't mention her without grinning," I say. "Have you noticed that?"

My husband says, "He stands in the door of my office and tells me what she's doing that day. She's going grocery shopping, then she has a dentist's appointment, then she's meeting her sister for lunch. I think he just likes saying her name."

There's a silence.

"My father seemed so old," I say, "didn't he? But sixty-one isn't old."

"No. It isn't."

"Did we think he was old because we were so young?"

"No," my husband says, "we thought it because he thought it."

Or maybe it's one of those nights when I've begun again, obsessively, to list the reasons for my father's death. The failing business. The expensive lifestyle that my parents couldn't afford. The anger in their marriage. His bad health. His horrific childhood. Clinical depression. I know that it wasn't any single thing, that it was all those things and something more — some way in which the combination or the relentlessness or the loneliness of all those things became unbearable.

My husband listens to me, and then he says, "There's something that happens in the ocean, called a double high tide." He tells me it's a phenomenon that occurs occasionally, during a bad storm. The winds and currents are so fierce that the tide comes in and never gets the chance to recede. It's trapped near the shore for hours and then the next high tide comes in on top of it. That's when catastrophes happen: boats, houses, and people swept out to sea.

"That's what killed your father," he says, "a double high tide."

Or it might be a night when I announce, out of nowhere, "My father was a selfish jerk."

"Yes," my husband says coolly.

We lie there for a while. Then I say, "But he wasn't."

My husband says, "I know."

Or maybe my husband has fallen asleep. I'm reading a novel, and suddenly I realize that one of the characters is going to commit suicide. There are ominous foreshadowings, hints that something violently beyond the pale is going to happen, oblique references to a note and a gun.

I've been enjoying this book, admiring and envying the writing, but now I shut it quickly and bury it under the other books on my nightstand. I don't want to read someone else's take on suicide.

I'm afraid the other writer will get it wrong. Make it too pat, or too melodramatic, or make it the backdrop for some other showy foreground plot—a love affair, a road trip across America, some redemptive literary conceit that purports to change the characters' lives and ultimately to heal them.

I am convinced that in real life suicide can't be the backdrop, dwarfed by something else. It is the foreground: itself inevitably the thing that changes people's lives. There is no other plot, and no resolution. And while some healing does happen, it isn't a healing of redemption or epiphany. It's more like the slow absorption of a bruise.

Another night. My husband is awake, and I am thinking of all the things he did after my father's death: wiping away the blood, arranging the funeral, getting papers to the lawyer, cleaning my father's study.

"You were great," I tell my husband, belatedly, years after the disaster.

And he, belatedly, squirms and says what I at first take to be the equivalent of *Aw shucks.* "No, I wasn't."

"Yes you were. You were amazing." I move closer and wrap an arm around him, put my head down on his chest. He lies there rigidly on his back. When he speaks after a moment his voice is sick with shame.

"I wanted you to think I was amazing. I liked the idea of being wonderful."

I don't find this confession of vanity disturbing; if anything, I am touched by it. "It doesn't matter. There were things that needed to be done, and you did them."

I can feel him, in the darkness, shaking his head. "It was just busywork." Then he says, "I couldn't really help you."

"You did," I say instantly, reflexively.

I think of a time, soon after my father's death, when my husband held me, murmuring over and over, "It's okay, it's okay," and how I finally drew back and said, "What the fuck do you *mean,* it's okay?"

And how he's never said it to me since.

And how I would have hated it if he had.

"You've been there," I say, and now his arms go around me. We are quiet for a while.

"Listen," I say, "can I ask you something?"

"What?"

It feels like a moment of perfect trust. I can ask, and finally, finally, he will tell me. I draw in my breath. "When you went to the house that night, was his body still there? *Did* you see him?"

He hesitates, and his arms loosen some, though he continues to hold me. Maybe he's deciding whether or not to keep lying, or maybe he's been telling the truth all along but is simply surprised, and sad, that so many years later I am still asking the same questions.

"No," he says, as he always has. "By the time I got there, he was gone."

graveyard

I am driving in Connecticut. I have spent the day with my mother. I took her and Doug out to lunch at a steak house. The steak set them off on an irritated, amused tirade about how the assisted living place was always running out of filet mignon because of the woman who ordered two steaks every night: one to eat, and one to take upstairs for later.

"Our theory is that she feeds it to her dog," Doug said.

They beamed at each other, and my mother said fiercely, "We're planning to form a grievance committee."

The route back to the highway takes me through the town where my parents used to live, past the town library. I grin, driving by, remembering how every September my mother would give several boxes of books to the annual library book sale, and my father would come home excitedly with a stack he'd bought. "Look what I found!" he would say, and my mother would look at the books in dismay: "Paul, I *donated* these."

See? I can smile now when I think of him, I tell myself.

At the same time, I'm aware that I can't smile about him without finding the smile noticeable, remarkable.

At the stop sign after the library, my eye registers a turnoff labeled DIAMOND ROCK ROAD. Familiar, I think.

Then I remember: sitting with my mother and sister in Ted Tyson's chic kitchen the day my father died, arguing about whether to bury his ashes in the graveyard my mother knew about, on Diamond Rock Road. The memory is vivid and leaden—not quite as vivid as if we're still sitting there, but almost. It's also sorry, wistful, laced with some compassion for those three sad shocked women of fifteen years ago.

I remember my sister saying, "There needs to be a place, so we can visit it."

My sister did visit it with her two children, my mother has told me; they went and put cherry tomatoes on my father's grave.

I remembered how my father loved cherry tomatoes, and how he always scattered his tomato plants among the flower beds, because he believed that proximity to the flowers made the tomatoes sweeter.

My mother asked me then, hesitantly, if I had ever visited the grave.

"No," I said, with more vehemence than I'd intended.

But today, for some reason—a benign, green, lush summer day, so many years after his death—I flick on my blinker and turn left on Diamond Rock Road.

Hills, curving and dipping. Stone walls, day lilies, barns converted to houses, houses nestled in real-estate-brochure acres and acres of emerald lawn. Big old trees. New trees laid out in geometric patterns, carefully mulched. Money.

The road is longer than I expect. But then, just when I think that perhaps I've remembered wrong, there it is: a green slope, flanked by woods, dotted with gravestones. I am glad and sorry to find it. I pull the car over into the dirt road at the edge of the graveyard and get out and start walking up the hill, reading the names on the stones.

The only other time I was here was the day we buried his ashes. It was springtime, a few months after he'd died. There was a small deep hole in the ground. The ashes were in a gray metal box, like the box we kept the cash in at my son's nursery school fair. We stood around in the graveyard, and my mother read the Twenty-third Psalm aloud. She was wearing shoes with high heels, and they kept sinking into the soft ground and she kept trying to pull them out, lurching each time, and all the while she kept on reading this psalm. Her voice was intense, emphatic, holy, and, when her shoe would unexpectedly sink again and throw her off balance, angry. It was the first time I'd ever heard anything remotely religious coming out of either of my parents' mouths. Both of them were atheists. I was calm, numb, looking at the sky, trying not to laugh. Weren't there families somewhere who could handle this sort of thing more straightforwardly? What were we doing here with my mother lurching all over the place reading from the Bible?

What I can see today, climbing slowly up the grave-studded hill, is that we were reeling. Suicide isn't just a death, it's an accusation. It's a violent, public declaration of loneliness. It's a repudiation of connection. It says, "You weren't enough to keep me here." It sets up unresolvable dilemmas of culpability and fault: were we to blame for being insufficient, or was he to blame for finding us so? Someone had been weighed and found wanting, but who?

No wonder none of us could figure out how we felt.

Today, wandering around this small green space, I can't find him. The graveyard is tiny but disorganized. Eroded stones from the nineteenth century jostle up against crisply engraved ones from a year or two ago. My memory from that long-ago spring day is reliable, but useless. I remember trees and a steep slope; the whole place is treed and sloping.

I do find him, eventually. His stone, pale granite, engraved on the left-hand side with his name and his dates, the right side left blank for my mother.

(Which, I can't help thinking, were the sides of the bed they slept in throughout their marriage. And I am reminded of an Etruscan tomb sculpture I saw once, in a museum in Italy: a couple, reclining, staring at each other in frank horror, as if to say, Oh my god, it was bad enough to go through life with you—are you telling me we're stuck together for *eternity*?)

There is his name, on a gravestone. He's really dead.

But I knew that already.

I cry for a while. I leave.

Italy

I am standing in a medieval church in a small town in Italy.

My husband is outside, sketching the facade. Our sons are nearby, in the main square. When they were younger, they made up a game on one of our Italy trips where they would draw imaginary swords, yell "ching!" (the sound of the sword coming out of its scabbard), and then chase each other around waving their arms, lunging, and arguing about who had stabbed whom first. Now, at eighteen and twelve, they're too old for public exuberance. They slouch around looking bored, but sometimes, when there are no other people around, I'll see them darting and scuffling in a brief silent version of their old game.

The church is empty; I'm alone. I move slowly up the aisle. It is neither dark nor light. A pale pearly dimness, like the receding shadowed interior of a seashell. The church smells of damp chalk: the smell of Europe.

Sometimes, when I was a child and my father and I were outside together, he would look up and say, "A European sky."

I never knew what he meant. It always looked like regular sky to me; there seemed nothing particular or unusual about it. And I thought, though I wasn't sure, that he said it about different kinds of skies.

"What makes it European?" I asked. "What does a European sky look like?"

He shrugged, and looked at the sky for a long moment. "Oh . . ." He would shrug again, and laugh, and never explain. I don't think he quite knew what he meant.

The air in the church is cold, and the draught is like someone breathing, cool quick breaths on my cheek.

I pass the altar and turn to go up the other aisle. Near the end of it, I stop. Candles burn on a spiky wrought-iron stand before a picture. It's a panel painting, fourteenth century I think, of the Madonna and child. Mary's head is bent, her cheek resting against her child's hair as she gazes sadly out at the viewer. The child is looking up at her, one hand wrapped around her neck, imploring her not to be sad, trying vainly to comfort her. Either he knows less than she does of what lies ahead for them, or far more.

I put some coins into the box and reach for a candle. It's an impulse: I'm not sure why I'm doing it. Touching the wick to a nearby flame, I set it burning on one of the few empty iron spikes in front of the Virgin. I close my eyes, and think of my father.

When I open my eyes, the flames dance and blur, each in its own pulsing halo of light. I'm not sure anymore which candle is his. All the flames flicker and bow in unison; there is nothing to distinguish the one I just lit from all the rest.

In this moment—dim, blurred by candlelight—I can stand and watch the white flames, the multitude, and think that I see him somewhere in their midst, restored to his place among the tall shining souls.

psychiatrist's office

I am sitting with my doctor, telling him about the church in Italy, about how I lit a candle there for my father. My eyes water a little as I describe it to him. "I think that's going to be the ending of my book," I say, "that candle, burning there with all the other candles."

He is shaking his head. His face is filled with—what? Pity, affection, knowing me very well. "That's not where you are," he says.

We sit for a while. I'm annoyed: what does he mean, that's not where I am?

But he's right. It isn't. It's where I wish I were. It's what I think is supposed to happen.

We sit together, looking at each other, silently acknowledging my fierce desire for a resting place, an ending, and the fact that we both know there isn't one.

"It's partly where I am," I say. "It's not untrue."

where I didn't go

I am driving in Connecticut again, after spending a couple of days with my mother.

Again I am passing through the town where my parents used to live. Again I'm at a stop sign—but a different one this time. This time, I notice a small blue sign that I've never seen before. An arrow and the words POLICE STATION.

There is no one behind me. I sit in my car for several moments, deciding whether or not to turn.

In that police station, I know, is a file on my father's death.

314

A file of papers, from the days before everything was computerized. It would be in deep storage by now: in a basement, or an attic, or an outbuilding—which, in a small rural town like this, could be an old barn, with swallows nesting in the eaves above rows and rows of rusty file cabinets.

But somewhere, that file exists.

In it are all the things I've seen. Copies of the death certificate, the autopsy report, the list of items the police removed from the house on the day of his death. A photocopy of the spreadsheet he left for my mother—that long, pathetically dwindled list of his assets.

That folder, I know, also contains something I've never seen. Pictures. Photographs of him dead in the armchair. Of his face, of his eyes open or closed. Of the clothes he was wearing, of the bib-shaped dark stain on his chest. Of his head, fallen back or slumping forward. Of his ankles, crossed on the footstool. Of the gun, wedged down between the cushion and the arm of the chair, or fallen underneath the chair itself (hidden somewhere, I know, since my mother said she never saw it when she was in the room with him). Of the blood on the woodwork, before my husband wiped it away.

Still no one behind me at the intersection.

Why this impulse, to turn my car to the right and drive to the police station and ask to see his folder?

Masochism?

An attempt to shatter the last persistent vestiges of numbness, to force myself once and for all to look, to see, to get it, to feel it?

A kind of preemptive bravado? A desire to bring all the possible other shoes raining down on my head at once, so that I'll never have to dread another one falling?

Sheer curiosity? A salutary desire for omniscience? A journalistic urge to have followed all the leads, uncovered all the mysteries, learned everything that is learnable, shied away from nothing?

A lurid instinct that this might be a sensational ending to the book: this poignant, dreadful tableau of me and the pictures?

This last thought decides me: I step on the gas and drive straight through the intersection.

This, reader, is where I draw the line and the curtain.

I could end this book in a lot of different places, just as I began by circling, over and over, back to the day of my father's death. I could end in bed with my husband, in the graveyard, in the church in Italy, in my psychiatrist's office.

Or in my house, that first morning, hearing the news from Ted Tyson and thinking, "Oh no," and "Of course."

Or I could end driving in Connecticut, toward the highway, away from the sign that says POLICE STATION. Knowing that I'll never know the whole story. Knowing that I'll never feel his death as fully and directly as I might wish to; and that perhaps as a result I'll never be done feeling it.

Knowing that if I could somehow get him back, rewind the tape, look into his eyes, and say, "Please don't do it," he might look away from me and do it anyway.

And knowing that wherever I am, I am always moving, and I will never be in one place for long.